LAW, POLICY AND DEVELOPMENT
IN THE RURAL ENVIRONMENT

ENVIRONMENT AND COUNTRYSIDE LAW

The Environment and Countryside Law Series provides a forum for the publication of studies and research relating to distinctly 'rural' issues. The Series has a strong focus on environmental law and nature conservation, and on related issues of rural land use. However, other well-established areas of legal study, such as criminal law and property law, also raise distinct problems when studied in a rural context, and the scope of the series also includes subjects such as rural crime, rural housing and access to justice in rural areas. The Series therefore seeks to promote and publish research into all aspects of the law as it applies in the countryside.

LAW, POLICY AND DEVELOPMENT

IN THE RURAL ENVIRONMENT

edited by

NICHOLAS HERBERT-YOUNG

UNIVERSITY OF WALES PRESS
CARDIFF
1999

© The Contributors, 1999

British Library Cataloguing-in-Publication Data.
A catalogue record for this book is available from the British Library.

ISBN 0-7083-1476-7

Typeset at Action Publishing Technology, Gloucester
Printed in Great Britain by Bookcraft, Midsomer Norton, Avon

Preface

The regulation of development and land use in the countryside raises a variety of policy concerns. In the past private law has been used as a vehicle for regulating land use – for instance through the use of restrictive covenants affecting land, and the law of private nuisance. In the twentieth century the focus has switched increasingly, however, to the use of regulatory legislation of a public law nature to pursue and enforce a diverse range of policy objectives. The 'public' interest encompasses a wide range of disparate (and often competing) policy objectives – the need to promote efficient agriculture and food production, to protect and enhance valuable wildlife habitats, to encourage greater recreational enjoyment of the countryside, to name but a few. Development control law has had an increasingly important role, not only in enforcing these policy objectives, but in providing a legal framework within which these competing land use priorities can be balanced and conflicts adjudicated. Development control policy has become increasingly sophisticated, and with it a complex body of jurisprudence has developed.

In this, the fifth volume in the Environment and Countryside Law series, Nicholas Herbert-Young has brought together a number of experts in planning and environmental law to provide a stimulating and diverse collection of essays. The contributions consider both the theoretical bases of planning law in the countryside, and also address specific policy concerns and their treatment in the planning process. In so doing it should, it is hoped, contribute greatly to our understanding of the role of planning law in the countryside and its use as a regulatory tool for implementing countryside policies – be they for nature conservation or for promoting economic regeneration of rural areas.

Christopher Rodgers
Centre for Law in Rural Areas
University of Wales, Aberystwyth

Note: The authors have sought to state the law applicable as at October 1998 and, in most of the chapters that follow, the law will be that in force on 26 April 1999.

Contents

The Contributors

Stephen Crow is Honorary Professor of Planning Policy and Practice at the Department of City and Regional Planning, University of Wales, Cardiff, where his research interests include aspects of statutory planning in all parts of the British Isles. He currently acts as Independent Inspector in the Isle of Man and in May/June 1999 chaired the public examination into draft Regional Planning Guidance for the south-east of England. Prior to 1994 he was Chief Planning Inspector for England and Wales.

Charles George QC specializes in administrative, planning and environmental law. In particular he is interested in, and has been extensively involved professionally with, issues relating to planning and transport law and policy. In addition to practising at the Bar, he is a Recorder of the Crown Court, Chancellor of the Diocese of Southwark and a member of the House Council of St Stephen's House, Oxford.

J. D. C. Harte is a barrister and Senior Lecturer in Law at Newcastle Law School, Newcastle University. His interests are divided between law and religion and environmental law, with a particular emphasis on conservation of the countryside and the built heritage. He has researched and published in both areas and is on the editorial boards of the *Ecclesiastical Law Journal* and of the *Rights of Way Law Review*.

Nicholas Herbert-Young has written on a range of planning law issues, for both academic and practical publications, and has lectured at a number of universities in the UK. He is a non-practising barrister and was a member of the Centre for Law in Rural Areas at the University of Wales, Aberystwyth, from 1993 until 1998.

Wendy Le-Las holds an Honorary Lectureship in the Kent Law

School, University of Kent. She convenes the Planning Law Working Party of UKELA, and is a member of the Nature Conservation Working Party. Since 1990 she has been planning consultant to the National Association of Local Councils.

George Meyrick is a lawyer at Clifford Chance where he practises in property law. His particular expertise lies in land management issues in south-west Hampshire and the Isle of Anglesey.

Denzil Millichap specialized in planning law at both undergraduate and postgraduate levels, before transferring to legal practice in the public sector. Since 1990 he has been in the private sector and is now a member of the Planning and Environment Group at Linklaters. He has a particular interest in conservation (both built and natural heritage) and the historical development of planning control in the UK and elsewhere. He has written extensively as contributor, columnist and editor on many aspects of planning and environmental law.

Charles Mynors is a barrister in private practice specializing in planning, environmental and ecclesiastical law. He is also qualified as a town planner and chartered surveyor, and is an associate of the Arboricultural Association. He is frequently asked to give lectures on the law as it relates to trees, and is the author of a forthcoming book on *The Law of Trees, Forests and Hedgerows*.

Michael Purdue is Professor of Law at City University. He is author of several books on planning law, such as *Planning Law and Procedure* (with E. Young and J. Rowan-Robinson) (1989), and *Negotiating Developments* (with P. Healey and F. Ennis) (1995). He is Assistant Editor of the *Journal of Planning and Environment Law* and Case-Analysis Editor of the *Journal of Environment Law*.

Jeremy Rowan-Robinson is Professor of Planning and Environmental Law at Aberdeen University and a consultant in planning and environmental law with Paull and Williamsons, Solicitors. He is the author or co-author of seven books on planning law and related matters and is currently working on the second edition of *Scottish Planning Law and Procedure*. He is a member of the Board of Scottish Natural Heritage.

Gerard Ryan QC is a barrister who has spent much of his working life promoting or opposing projects which have substantial environmental effects. In private life he is both a philosophical and practical conservationist. Years ago he co-authored *An Outline of the Law of Common*

Introduction

Development and the Rural Environment

NICHOLAS HERBERT-YOUNG

The title of this book, it is hoped, captures the scope of its concerns with reasonable accuracy. It is now commonplace to acknowledge that private and public law have had a long-standing role in the regulation of rural land use and development; from a historical perspective, the doctrine of tenure and recognition of the enforceability of restrictive covenants and schemes of development, together with a balance achieved by the law of nuisance between the rights and liabilities of landowners and occupiers, created more than a modicum of mutual regulation. Legislation contributed to this regulatory patchwork at least as early as 1589, for example, providing some restriction on the erection of housing by linking housing supply to occupancy needs. The first specific planning legislation arrived at last on the statute book in 1909; planning law itself has developed and interacted with private and public law to affect town and country in Britain since 1932 and it is not difficult to identify either the interactions between planning law and the law of nuisance (see, for example, chapter 8 on statutory land compensation provisions and nuisance criteria) or limitations in planning law on the provision of housing through occupancy requirements (see, for example, *Fawcett Properties Ltd* v. *Buckinghamshire County Council* [1961] AC 636).

The twentieth century has, however, made diverse, often contradictory but well-known demands of the rural environment. Scientific and preservationist goals of nature conservation and landscape protection have been pursued at the same time as economic and social 'demand', or 'need', for the provision of food, raw materials, amenity, recreation, employment and housing; that interesting hybrid, the custodian farmer, embodies the rapprochement attempted by Parliament (if this is not to put it too highly) between such apparently inconsistent aims. To these traditional aims we must add now the notions of biodiversity and sustainable development, hoping that we are not simply applying a spurious gloss.

Development in the rural environment provokes fundamental questions of, and about, the law and policy relating not just to particular areas, such as National Parks and SSSIs (Sites of Special Scientific Interest), important though they are, but to the British countryside as a whole. So, the adequacy of area designation, for example, is discussed in this book (at the time of writing, an attempt to secure National Park status for the South Downs has just failed, as it did in 1949). As for law and policy on development in the countryside as a whole, a number of chapters in this book consider, for example, the impact of s.54A of the Town and Country Planning Act 1990, the use of management agreements in development control, the scope for, and adequacy of, legal provision for representing individual interests in the development process and the reform of local government and development planning in rural areas. The history of recent cases concerning the lack of compensation for off-line planning blight in parts of rural England stands as a sobering record of the legal problems afflicting those whose rural property interests fall just outside the bounds of current legislation and of the technical, and policy-based, faults of recently amended legislation. To adapt Santayana's adage to town and country planning: we do not forget the past, but we seem condemned to repeat it (often).

1 Plan-Led Development and the Rural Environment

The insertion of s.54A into the Town and Country Planning Act 1990 has been one of the more significant changes to statutory planning during the 1990s and it is a powerful example of the extent to which planning law and policy interact. The impact of s.54A upon the processes of statutory planning has been extensive. A number of contributors to this book have taken the opportunity to comment on s.54A and development control.

Wendy Le-Las highlights what she considers to be the planning system's 'bias in favour of development' in her chapter on biodiversity, development and the planning system (chapter 4), arguing that this lies at the root of statutory planning in Britain, that it limits the ability of the planning system to protect biodiversity against development motivated by social and economic considerations. S.54A requires the making of planning determinations in accordance with the development plan and so could be said to support the Le-Las view. The support that s.54A might give to the needs of biodiversity turns entirely on the policy content of the appropriate development plan and/or the materiality of biodiversity considerations without it (see also Warren, chapter 5). By this reckoning, a local planning authority might even find itself granting planning permission for a development that maintains or improves rural biodiversity, and so accords with the development plan, or refusing permission that does not maintain or improve rural biodiversity in accordance with the development plan.

Le-Las points out, however, a major problem of the alleged pro-development bias that cannot be ameliorated by the terms of s.54A, namely the lack of a statutory right of appeal in third-party objectors to a grant of planning permission. We should not ignore s.54A in this context; Stephen Crow points up the importance of local plan and unitary development plan formulation, noting the rural context of many local plans in England and many unitary development plans in Wales (chapter 9). Potential third-party objectors may need considerable prescience, but s.54A could reward in due course careful attention paid to development planning, and participation in the plan-making process, in order to establish the materiality of third-party concerns, preferably in the policies of the development plan, and so mitigate the lack of third-party appeal rights at the application stage (see *British Railways Board* v. *Slough Borough Council* [1995] JPL 678 for an early example of judicial awareness of this point).

S.54A is of at least as much importance to that part of the rural environment adjoining urban peripheral areas (Green Belt or otherwise) as it is to the deeper countryside. Michael Purdue, in chapter 2, focuses on the place of s.54A in determining the legal status of Green Belt policies in development control decisions. S.54A can be understood readily to affect planning determinations relating to the Green Belt as Purdue, like Denzil Millichap in chapter 1, highlights the consequences of the policy status of the Green Belt: the Green Belt 'depends for its implementation completely on the development control system. It is the power of local planning authorities to refuse development, which is inappropriate to the Green Belt, which makes the policy stick.' S.54A affects the legal status of those Green Belt policies *not* to be found in the development plan most directly by altering, though not eliminating, the twofold test set out in *Pehrsson* v. *Secretary of State for the Environment and the Royal Borough of Windsor and Maidenhead* (1991) 61 P & C R 266, so elevating consideration of the development plan over consideration of the appropriateness of the proposed development in the Green Belt. National policies on the Green Belt, such as those in Planning Policy Guidance Note (PPG) 2, *Green Belts* (January 1995), may be reflected in the development plan itself, of course; even if they are not, such policies may be material considerations. Purdue illustrates the difficulty in establishing a clear test, following the introduction of s.54A, by pointing out the opposing views of Roy Vandermeer QC and Sedley J.

Plan-led development may impact upon the use, and the treatment, of planning obligations, themselves another change in planning legislation during the 1990s. Policies involving the use of planning obligations are common to development plans in rural England and Wales, and often address such issues as local occupancy and affordable housing (see chapter 11), so providing a means for translating plan policies into practice through negotiation between a local planning authority and a developer. Jeremy Rowan-Robinson and Anne-Michelle Slater discuss in chapter 3 two Scottish examples of planning agreements, made under s.75 of the Town and Country Planning (Scotland) Act 1997 (as distinct from, for example, the creation of management agreements for environmentally sensitive areas and other management agreements not linked with development proposals. The authors point out that much of their discussion is relevant to planning obligations in England and Wales in spite of the different terminology). The two planning agreements were made pursuant to a grant of planning permission in order tò secure the managed implementation of the local planning authority's lowland crofting policy in the West Lothian area of Scotland, the local plan identifying 'principal matters to be covered by an agreement'. As the authors point out, such use of the planning system may have a considerable role to play in anticipating and resolving development-related conflicts in the countryside, helping thereby to achieve 'shared responsibility' for the environment and to improve degraded rural areas. The legal requirement of plan-led development in England and Wales, at least, could influence local planning authorities to pursue positive environmental goals as 'principal matters' to be agreed with potential developers, or to be undertaken by the latter, when seeking planning permission. Local planning authorities, already subject to statutory environmental requirements in the formulation of development plans, might also draft policies specifically to make more material environmentally positive planning obligations in the determination of rural planning applications generally, and of those applications relating particularly to degraded rural environments.

2 Development and the Green Belt

The Green Belt may be seen as one of the earliest, and most enduring, aspects of the statutory planning system in those parts of the countryside peripheral to urban/suburban areas. Denzil Millichap describes 'the Green Belt regime' as 'perhaps the one aspect of UK planning practice that is known throughout the planning world' (see chapter 1). There is no designated Green Belt in Wales at the time of writing, however, though the Welsh Office appears to have assumed the existence of Welsh Green Belts when it issued Planning Guidance (Wales), *Planning Policy* (May 1996), and acknowledged the error in the first draft amendment thereto in 1997; the present government has exhorted local planning authorities in north-east and south-east Wales to designate areas of Green Belt.

Millichap provides a timely reminder of the evolution of the Green Belt concept, its origins, purposes and policies, because 1998 marked the centenary of the publication of Ebenezer Howard's *Tomorrow: A Peaceful Path to Real Reform*. Millichap raises again, in a rural context, some fundamental issues, including private and public interests and distinctions in the disposition of planning responsibilities and property rights (cf. the 'shared responsibility' features of planning agreements in Scotland – see Rowan-Robinson and Slater, chapter 3); the farmer as custodian of the countryside (cf. Warren, Ryan and Meyrick, and Mynors at chapters 5, 6 and 7, respectively) and the status of the Green Belt in policy and, potentially, as the subject matter of specific legislation (cf. Purdue, chapter 2).

Millichap explores also his community-rights thesis in the context of the Green Belt and 'public interest' as the rationale for the present planning system, looking to the Housing, Town Planning, etc., Act 1909 as the basis of his argument for replacing the notion of the public interest as the foundation of statutory planning, and arguing instead for a community-rights approach, modelled on the 1909 Act. As Stephen Crow points out, however, the 'country' was not an express concern of statutory planning until 1932 but Millichap, insofar as he applies his interpretation of community rights to the Green Belt, does not stray far beyond those areas identified in the 1909 Act. Millichap's thesis, whether one agrees with it or not, may yet prove to be highly attractive to planning and environmental pressure groups, as well as rural communities and their (New Labour?) representatives in local government and Parliament, should levels of housing demand, for example, increase development pressure upon Green Belt land in spite of sustainable development considerations (cf. Le-Las, chapter 4).

Should the Green Belt have its own statutory recognition akin to that conferred upon listed buildings and conservation areas? Purdue thinks not, given the potential complication of an already complex system of development control. In chapter 2, Purdue considers judicial contributions to the understanding, and application, of Green Belt policies, given s.54A and recent cases. Purdue argues that the scope afforded by the courts to local planning authorities in construing Green Belt documents, especially where words may 'properly' have more than one meaning, suggests a 'judicial deference' to decision-makers and a judicial reluctance to overcomplicate planning administration by challenging policy interpretations and applications made locally. This phenomenon of deference or reluctance has been evident more generally in planning cases during the 1990s, in town or country situations, or in such cases as *R. v. Swale Borough Council, ex parte Royal Society for the Protection of Birds* [1991] JPL 39 and *Tesco Stores Ltd v. Secretary of State for the Environment and Others* [1995] 1 WLR 759; in the latter case Lord Hoffmann's judgement may be seen to show the phenomenon as a response to earlier judicial interventions in local authority decision-making, notably the decision in *Hall & Co. Ltd* v. *Shoreham-by-Sea Urban District Council* [1964] 1 WLR 240.

Purdue comments also on the accountability of local planning authorities and inspectors for their decisions; the construction and application of Green Belt policy by decision-makers may be an area where the courts are loath to intervene, but it is unlikely that demands for greater accountability will disappear as conflicting pressures grow over the designation and integrity of Green Belt areas.

3 Planning, Nature Conservation and Biodiversity

The Green Belt, nature conservation and biodiversity are linked matters, of course; if the Green Belt is the one aspect of the planning regime known throughout the world, nature conservation and biodiversity issues have become such prominent concerns globally that international and European influences, in addition to domestic considerations, have affected planning law and policy in Britain during the 1990s. Many of the chapters in this book touch upon the contribution of these concerns to planning law and policy, over and above that body of law and policy established in Britain by the mid-1980s to deal with long-standing and conflicting demands of preservation and conservation, recreation and amenity, agriculture and afforestation. The range of the issues raised in these chapters is too vast to allow for any significant discussion here: suffice it to state that lawyers and others may continue to anticipate a flow of planning-based litigation (cf. Ryan and Meyrick, chapter 6). Examples of traditional nature conservation weaknesses in the planning system are illustrated and explored and may temper optimism arising from the success of recent examples of environmental co-operation between developer and local authority – who can forget the farmer as custodian of the countryside, the vulnerability of protected areas, the definition of 'development' in town and country planning legislation and its connection with the problems of agricultural land use and afforestation?

The scope for planning litigation might even expand. The Cairngorm funicular railway scheme, discussed by Rowan-Robinson and Slater in chapter 3, was the subject of a legal challenge mounted by the WWF (World Wildlife Fund) and the RSPB (Royal Society for the Protection of Birds) on habitats designation, in the Court of Session at the time of writing. Changes introduced to decision-making criteria for National Park authorities in discharging statutory functions could echo the type of confusion aroused by the introduction of s.54A of the Town and Country Planning Act 1990; the 'patchwork quilt' made of legislation on public access to the countryside over the last fifty years has been added to by the elevation of the conservation and enhancement of 'extensive tracts of country in England' over opportunities for their understanding and enjoyment by the public (see ss.11A and 5 of the National Parks and Access to the Countryside Act 1949, as amended, and Ryan and Meyrick, chapter 6). The expansion of planning law and policy in the 1990s under international, European and domestic influences to include regulations on environmental assessment, habitats and hedgerows, for example, has legal implications not only for decision-makers but also for developers, landowners and other concerned parties (see Le-Las, Warren, Ryan and Meyrick, and Mynors at chapters 4–7). Can one reasonably hope that models and arrangements cited by Rowan-Robinson and Slater, and Ryan and Meyrick are good indicators for the future?

4 Planning: Public and Private Interests

The successful co-ordination of certain public and private interests in rural development through such planning devices as s.106 obligations and Grampian conditions (see, for example, chapter 3), and such private law means as restrictive covenants (see, for example, J. D. C. Harte's comments in chapter 10), cannot wholly mask the existence of what Stephen Crow calls 'the rural battleground' of conflicting and competing interests, nor should it be thought to do so.

Crow points out a limitation of the planning-appeals system in its failure to provide for a statutory right of appeal for third parties against grants of planning permission by local planning authorities. Charles George QC provides a particularly contemporary and disturbing example of prejudice to private interests under the operation of the planning system (see chapter 8), namely the issue of uncompensated loss from off-line planning blight in the countryside. Faults in the recently amended legislation, and their consequences, are illustrated by reference to particular examples of loss associated with highways schemes in Gloucestershire and Norfolk, and by discussion of generalized off-line blight in rural Kent caused by the Channel Tunnel Rail Link project: off-line blight 'is at its most acute where public works conflict with the seclusion that has been sought (and found, often at high price) in the countryside'. The chapters by Crow and George question the status of private interests in the planning system, their recognition, protection and treatment as rights deserving standing and/or compensation, not least because of contemporary calls for a third-party right of appeal, however limited, and the inadequacy of s.62 of the Planning and Compensation Act 1991 in reforming compensation law; and yet the compensation issue also betrays the persistent influence of tort in planning law (through legislative reference to nuisance in compensation criteria – see chapter 8). Perhaps the most difficult aspect of the compensation issue is the public authorities' use of statutory discretion whether or not to make an award, and it is particularly interesting to note the comments of Sedley J (given in chapter 8) on discretion and local authority funding considerations. If comfort is needed on the blight issue, there is some (admittedly cold) to be found in George's observation that our current domestic law on compensation is more sympathetic to property owners than the law of a number of other European states.

In chapter 9, Crow describes the contribution of 'rural battleground' appeals to the development of contemporary planning law and the appeal system; he notes also that appeals in rural areas frequently present 'the greatest challenges to the professional skills of an inspector'. Incidentally, note Crow's reference to Sedley J's view on the matter of standing in *R. v. Somerset County Council and ARC Southern Ltd, ex parte Dixon* [1997] JPL B 138. It is apparent from the number of references in chapters of this book alone that Sedley J is a judge who may yet exercise considerable influence over the development of town and country planning law.

5 Rural Planning Administration

The administrative structure of town and country planning has been subjected to considerable changes recently, and faces more in the near future, at central, regional and local levels. Central government planning responsibilities have shifted, not least with the creation of the Department of Environment, Transport and the Regions in 1997 and the transfer of the listing of historic buildings to the Department for Culture, Media and Sport via the now-defunct Department for National Heritage. A major issue for rural planning and development has been the annual transition of tranches of local government from two-tier status to unitary status and its consequences. Some enlightenment on the transitional aspect of local planning may be found in the orders creating new authorities and, for example, in England, the Department of the Environment (DoE) Circular 4/96, *Local Government Act 1992 and Town and Country Planning Act 1990: Local Government Change and the Planning System.*

Confusion may arise not only over the identity of local authorities and applicable development plans from case to case, but also from the differences in administration between rural areas in Wales and those in England (over and above the 'solo' status of the Welsh Office in creating planning policy) because transition to unitary-authority status, with a view to the creation, *inter alia*, of unitary development plans, is required throughout rural Wales but not throughout rural England. Other relevant difficulties, at least in the Welsh rural context, are considered in chapter 11, including the point that the Welsh Assembly may introduce its own planning policies and secondary legislation for rural Wales.

Another aspect of planning administration in rural areas is the subject of J. D. C. Harte's chapter which focuses on the role of the Church of England as rural landowner and developer and on its relationship to the secular planning system (see chapter 10). This relationship has been affected during the 1990s by the Ecclesiastical Exemption (Listed Buildings and Conservation Areas) Order 1994 (Statutory Instrument No.1771), as has the relationship between secular planning and other religious bodies. Harte points out the diversity of roles that the Church of England has in the development of its own and others' land across over 28,000 parishes; he highlights also the extent to which the Church's own systems of development control interrelate with planning law and other secular systems (often concerning heritage protection), particularly the Church's faculty jurisdiction, the criteria by which decisions are made under it and the role of that jurisdiction in conserving the Church's built heritage as 'an important visual focus for the surrounding community and landscape', especially in rural areas. Detailed study could be made of the extent to which decision-making criteria upon applications for faculties reflect secular planning concepts, particularly given the long-standing links between the Planning Bar and the body of diocesan chancellors, whether or not planning permission and other planning consent is required from case to case. Suffice it to state that the diverse nature of the Church of England's interests in land, and its particular significance among rural communities, merits its inclusion here both as a modern and important form of planning administrator, legislator and adjudicator, and as an often key player, through its use of public and private land-law rights, in shaping the rural environment.

Finally, a brief reference to the Nolan report on standards in local government (see further chapters 3 and 11). The fact that the administration of planning by local government constituted a major area of inquiry for the Nolan Committee, and a large part of its report, could be taken to speak for itself. Aspects of the report are considered in this collection and there can be little doubt of its relevance to the implementation of planning law and policy in the rural environment. If, as this collection of essays may show, developers are the main beneficiaries of the planning system, its law and policy in the rural environment, how long will it be before a new report is needed to address not just local government standards but the fundamentals of the statutory town and country planning system itself?

1

Green Belt Policy and Law: A Study in Transitions

DENZIL MILLICHAP

1 Introduction

The Green Belt regime is perhaps the one aspect of UK planning practice that is known throughout the planning world. It is also of particular interest to the UK planning professions as its genesis lies in the work of the pioneering work of Ebenezer Howard and his notion of the garden city. Ebenezer Howard's *Tomorrow: A Peaceful Path to Real Reform* first published in 1898 and subsequently in 1901 under the better-known title *Garden Cities of Tomorrow* is the main source for his views on garden cities. The version most readily available is *Garden Cities of Tomorrow*, edited by F. J. Osborn (London: Faber and Faber, 1965). As 1998 was the centenary of his seminal work some reference to his thoughts is appropriate in a discussion of Green Belt and development in rural areas. The aim of combining the benefits of both town and country for the inhabitants of the garden (or 'social') city was to be achieved, in Howard's view, by ensuring that rural areas were protected for rural uses. The 'agricultural zone' was, as shall be shown, the concept that was transformed into the notion of the Green Belt that is now more famous than its originator. Yet these garden-city roots of the Green Belt idea, the following suggests, should not be overlooked if a critical account of the concept's implementation is to be attempted. The garden-city idea thus provides the important context for understanding what the original role of Green Belt was intended to be. The following will thus dwell on the changes which produced a form of Green Belt that is now distinctly different from that which Howard originally envisaged. In doing so the following will also illustrate how policy, law and practical action underwent transitions as the vision of Howard was transformed into reality.

2 Green Belt's Roots: Howard and the Social City

2.1 Introduction

The roots of our present Green Belt regime can be traced back to Ebenezer Howard and his conception of the social city – more commonly referred to as the 'garden city'. This conception was developed by Howard in order to provide a solution to the fundamental dilemma facing the communities living in the urban and rural environments. The problem that Howard sought to resolve was how to tackle both the overpopulation of Victorian cities and the underpopulation of rural areas. For Howard this required a new sort of urban form – the social city. The social city would maximize both accessibility to economic opportunities and social/environmental goods. The result, to use modern terminology, would be a better quality of life for all – avoiding the evils of both rural and urban as then revealed in Victorian Britain.

2.2 The social city: a radical solution

Underlying the concept of the 'social city' was a radical approach. The urban and rural components (including the agricultural belt that was to provide the city with its produce and much of the clean air and green environment to be enjoyed by citizens) of the social city were to be collectively owned by the communities forming the social elements of the social city. This is town planning at its most interventionist: the community takes direct control of the land. Community ownership would enable the constituent communities of the social city (communities in the 'urban' parts and those in the 'rural' parts) to enjoy the benefits of both rural and urban environments. The evils of the city (environmental stress etc.) and the evils of the rural areas (low wages etc.) would be eliminated.

The social city's boundaries were to be established by the agricultural belt. Howard and his followers seemed to think of the agricultural belt as the primary source of agricultural goods for the social city it encompassed. This agricultural belt is the germ of the idea that was to become the Green Belt regime of the post-war era. Howard's conception of the agricultural (Green) Belt can clearly be seen to be a subsidiary element in his general prescription for curing the social and economic ills of the unsocial cities created by Victorian urban growth. His Green Belt was also meant to secure sufficient room between social cities – to avoid damaging 'accessibility' to town and country by reason of over-large conurbations. It too was to be owned by the collective entity: this would then ensure that access to such land for recreational/amenity purposes could be secured. So when the Howardian conception, that forms the root of the Green Belt concept, is under examination the distinctive characteristics of the Howardian vision must be kept firmly in view. Howard's Green Belt was to perform an important economic and spatial role. It was to enable both rural and urban communities to be mutually supporting (and not lead to one community benefiting at the expense of the other). Indeed, the first garden city at Letchworth was said to have achieved this 'marriage' of town and country.[1] So Howard's Green Belt comprised agricultural land whose location and extent meant that it was to be protected (via community ownership) for the good of the community – rural and urban. Individual interests (whether social, economic or spatial) would be subordinated to those of the collective entity. The agricultural zone would not be in private ownership – except to the extent that tenant farmers etc. held leasehold interests. Amenity and other such benefits were to be kept available for all – and not to be captured by the private landowner.

The integrative purpose of the Howardian Green Belt was its first important characteristic. A second important feature of the Howardian Green Belt was its size. The social city was limited in size – on account of the need to maintain accessibility – for both the rural and urban populace. Thus the area of land that was later to earn the description of Green Belt was, in Howard's conception, a narrow (approximately two or three miles wide) area of open land between a garden city and its neighbouring garden cities or rural hinterland.

A third element in Howard's conception was that it was concerned with new settlements – not (directly) with addressing the problems of existing cities. Howard's conception was not aimed at a sticking-plaster approach to deal with existing overblown urban areas. He was concerned with 'real reform' (as the title to his book suggests) – not ameliorating an existing situation that, for many cities, may have posed an intractable problem.

Fourth, Howard's vision encompassed an integrated land-use planning and transport system. Only by integrating land-use and transportation policies could communities reap the benefits of both town and

---

[1] See C. B. Purdom, *The Building of Satellite Towns* (London: Dent, 1949), 146 – where the agricultural belt is discussed.

country. Howard had witnessed the unrestrained growth (around existing urban centres such as London) and was anxious to address the problems that this created. The lack of access to green open spaces for the urban masses, the difficulty of agricultural enterprises in servicing such areas – these could be addressed by tackling the lack of 'accessibility'. But growth was not itself bad – the social city channelled that growth into the appropriate locations. At the point where expansion might otherwise lead to the development of the vicious circle that affects an existing town 'accessibility' is maintained by the establishment of a new social city in a location removed from the 'agricultural estate' of that existing town. The new city would be created on a 'greenfield' site – again on land (forming both the civic and agricultural estate) wholly owned by the collective entity. New settlements (as long as they reflected 'social city' principles) were thus not outlawed by Howard – new settlements positively promoted his ideals. A moratorium on development in the rural hinterland was definitely not one of Howard's aims.

The key elements described above (not an exhaustive list) show that Howard had an integrative vision where collective ownership of the land needed to establish the social city (including its agricultural belt) was a central tenet. Howard did not want to preserve the rural environment for its own sake: rural depopulation, social and economic stagnation were just as evil as urban squalor and overcrowding. It is the good of the community (existing and future) that concerned Howard – and that was to be achieved by the appropriate 'marriage' of the two communities by means of the social city. The Green Belt was the wedding ring that gave the union a solid economic protection. (See also Purdom, *Satellite Towns*, p.442 and chapter V generally on the role played by 'agricultural belts'.)

3 Early Garden Cities, Green Belt and London

3.1 Letchworth

The first example of the agricultural belt being put into practice comes with the first attempt at creating a social city. This is where Letchworth takes centre stage. Letchworth was the first garden city established by Howard and his crusading band. In terms of that key element of his vision (collective ownership), it is clear from one contemporary writer (and supporter) that Letchworth's fundamentals were along 'garden city' lines. Thus both the city and agricultural estates were owned by the collective entity – First Garden City Ltd (established in 1903 – the year when the land was acquired to start the project). Thus Charles

Ashbee, in *Where the Great City Stands*, focuses on the ownership
issue when discussing, in chapter XII, the 'The garden city idea'.[2] On
p.43 he states that the garden-city concept reflects the principle that
'the profits resulting from the increase of population and people's
improvements shall go back to the people'. As the agricultural belt was
an integral element of the garden-city idea, it was necessarily also
owned by the collective entity. Yet there are suggestions in the literature that even Letchworth failed to conform on a number of points with
Howard's garden-city principles. The company secretary of First
Garden City Ltd and former secretary of the Garden City Association
(GCA), Thomas Adams, accepted the need to gain widespread support
for the project. However, he acknowledged that this was achieved at
some cost.[3] 'He pointed to differences in methods of raising capital,
administration, ownership of the sites and public services, land tenure,
the size of the estate, the proportion reserved for agriculture, restrictions on growth, layout and the system of distribution.'[4] Such
comments should give us pause when considering the development of
the concept of Green Belt: if garden cities in practice were diverging
from the Howardian vision then agricultural/Green Belts were far from
safe. Yet Letchworth was, in terms of its agricultural belt, very much
closer to the aims of Howard than Welwyn was to be. Purdom, writing
in 1949, notes that 'Letchworth has a town area of 2,182 acres for
35,000 persons and an agricultural belt of 2,380. Welwyn has a town
area of 3,282 for its projected population of 50,000, and nothing worth
calling an agricultural belt.'[5] If this was an accurate assessment then
the Green Belt's central role in promoting the objectives of the social
city was forgotten when Welwyn is examined. However, the immediate
post-war era was also to see legislative recognition of the garden-city
concept.[6]

3.2 The Housing (Additional Powers) Act 1919

The 'homes for heroes' clarion call of the immediate post-war era was
the occasion perhaps for central government to adopt the Howardian
social-city concept – and make provision for public funding of such
projects. This was signalled in 1919 with the Housing (Additional
Powers) Act ('the 1919 Act') of that year. Cabinet interest in dealing

---

[2] Charles Ashbee, *Where the Great City Stands* (London: Essex House, 1917).
[3] See Dennis Hardy, *From Garden Cities to New Towns* (London: E. & F. N.
Spon, 1991), 53.
[4] Ibid., 55.
[5] Ibid., 448.
[6] Ibid., 145.

with the housing issue had led it to investigate garden cities on the Continent: so lobbying for legislation for garden cities was not without disappointment. (The same year also witnessed Howard's embarking on the second garden-city project – Welwyn Garden City.) Powers (subject to central government consent) were thus made available by way of s.10 of the 1919 Act for the public acquisition of land for the purpose of garden cities. (Calls by the GCA for compulsory acquisition powers to be actively promoted by central government were not take up.[7]) These powers were to be repeated in subsequent 'planning' legislation – first as s.16 of the Town Planning Act 1925 ('the 1925 Act') and then as s.35 of the Town and Country Planning Act 1932 ('the 1932 Act'). The scheme of these legislative provisions encompassed the 'collective ownership' approach found in the philanthropic/private-sector approach of Letchworth. They envisaged that 'authorized associations' (or local authorities – bringing the public sector into the picture) could be given help in achieving particular objectives – namely, to establish or extend garden cities. Such help would comprise the use of compulsory purchase powers 'on behalf' of such associations or authorities: here was the important public-sector funding element. The land would then be vested in such bodies by the Minister of Health. S.16(5) of the 1925 Act expanded on the term 'authorized association' – this covered 'any society, company or body of persons approved by the Minister whose objects include the promotion, formation, or management of garden cities (including garden suburbs and garden villages), and the erection, improvement or management of buildings for the working classes and others . . .'

The language and mechanisms appearing in s.16(5) also show how the Howardian conception was already being altered to suit popular understanding of garden cities. The legislative recognition of 'garden suburbs' (a term often applied by developers to market residential housing schemes that were far from the Howardian pattern of a self-contained community) was hardly fulfilling the Howardian vision of integrative communities marrying town and country. 'Garden villages' were another example of the bowdlerization of the concept. So although the Howardian idea of community ownership was reflected in legislation (though supplemented by a public-sector version), it was clear that 'populist' conceptions were already hijacking the garden-city conception. The Howardian concept of the agricultural belt (an integral element of his social-city concept) was absent from this idea: sprawl was the unspoken implication of 'garden village' development – sprawl was clearly one of the evils of unrestrained urbanizing development

[7] Ibid.

that Howard wanted to prevent by way of, *inter alia*, his Green Belt. It is also unlikely that those developers promoting 'garden villages' shared Howard's emphasis on collective ownership! The agricultural belt as described by Howard thus had no role in such locations. Agricultural belts in the Howardian sense thus had no place in the marketing of the new suburbia. It could even be said that the government's 'housing' aims for the 1919 Act foreshadowed the Green Belt situation that we know today. Instead of a mechanism ensuring an integrative community based on social-city lines we have instead one which provides an amenity enjoyed by landowners: the modern Green Belt is not the resource (producing agricultural products and amenity benefits for the common use and enjoyment of all) that Howard had intended. It has become an aspect of home ownership and an asset which supports the economic investment made by private property owners. The 1919 Act's link with housing was to surface in a similar way throughout the following decades as the institution of the Green Belt matured. In fact it might be said that Green Belt only became institutionalized and embedded in the popular mind when it came to support suburban housing values: the link between developers' hyperbole, the bowdlerization of the Green Belt and garden-city concepts can thus be seen at an early stage in the history of planning. Howard's vision was not, however, entirely dead. Collective/public ownership of agricultural land on the urban fringe was to figure in the most obvious legislative manifestation of Green Belt thinking. The Metropolitan Green Belt legislation was a step back to the Howardian vision.

3.3 London Green Belt legislation

Although 1919 and a desire to address the housing problem did mark a (rather hollow) victory for the GCA, it was in the metropolis that one element of the garden-city ideal (the agricultural zone) received particular, and more fruitful, attention. Again the impetus seems to have come from central government. In 1927 Neville Chamberlain, the Minister of Health (and so the person in charge of the national planning system originally established in 1909 by the Housing, Town Planning etc. Act ('1909 Act') of that year), set up the Greater London Regional Planning Committee. At the first meeting of this body one of the issues he raised with them was clearly inspired by the Howardian vision. He asked whether London should 'be provided with something which might be called an agricultural belt, as has often been suggested, so that it would form a dividing line between Greater London as it is and the satellites of fresh developments that might take place at greater distance'.[8] In order to address these issues the Greater London Regional Planning Committee (GLRPC) appointed a technical adviser

(Sir Raymond Unwin) to explore and report on an appropriate strategy. He was not to suggest a full-blooded use of the garden-city powers recently established by the 1919 Act. (These powers were, in fact, never used: the housing objective, which had been the basis of government support from the garden-city provisions in the 1919 legislation, was to be promoted by other means.) Unwin focused on the interests of the inhabitants of the metropolis and the deficiency of open space and recreational areas.

3.4 Recreation and the Green Belt

The challenge set by Chamberlain used the language of garden/satellite cities. This was, because of the unique challenge posed by London, to lead to a view of Green Belt that was somewhat removed from the approach by Howard. Yet there are some notable similarities between Howard's utopian position and the pragmatic solution that was to develop under Unwin's guidance. Howard was keen to ensure that the urban populace was given effective access to the benefits of the rural environment – an aspect of the 'marriage' between the rural and urban community. One aspect of this was the provision of access to recreational areas. This is a theme that had a wider constituency than merely that of the planning fraternity: in fact a concern for 'healthy' entertainment etc. had been a concern of Victorian social reformers since the time of Chadwick and the first public-health legislation. Providing space for playing fields etc. near to the urban population of London was therefore something which naturally fitted in with a general concern for controlling urban sprawl. It is not surprising then that this 'recreational' aspect of Green Belt policy gained an important place in the work of Unwin. No doubt his focus on this lay behind the expression, in 1935, of the 'recreational' purpose underlying the strategy he proposed. This was a strategy that still kept close to the Howardian vision: the Parks and Town Planning committees set out the objectives of the strategy in these terms: 'to provide a reserve supply of public open spaces and of recreational areas and to establish a Green Belt or girdle of open space lands, not necessarily continuous, but as readily accessible from the completely urbanised area of London as practicable'.[9] Such was the basis for meeting the challenge set by Chamberlain. The quoted excerpt also shows a close link in another important respect with Howardian conceptions of the Green Belt. Collective/public ownership is a key

---

[8] Quoted in Department of the Environment, *The Green Belts* (London: HMSO, 1988), 10.
[9] Ibid.

feature: yet, there are some differences. The private-sector philanthropy that was a key element of Howard's whole approach has been replaced by an avowedly public-sector-dominated response (unsurprisingly, perhaps, given the genesis of the proposal and taking into account the 1919 Act's approach to the use of compulsory purchase powers for acquiring land for the garden city). This conception also clearly differs from that of Howard in terms of the 'discontinuity' element. The GLRPC's version of the Green Belt does not envisage a continuous zone in which agricultural production will be protected and space denied to urbanizing development. There was no commitment to keeping urban areas separated by a continuous zone of rural land. Thus the 'separation' function (an element in Howard's conception, as it was essential to preserve accessibility) appears to have been lost. Ensuring easy and affordable access to the amenities of the (social) city has also, as with the earlier statement, been left out of the equation. So of the elements that can be used to define (for the purposes of this discussion) Howard's conception, we are only clearly able to identify in the GLRPC model the key issue of collective ownership – and this has become 'nationalized' ownership (rather than ownership by the collective entity comprising individuals living in the area concerned). The influence of Herbert Morrison may have been relevant here: the Labour Party gained control of the LCC (London County Council) in 1934. (Initially land was acquired under existing powers and in concert with the relevant local authorities to whom the LCC made grants available. The complexity of this and a concern that permanent preservation might be difficult to guarantee led to the LCC introducing a Bill to safeguard the acquired land and put the process on a firmer statutory footing.)[10]

3.5 Green Belt (London and Home Counties) Act 1938

The fruits of LCC's efforts comprised the Green Belt (London and Home Counties) Act 1938 ('the 1938 Act'). The long title to the 1938 Acts reads as follows: 'An Act to make provision for the preservation from industrial or building development of areas of land in and around the administrative county of London . . .' This suggests that

[10] David Thomas, *London's Green Belt* (London: Faber and Faber, 1970) provides a full account of the genesis of London's Green Belt – noting the ideas put forward to the Parks and Open Spaces Committee of the LCC by Lord Meath (1890) and William Bull (1901) for open spaces etc. around London; George Pepler proposed a 'parkway' round London in 1911; in 1924 the LCC resolved to ask its Town Planning Committee to consider 'whether or not the preservation of a green belt . . . is desirable'. Thomas suggests that this was the first recorded use of the term 'Green Belt' in the London context. Lord Meath was the first chairman of the Metropolitan Public Gardens Association – which was responsible for the open-spaces legislation.

being a favourite target of people such as Abercrombie and others in the late 1920s and 1930s) thus bore fruit with an emphasis on protecting rural amenity. The Howardian emphasis on agricultural productivity could also be said to have resurfaced – though perhaps this was more of a reaction to the crisis in general capacity than a concern for keeping agriculturally productive areas close to urban populations. So it is not surprising that the Scott Committee strongly recommended that agricultural land should not be turned over to urban uses unless there was a demonstrated case based on national interest for so doing.[13] The committee also emphasized the importance of allowing the planning system to operate to the fullest extent possible by ensuring that 'all considerations affecting land use be taken into account in land planning'. (Here we can glimpse the language of 'all material considerations' as found in the development-control provisions of the planning legislation of today.)

But did the Scott report reflect Howard's emphasis on collective ownership of the agricultural belt? It did not. Scott laid the basis for a privately owned but subsidized farming system that only now is being questioned. Public ownership of Green Belt land and securing access to it for recreational/amenity purposes were not among the recommendations made by Scott. Scott was much nearer the position sought by that relatively new pressure group, the Council for the Preservation of Rural England – whose chairman, Abercrombie, was to be very influential in the development of early Green Belt policy. Thus Scott did not threaten the CPRE's power base (rural landed interests were a significant element) when it emphasized that the farmer would continue to control land in the Green Belt as he was 'the normal custodian of the land'.[14] Scott thus implied that the farmer was already acting in the wider interest and so could be trusted to act in accordance with public policy aims. In another passage in the text of para.202 reference is also made to the 'forester' and the farmer acting as the 'custodians and managers of green belts'. Green Belts are thus seen by Scott as compromising good farmland which

> may be used for the supply of fresh market garden produce to the towns or, in other cases, of securing the reservation of woodland which can be both scenically attractive and economically productive – in other words the farmer and forester can well act as the custodians and managers of green belts.

This was not in line with Howard's thinking: landowners could only

[13] Ibid., paras.232–3.
[14] Ibid., footnote to para.202.

take leasehold interests in land in the green belt – the community was to own the freehold and so be capable of ensuring that the community reaped the economic and other benefits that were due to the community. The distortion of Howardian concepts (by others) was, in fact, an issue noted by the Scott report. The footnote to para.202 also noted that although the term Green Belt

> is of comparatively recent introduction it seized the public imagination and has become not only widely used but still more widely misused. It is a townsman's expression which embodies a townsman's point of view and has come, unfortunately, to mean a belt of open land – of commons, woods and fields – to be 'preserved' from building . . .

This footnote concludes with the terse definition – 'in essence the green belt is just a tract of countryside'. The following paragraph (203) then discusses 'Garden Cities and Satellite Town' – noting the 'erroneous views' frequently held about the aims of the garden-city movement. However, the Scott characterization of Green Belt 'as just a tract of countryside' could, from the Howardian perspective, be said to be another 'erroneous view'. It omits the important element of public ownership as a means of securing amenity and other benefits for the urban populace. Scott was thus, in one sense, to help the 'townsman' (whose perspective the report criticized) gain a slice of the Green Belt. The Green Belt was left in the hands of 'forester and farmer' – but the suburban property owner could buy an adjacent site (when buying his residential property) and enjoy the amenities so provided. The 'townsman's' view of Green Belt criticized by Scott was thus to be the basis of popular support for a Green Belt regime that benefited one element of the community – by increasing domestic property values and allowing such owners privileged access to its amenities.

The nearest that we come to the Howardian notion of collective ownership is to be found in one of the other significant reports of the time – the Uthwatt report.[15] Paras.348 and 349 set out an approach which has some resonance with the Howardian thinking on land ownership – another response to the long-standing 'land question':

> 348. The proposal submitted to us for the unification of the reversion of land is as follows:

> That all land in Great Britain be forthwith converted into leasehold interests held by the present proprietors as lessees of the State at a peppercorn rent for such a uniform term of years as may reasonably, without payment of

[15] *The Final Report of the Expert Committee on Compensation and Betterment*, Cmd. 6386 (London: HMSO, 1942): see generally paras.348–51.

compensation, be regarded as equitable, and subject to such conditions enforceable by re-entry as may from time to time be applicable under planning schemes.

349. The immediate result of the adoption of the scheme would be that the State as landlord would enforce town planning restrictions in the same way as is common under the long leasehold system in England and Wales. If the covenant is broken, the State should be given a power of re-entry. But that power of re-entry, just as in the case of a private landlord, would be subject to the jurisdiction of the Court to give relief. The practice of the Court in freely giving relief is settled and well known.

This method of securing compliance with town planning restrictions would have the effect of impressing upon landowners that landholding involves duties as well as rights.

Uthwatt would have perhaps been less impressed by the farmer's claim to be the 'custodian' of his land. Uthwatt has much stronger links with the Howardian approach: private owners should only have leasehold interests – allowing the freeholder (in Howard's conception, a private charitable trust) to maintain broad control for the good of the community. The collective entity was the better custodian of land – to use some of the language of Scott but the approach of Howard/Uthwatt. Under the Uthwatt proposal this 'new' form of ownership was to apply to all land – not just that meant for new development. It was not implemented – though the fact that it was put forward is testimony perhaps to the continuing pull exerted by Howard (and others before him such as Henry George who had argued for substantial land reform/redistribution).

4.2 Reith and Barlow

The 'social city' conception of Howard had its most enduring impact in post-war Britain with the birth of the New Towns. The Reith Committee on New Towns (in its three reports) looked in detail at the creation of a large-scale New Towns programme.[16] This had a remit beyond that of dealing with the problems caused by London's proliferation. New Towns were proposed in all regions of the UK (though most of the early designations were in the south-east) – as mechanisms for promoting a better form of urban growth and development. This supplemented the work of the Barlow Commission, which focused on congestion in the established urban areas and proposed redevelopment of existing urban areas and decentralization and dispersal of industry

[16] *Report of the Royal Commission on the Distribution of the Industrial Population*, Cmd. 6513 (London: HMSO, 1940).

and population away from them.[17] However, as far as the Howardian
agricultural belt or the modern Green Belt are concerned New Towns
may have been new urban settlements – but they were not to be the new
integrative communities as envisaged by Howard. Their actual growth
generally meant that little restraint by way of a Green Belt was needed.
For activity on the Green Belt front we need to return to London, its
rural hinterland and the proposals of Abercrombie.

5 Abercrombie's Green Belt Conception

The Green Belt concept of Abercrombie was somewhat eclectic. His
proposals for a 'family' of Green Belts for London envisaged a tripartite approach.[18] They also indicated a further distancing from the
Howardian notion that was based on public ownership and the protection of the agricultural estate for both recreational and production
purposes: the CPRE's particular slant on preservation was no doubt
pertinent here. Abercrombie's proposals included a large area of Green
Belt that was formed not by a narrow green girdle but by a ten-mile
wide Metropolitan Green Belt. This separated the metropolis from its
rural hinterland. The depth of the Metropolitan Green Belt as envisaged
by Abercrombie could perhaps be justified as a special form of
Howardian Green Belt in that the difference in width (ten miles instead
of two) reflected the need to protect a larger area of agricultural land in
the belt. Such an area of land was exceptionally required for London
because it was clearly not of the social-city scale. (Whether the width
chosen by Abercrombie was so determined is not something which this
writer has established – but it could be an argument supporting the case
for Abercrombie, at least as regards this member of his Green Belt
family, being close to the Howardian notion of Green Belt.) The
second member of Abercrombie's Green Belt family comprised a
number of local Green Belts around established (and new) urban areas.
This is arguably more in keeping with the Howard conception, as the
new urban areas so enclosed by such belts would appear to have some
links with the social-city concept. Abercrombie, however, favoured the
Scott report approach and did not suggest public ownership and securing access to such areas for recreational/amenity purposes. On this
point he differs fundamentally from Howard and the Unwin approach.
   The third element in this loose family of Green Belts comprised a
Green Belt designation for 'scenic areas': this is where the 'family'
certainly becomes a rather extended one – perhaps as a result of his
concern for preservation of rural amenities from sprawl. Features such

[17] The final report was produced in 1946 – Cmd. 6794.
[18] See his *Greater London Plan: 1944* (London: HMSO, 1945).

as the Chilterns and North Downs were covered by this type of Green Belt. The purpose of this designation was to protect the amenity of the (rural) area so designated. Development was to be restricted to the foothills and immediate surroundings of such areas.[19] This type of preservation had already been promoted in the hinterland of other cities. It was not something which Abercrombie invented for the purposes of improving the London environment – it was a response to a common issue confronting many who were similarly concerned about sprawl. An example is to be found in the use of powers under the 1932 Act to restrict the use of rural areas of scenic value around Cambridge. The mechanism used was the 'planning agreement'. According to the *Cambridgeshire Regional Planning Report* (prepared for the Cambridgeshire Joint Town Planning Committee), the powers under the 1932 Act had been used to achieve some of the aims for the 'proposed open belt around Cambridge' – as the heading in chapter V – 'Open Spaces – National – Regional – Local' puts it.[20] In order to 'preserve any of the natural beauty of the background of the town a chain of reservations is proposed which would, in effect, keep a generally open belt of country encircling Cambridge'.[21] The report thus noted that the Grantchester area

> has been sterilised by covenant under the Town and Country Planning Act, 1932, between the owners, King's College, Cambridge, and Merton College, Oxford, and the Borough Council. This is one of the first agreements in the country to be entered into under section 34 of the Act. The Cambridge Preservation Society through a further gift of £10,000 from the Pilgrim Trust, was able to secure completion of this agreement.[22]

Page 84 of the report refers to the Cam Valley and talks of 'open belt' and 'recreational belt' areas. The protection of 'scenic' value attaching to rural areas around cities was thus seen as an important element in activities of charitable trusts and public authorities in various parts of England.[23]

Protecting 'scenic' values was thus a popular use of interventionist powers among property owners and those able to visit such beauty

[19] Martin Elson, *Green Belts* (London: Heinemann, 1986), 8.

[20] W. R. Davidge, *Cambridgeshire Regional Planning Report* (Cambridge: Cambridge University Press, 1934), 81. Thomas (above n.10, p.51) cites Davidge's regional plan for Hertfordshire as one which designated proposed open spaces – including a 'Middlesex boundary green belt'.

[21] Ibid.

[22] Ibid.

[23] See Ministry of Housing and Local Government, *The Green Belts* (London: HMSO, 1962), 4 and Elson (n.19).

spots. It was one way of garnering support for both Green Belt and planning in general. Even if that support was bought at the expense of Howard's vision of integrative communities where rural and urban elements would be mutually supporting, it was probably a price worth paying. The integrative vision may have been much too radical for Abercrombie and his various allies – as well as those cities etc. for whom he produced many of his plans in the years surrounding the Second World War. Abercrombie was being pragmatic. He helped to promote a practical model of Green Belt – a model that was later to be reflected in the post-war regime that is largely identifiable to this day. However, that support was bought at a cost – and not merely the loss of Howardian themes (an issue addressed below).

The 'scenic' Green Belt as envisaged by Abercrombie for certain areas is perhaps best seen as coming to fruition (on a national scale) in the post-war regime introduced by the National Parks and Access to the Countryside Act 1948 ('the 1948 Act'). The areas of high scenic value described in Abercrombie's third form of Green Belt (the Chilterns and North Downs) were in fact designated under the 1948 Act as Areas of Outstanding Natural Beauty – a designation one step down from 'National Park' status which was also introduced into the planning regime by the 1948 legislation. The links between the Howardian Green Belt concept and National Parks is evident in the stress on 'access' found in the Dower report's definition of a National Park.[24] This definition has as its second element the notion that 'access and facilities for the public's open air enjoyment are amply provided'. Public ownership as a basis for an integrative community comprising both town and country was not, however, part of that vision.

In terms of national policy the Green Belt family proposed by Abercrombie was split up, and two siblings were adopted by the way of the 1948 legislation. The support for that family was, however, strong enough to sustain the national Green Belt policy initiative of 1955 – given expression in Circular 42/55.[25] The protection of 'scenic' values became a selling-point for the Green Belt concept. Another solid vote-winner was the ability of the Green Belt to constrain urban growth and so protect the countryside. Accessibility to Green Belt was forgotten. This effectively meant that the mass of the urban population was ignored as Green Belt policy took off. The real winners were those who could afford accessibility – either by reason of home ownership on the urban fringe or by reason of private transport. So Abercrombie's approach was in fact to favour a much narrower community than that

[24] *National Parks in England and Wales*, Cmd. 6628 (London: HMSO, 1945).
[25] Ministry of Housing and Local Government, *Green Belts* (London: HMSO, 1955).

envisioned by Howard or even Unwin. Instead of a system informed by
an integrative vision that would seek to promote both rural and urban
interests, we have produced one that, fundamentally, is weighted
towards suburban and urban fringe communities – and those within
such communities who have the economic power to make most effective use of the Green Belt's amenity.

6 The Post-War Green Belt

Legislation, in one form or another, thus (imperfectly) reflected some
important themes of the social-city idea: however, legislation was not
favoured as the means of attempting to implement the Green Belt
concept that was so enthusiastically promoted by those who developed
Howard's ideas in the inter-war era and after. This anomaly is, at first
sight, puzzling. We have legislation for the metropolitan area that
seemingly could have been adopted on a national basis. It was, in
conception, quite close to the Howard ideas of maintaining an agricultural 'estate' for urban areas and promoting access to such open land
for the benefit of the urban populace. In a new post-war context where
the agricultural industry was subsidized the cost implications, however,
would have been very significant. Another factor may have been the
more practical political problems that would face such a strategy of
nationalization. The new deal for the farming community promised
them subsidies and support: to threaten compulsory purchase would
have not been an acceptable strategy. Instead the 'amenity'-protection
rationale could be achieved in tandem with the support for farming.
This rationale could be furthered by policy, as it was now possible to
institute (with little threat of compensation being payable) the broad
Green Belt concept of Abercrombie's regime by using the wide planning powers granted to the Minister in the 1947 legislation. When
compensation rights were limited by the Conservative government the
financial disadvantages of using the planning system were effectively
removed. Planning, by way of development-plan designation, could
thus implement a national Green Belt policy. The circular offered the
obvious route for starting the process. It was a method long used by
central government: Ministry of Health circulars were common in the
1920s as a means of informing local authorities about the basic operation of the planning regime as it evolved in the inter-war era. Circular
42/55 was to be the answer. The circular's advice was gradually
utilized by local authorities (under central-government supervision)
using zoning controls under the development-plan system. Circular
42/55 was soon supplemented by further advice (Circular 50/57) on
Green Belt boundaries and the publication by the Ministry of an
explanatory booklet on the Green Belt. There was no special legislation

such as that which created the regimes for National Parks, listed buildings, conservation areas or other conservation policies – all with,
arguably, less draconian restrictions than those of the Green Belt
regime. Green Belt on a national scale thus started life on the basis of
ministerial fiat – with no discussion in detail by Parliament.

The details of that policy changed over time according to the political
pressures of the day. In 1955 the first circular on Green Belt focused
on growth management of the larger urban areas. The three reasons set
out to justify the establishment of the Green Belt were (a) to check the
growth of a large built-up area; (b) to prevent neighbouring towns from
verging into one another; and (c) to preserve the special character of a
town. The first two can clearly be seen as 'growth management' objectives. Since then we have had piecemeal expansion – with the current
policy in PPG 2 containing an incoherent mixture of 'purposes' (setting
out the basis for putting land in Green Belt) – five are listed and range
from growth management to urban regeneration and protection of the
built heritage. Para.2.1 then states the 'essential characteristic' of
Green Belts – their permanence. However, inappropriate development
can be permitted in 'very special circumstances' – which now merely
seems to require a demonstration that 'the harm by reason of inappropriateness, and any other harm, is clearly outweighed by other
considerations' (para.3.2). In terms of supplying a concise and logical
statement of the purposes of the regime, such language is not terribly
clear. (The revised policy has removed some of the problem language
that previously generated litigation, but the evident difficulty in accommodating a wide range of interests in order to maintain the veneer of
support for Green Belt is still marked.) In trying to accommodate a
wide range of interests the policy-makers may have seemingly created
problems well into the future. However, given the degree of flexibility
afforded by the 'very special circumstances' test, local authorities, and
particularly the Secretary of State, continue to enjoy very real discretion in deciding individual cases. A good example is to be found in an
appeal decision where this term (as with many such appeals) was the
crucial criterion. The appellants proposed a new medical research facility on land which already had existing research buildings on it. The
Secretary of State said that he considered that

> the advanced scientific nature of the work undertaken and the contribution
> to the health of peoples all over the world which may be expected to be
> derived from it are sufficient to justify an exception, on the basis of 'very
> special circumstance', being made to the presumption there is against devel-
> opment in the Green Belt.[26]

[26] Appeal reference – T/APP/W1525/A/87/074543, see the edited version in
[1989] *Journal of Planning and Environmental Law* 57.

Such a concern for community-welfare issues of a global nature is commendable – although somewhat unusual in the context of a planning decision. I am not aware of a refusal to grant permission on appeal because of the harm that might be done to the health of others in other countries. The fact that the company at issue was shortly to be privatized was, of course, irrelevant.

Such a capacity for capricious decisions is a direct consequence of the policy. (The possibility of creating a legal regime for designation and development control in the manner of listed buildings and conservation areas is clearly an issue – but one which is outside the scope of this paper.) The benefits of having a Green Belt policy have been sold to a range of interests – with each seeing in the regimes the objectives that each wants to emphasize. However, this can often mean that decisions have no consistent basis to them. There is no real sustenance given to transparency and accountability. This is partly due to the weak rationale explaining the role of planning – the 'public interest' rationale. Development on the urban fringe that involves the once-and-for-all transition from rural to urban uses involves a range of issues that should be fully discussed in an open manner. All the communities affected should have their interests properly examined – and that is much more likely to arise where the underlying rationale demands a transparent and accountable process for describing how those different communities are affected. This is quite different from a 'public interest' rationale that supports decision-makers without really making them accountable. Perhaps a legal regime for Green Belt should be instituted – setting out for all to see the key factors and legislative weight (if any) to be given to its protection. What may also be needed is a better rationale for planning – one that avoids the overgeneralizations of 'public interest' and opts for a richer and yet more demanding standard – 'community rights'. Such a rationale also has its (forgotten) roots in the inter-war era – when the Howardian vision of garden cities and Green Belt was still discernible in law and policy.

7 Community Rights and Green Belt Decision-Making

If we return to the inter-war era and the years when Howard's integrative vision could still be glimpsed (in Letchworth and Welwyn for example), we find case law that parallels Howard's focus on the community. The case in question arose out of a proposed planning scheme (under the 1909 Act). That scheme (one of the first in the country) was addressing new suburbanizing development on the outskirts of London (in Ruislip). One landowner objected to various elements in the planning scheme.[27] In examining the legislation from a

[27] *Re Ellis and the Ruislip-Northwood Urban Council* [1920] 1 KB 343.

broad perspective, Scrutton LJ had this to say of the implications of the
new regime for the property owner (at p.372): 'I can quite understand
that Parliament may have taken a view that a landowner in a community
has duties as well as rights, and cannot claim compensation for refrain-
ing from using his land where they think that it is his duty so to refrain.'
His pithy comment that the landowner now owes duties to the community as a result of this legislation could be said to encapsulate the key
feature in the Howard vision of the social city (and, of course, the agri-
cultural/Green Belt). (It also provides a pre-echo of the Uthwatt
language quoted above.) All landowners in the social city (including the
agricultural/Green Belt) were subject to the limitations imposed under
their leases: the collective entity, their landlord, controlled their use and
occupation for the good of the community. Under the 1909 Act the
landowner was subject to limitations by virtue of the planning scheme
(rather than the lease). These limitations, expressed by Scrutton LJ as
the duties owed to the community by the landowner, were to prevent
the urban ills of Victorian speculative development – from both the
'sanitation' and 'amenity' perspectives. We can view these 'landowner
duties' as giving rise to 'community rights' – Lord Justice Scrutton is of
the view that those duties were owed to the community. So Lord Justice
Scrutton could be taken as saying that planning was the process by
which the local authority defined and enforced those 'community
rights'. This link between the early planning case law and the roots of
the planning legislation thus emphasizes the central role of concepts
such as 'community', 'rights' and 'duties'. However, just as Howardian
conceptions of the Green Belt were largely jettisoned after the Second
World War so too was the 'community rights' approach displaced by a
'public interest' rationale for planning. The transition was not immediate. Elements of the 'community rights' approach can be seen in
Buxton.[28] Here the role of the public authority as 'guardian' of the
public's interests is noted. This suggests that the 1909 Act (and later
planning legislation) also imposed a duty of guardianship (we might
prefer the equivalent term of 'trusteeship') on public bodies. So putting
flesh on 'community rights' would also involve ensuring that public
bodies acted fairly and openly – meeting a public-law equivalent of
'utmost good faith'. This (procedural) duty to the community would
most commonly involve giving clear answers to two important issues –
'which community' and 'whose rights'? Within the context of a rights-
based dialogue (established by a 'community rights' rationale) the
decision-maker must therefore meet standards of transparency and
accountability in carrying out his duties. So 'community rights' means

[28] *Buxton* v. *Minister of Housing* [1960] 3 All ER 408 at 411.

that the decision-maker has to focus on and give expression to the assessment as to the various 'communities' and their 'rights' which are relevant to the decision in question.

The *Re Ellis* approach – as applied particularly to Green Belt decisions – would mean a much more demanding standard of decision-making than that required by the vaguer 'public interest' rationale. If the context for decision-making is based on the 'public interest' perspective then this all too easily leads to a self-justifying basis for the decision. The courts, once they have accepted the broad discretionary powers granted to public bodies under the planning system, have then little incentive to go further and impose more active duties on the decision-maker. If a decision-maker asserts that he is the best judge of the 'public interest' then the court is unlikely to intervene. However, if 'community rights' is the starting-point the courts are more likely to require greater transparency in the decision-making process. Without answers to questions such as 'what rights?' and 'which communities?', how can we be sure that the decision-maker has properly performed his duties? With Green Belt this means focusing on the rural and urban communities whose interests are clearly at stake where urbanizing developing in the Green Belt is being proposed. It forces the decision-maker to be open about the conflicts – economic development as opposed to amenity preservation. With this approach the decision-maker cannot so easily avoid his political obligations (for example, to express his views on such vital preliminary issues).

With 'public interest' language such issues hardly ever surface. 'Public interest' maintains a veil of unknowing over such factors. It may be a rationale that once had some utility in justifying the planning system in general – but it is not a rationale that easily generates demanding operational principles for decision-making. It may warn decision-makers against the temptation (especially prevalent at local level) of supporting local economic interests: this is largely the focus of the 'public interest' discussion in policy guidance.[29] But in terms of producing a positive set of principles to implement planning in its fullest sense (as expressed by Howard and *Re Ellis*) the 'public interest' principle is woefully deficient. As Uthwatt suggested (in an echo of *Re Ellis*) it was important that landowners appreciate their position in the new world of planning control. For Uthwatt the 'Crown reversionary interest' approach would have had the effect of 'impressing upon landowners that landholding involves duties as well as rights'. This is very much in line with the approach suggested by *Re Ellis*. However,

---

[29] See Department of Environment, *Planning Policy Guidance Note 1: General Policy and Principles* (London: HMSO), para.64.

history shows that this support for the Howardian vision of planning
for the community was not to survive that long. The much less rigorous
'public interest' rationale was to take hold. Green Belt policy was also
to abandon its links with Howardian principles and thus was to become
a tool of sectional interests. (A fuller discussion of the 'community
rights' rationale and its eclipsing by 'public interest' is provided in a
chapter of a textbook on Land Law.[30])

8 Conclusions

The early story of the Green Belt illustrates how Howard's vision for
the rural and urban community was partly reflected in legal mechanisms and case-law comments – only to be lost to the vicissitudes of
political expediency. The communities which Howard sought to integrate remained polarized – a feature accentuated by a Green Belt
mechanism that had originally been a key element of Howard's integrative strategy. The inter-war period reflected some positive moves in
terms of the London Green Belt legislation and the expression of a
nascent 'community rights' rationale. Yet before this period ended the
seeds of a less radical, less integrative and less open system were
sown. Abercrombie's efforts to broaden support for Green Belt led to a
less coherent conception of Green Belt and also foreshadowed a form
of Green Belt (and planning system) that was not so threatening to
landed interests. It was also a system that could be moulded to suit the
political ends of those in power at the time and cloaked decision-
making with a patina of propriety. Policy ambivalence rather than
legislative principle was the framework for Green Belt decision-making
after the Second World War. The benefits of the policy would largely
be retained by those able to afford the price commanded by those edge-
of-urban locations where Green Belt served to protect their amenity.
The urban fringe would be a battleground of competing interests –
rather than an economic and recreational asset that could be of mutual
benefit to both rural and urban communities. Green Belt became no
more than a political slogan and marketing catchphrase serving short-
term political ambitions and economic ends. Howard's social city and
agricultural belt had passed into oblivion – they were too radical for
politicians, landowners and the populace. The result was that urban and
rural communities continued to be treated as separate communities.
Howard's integrative model might even be said to have foundered on
the exclusive barrier of post-war Green Belt. Planning was also to

[30] Denzil Millichap, 'Real property and its regulation: the community rights rationale for town planning', in Susan Bright and John Dewar (eds.), *Land Law: Themes and
Perspectives* (Oxford: Oxford University Press, 1998).

abandon its development of a 'community rights' rationale as the transition from the inter-war system to the post-war regime was completed. 'Public interest' served to justify and mask decisions made with little regard to transparency and the effects on different communities (urban and rural). Planning had completed its transition from vision to reality.

2

The Legal Status of the Green Belt Policies and the Role of the Courts in their Construction and Application

MICHAEL PURDUE

1 Introduction

Despite the longevity and importance of the concept of the Green Belt (it can be traced back to the proposal made by the Greater London Regional Planning Committee in 1935 and has arguably had the most impact on post-Second World War town and country planning of any policy), it is important to remember that it only has the status in law of a policy. It depends for its implementation completely on the develop-ment-control system. It is the power of local planning authorities to refuse development, which is inappropriate to the Green Belt, which makes the policy stick. Of course, it can be pointed out that legal tools or powers are in themselves useless without policies to drive and direct their use: the two interconnect. Yet, it is crucial in legal terms to remember the status of the Green Belt as a policy, or more correctly as a package of policies. One immediate issue is the relationship between the policy on the Green Belt and the even older policy that there should be a presumption in favour of granting planning permission. This leads to the difficulty of locating what Lord Donaldson has described as the 'onus of persuasion'[1] or what can be termed the battle of presumptions.

The policies on a particular stretch of Green Belt are not to be found in one authoritative document and this has been the cause of some

---

[1] See *Pehrsson* v. *Secretary of State for the Environment* (1991) 61 P & C R 266 at p.267.

problems. The three main sources are Planning Policy Guidance Notes, Regional and Strategic Planning Guidance, and the development plans. Planning Policy Guidance Note 2 on Green Belts (PPG 2), the present version of which was issued in 1995, sets out the government's policy on the Green Belts and itself explains that regional and strategic planning guidance set the framework for Green Belt policy, while the Green Belts themselves are established through the development plans.[2] This statement suggests that there is a clear hierarchy of policies, which should ensure that the detailed boundaries of the Green Belts found in the local plans conform with the structure plans, which in turn conform with the regional policies and so on. This hierarchy however is complicated by the fact that it is only the development-plan policies which have an express statutory status under s.70 of the Town and Country Planning Act 1990. Until the advent of s.54A, this was not really a problem as s.70, as well as requiring regard to be had to the policies in the development plan (where relevant), also required regard to be had to any material considerations, and the courts have for some time held that government policies, at least when set out formally in published documents, are material considerations. S.54A, by giving a presumption to the policies in the development plan, produces the situation where, if there is a conflict between the development plan and government policies, the development plan is at least the first consideration.[3] Further complications arise when the development control decision is being taken at a time when both government policies and the development plans on the Green Belts are being revised, as again it has for a long time been settled law that both draft PPGs and draft development plans are capable of being material considerations.

Following from the difficulty of ascertaining what are the relevant sources of Green Belt policy and how they interrelate as a matter of law, there is the fundamental issue of determining the meaning of the policies and which body (the planning authorities or the courts) is to be the final determinator of that meaning. This issue in constitutional terms relates to the separation of powers between the executive and the judiciary and is central to the scope of judicial review of administrative action. It therefore has a significance beyond the Green Belt and planning law generally, though as Sedley J pointed out in *R.* v. *Teesside Development Corporation ex parte William Morrison Supermarket*

[2] See para.2.2 of PPG 2.

[3] The House of Lords decision in *City of Edinburgh Council* v. *Secretary of State for Scotland* [1997] 1 WLR 1447 has made clear that the development plan is not paramount and that it is still up to the decision-maker to decide whether there are material considerations of sufficient weight to justify not making the determination in accordance with the development plan.

PLC[4] planning law, perhaps because of the intensive litigation over its application, tends to develop its own jurisprudence of judicial review. Indeed, it is clear that the courts are willing, even keen, in certain areas of administration to give the decision-maker more autonomy and independence, than they are in other areas. The division of labour as well as the division of power will vary.

This chapter will now attempt to analyse these points in more detail and to address the consequences.

2 The Source and Status of Green Belt Policies and their Interrelationship

2.1 The position prior to the enactment of section 54A

As indicated above, most of case law on the Green Belt, not surprisingly, has turned on whether a particular development was or was not an appropriate use in a Green Belt and, if it was not appropriate, whether there existed any very special circumstances to justify granting permission. The Court of Appeal in the case of *Pehrsson* v. *Secretary of State for the Environment and the Royal Borough of Windsor and Maidenhead*[5] laid down the following rules as to what was the correct approach; what can be termed the *Pehrsson* approach. All three of their lordships agreed that there were two distinct stages. First it had to be decided if the development was appropriate according to the policies for the Green Belt. This first judgment then determined how the second stage should proceed. Stuart-Smith LJ put the approach most succinctly when he stated:

> The first consideration is whether the development is appropriate for the Green Belt. If the answer is yes, then the general presumption applies in favour of the development, unless there is demonstrable harm to interests of acknowledged importance, other than the preservation of the Green Belt itself. If the answer is that the development is inappropriate then the second stage is to consider whether there are very special circumstances which justify the particular application. In my judgment the reason for this is that the preservation of the Green Belt is an interest of acknowledged importance and if the development is inappropriate it is harmful to that interest. (p.272)

Or, to adopt Lord Donaldson's approach, the onus of persuasion varies, depending on whether the development is deemed appropriate or inappropriate. If it is appropriate, the policy that there is a presumption in

---

[4] [1998] JPL 23.
[5] (1991) 61 P & C R 266.

favour of granting permission operates, so that the planning authority must be persuaded that the development will nevertheless damage an interest of acknowledged importance. If it is not appropriate, the presumption is the other way round and the onus is on the developer to point to the very special reasons why the permission should be granted.

At the stage of deciding whether a development is appropriate, the local planning authority will obviously have to examine and apply both government policies and their own development plan. If there should be a conflict between the development plan and government policies, the courts, at the time of the *Pehrsson* decision, seem to have accepted that the Secretary of State as a matter of policy is entitled to give more weight to his own policies. *Pehrrson* was decided just before the important change of policy that development control should be plan-led rather than appeal-led. Lord Donaldson in this regard referred in his judgment to the statement in Circular 14/85 that the development plan was only one of the considerations which had to be taken into account in dealing with planning applications. That circular then went on to state that the development plan should not be taken to override material considerations. In doing this, Circular 14/85 echoed the statement in Circular 16/84 that permission should not be refused just because the development was contrary to the development plan. So Lord Donaldson would appear to be accepting that there was nothing legally improper in giving priority to government policies. The flexibility of the pre-s.54A position was summed up well by May LJ in *ELS Wholesale (Wolverhampton) Ltd* v. *Secretary of State for the Environment*[6] when, having set out various government policies (including the statement that the permission should not be refused just because of the development plan), he stated:

> In one sense the indications given in the circulars did no more than repeat what was set out in various sections of the 1971 Act: that in deciding whether or not to grant planning permission the planning authority or the Secretary of State should have regard to the terms of any development plan, and to any other material considerations. The circulars indicated from time to time the approach to be adopted in general terms to applications, and also indicated what might from time to time be the more important or the less important 'material considerations'. (p.77)

More important at this first stage is the extent to which the decision-maker must give reasons why the development is considered to be or not to be appropriate. Here, at first appraisal, there would seem to be two conflicting Court of Appeal decisions. In *Pehrsson* the inspector

[6] (1988) 56 P & C R 69.

had held that the change of use of a disused cricket pavilion in the grounds of a large residence to a residential use by employees of that residence, did not come within the general category of uses appropriate to a Green Belt. The majority (Lord Donaldson and Stuart-Smith LJ) held that the inspector had failed to give adequate reasons why she had come to this decision. Staughton LJ in contrast stated that whether or not a development was appropriate was a question of fact and planning judgement with which the courts should not interfere. Lord Donaldson laid down the principle as follows:

> *The giving of reasons*
> The decision-maker should give reasons sufficient to show what was the chain of reasoning. As applied to Green Belt applications, this had to involve saying why the proposed development was or was not appropriate to the Green Belt. (p.268)

Yet in a later Court of Appeal decision, in *Stewart* v. *Secretary of State and Vale Royal District Council*,[7] Purchas LJ in a judgment (with which the rest of the bench agreed) held that the Secretary of State, in disagreeing with his inspector that it was important to preserve an existing open space between the new and older parts of a village in the Green Belt, did not have to give more specific reasons. As Purchas LJ expressly adopted Lord Donaldson's statement in *Pehrsson* concerning the need to give reasons, he cannot have been diverging from that need. The decision, however, can be explained on the grounds that the Secretary of State had given reasons for the inappropriateness of the development; the destruction of the existing open space. Therefore what the court was holding was that there was no duty to go further than that and to spell out why he disagreed with the inspector on the need for the open space. So, it is submitted that it is not sufficient for the decision-maker simply to find that the application is inappropriate. She must at least explain in what way it is inappropriate to the Green Belt and also how it is damaging to the objectives of the Green Belt. In this sense there would appear to be no such thing as a completely technical breach of Green Belt policies. The result is that, although inappropriateness is deemed to be damage to interests of acknowledged importance (and so can defeat the presumption in favour of granting planning permission), to show inappropriateness you must explain how harm will be caused.

The need to show harm is taken further by Lord Donaldson in *Pehrsson* when he goes on to the next stage of deciding that, even though the development is not appropriate, there may be very special

---

[7] [1990] JPL 48.

circumstances for allowing the development. This is because he states that:

> If it was considered to be inappropriate to the Green Belt, the decision-taker had to go on to express a view on the weight of the damage which would be done to the Green Belt if permission were granted and the weight or lack of weight which he attached to the countervailing consideration based upon the alleged advantages which would stem from allowing the development to proceed. (p.268)

So a balance has to be struck between the extent of the harm to the Green Belt and the planning advantages which would flow from the development. Yet the phrase 'very special circumstances' would seem to indicate that the damage to the Green Belt would have to be very small and the advantages very great to merit that description. Indeed in a speech in 1989 to the London Green Belt Council the then Secretary of State for the Environment, Christopher Patten, said that by their nature special circumstances will be rare.[8] Yet in *Pehrsson* Lord Donaldson failed to emphasize the special weight to be given to the Green Belt when carrying out this balancing exercise, though he did accept that if there was a state of equilibrium the application should be refused.[9]

Later case law has, however, qualified Lord Donaldson's statement and emphasized the extent of the burden in finding 'very special circumstances'. First in *Vision Engineering Ltd* v. *Secretary of State for the Environment*[10] Roy Vandermeer QC sitting as a Deputy Judge, stated that if there were no benefits then the application had perforce to be refused. He then stated that if there were planning benefits, in carrying out the balancing exercise, the decision-maker had 'to ask himself whether the overall situation amounted to very special circumstances that justified setting aside the normal presumption against inappropriate development in the Green Belt' (p.953).

Further clarification was provided by Auld J in *Tesco Stores Ltd* v. *Secretary of State for the Environment and Hounslow London Borough Council*.[11] He pointed out that neither Stuart-Smith LJ nor Staughton LJ had adopted Lord Donaldson's approach of simply balancing harm and advantage. He then adopted the test that permission should only be granted if: 'those circumstances [the claimed planning advantages] so

---

[8] See Elson and Ford, 'Green Belts and very special circumstances' [1994] JPL 594 at p.595.
[9] At p.268.
[10] [1991] JPL 951.
[11] [1992] JPL 268.

outweighed the harm as, in his view, to amount to very special circumstances justifying the grant of permission' (p.270).

Auld J (as he then was) is therefore making clear that, in terms of weight, the inappropriateness of the development in the Green Belt is to be given a lot more weight than any other planning advantages. Of course, this does not directly conflict with Lord Donaldson's approach, in that at the end (to continue the metaphor of scales), you are still looking to see whether the scales tip in favour of the Green Belt policies or the countervailing planning advantages. The approach of Roy Vandermeer and Auld J, however, is less misleading as it emphasizes the strictness of the Green Belt policies. Auld J's approach in particular also suggests that, for there to be very special circumstances, the planning advantages clearly have to outweigh the damage to the Green Belt: it is not enough that they should just tip the scales in favour of granting permission.

Another consequence of the *Pehrsson* approach is that, at least where there are planning arguments in favour of the application,[12] the decision-maker will have to examine closely just what harm the development will do to the Green Belt policies. Thus in *Barnet Meeting Room Trust* v. *Secretary of State for the Environment and Barnet LBC*,[13] Auld J accepted that in calculating the amount of harm to the Green Belt policy it was proper to consider the extent to which the Green Belt objectives would be undermined by the proposed development. In that case the inspector had concluded that the development 'would not detract from the character and appearance of the area nor significantly affect the integrity of the Metropolitan Green Belt'. It was the failure of the Secretary of State adequately to explain if and why he disagreed with this finding that was one of the grounds for quashing the decision.

The danger of this approach is that it will encourage developers to rerun previous arguments as to whether the land contributes to the Green Belt. However, it can be pointed out that the same principle applies to the application of s.54A, as in *R.* v. *Canterbury City Council ex parte Springimage Ltd*[14] it was accepted that a development which was contrary to the wording of the development plan could, nevertheless, be granted on the grounds that it would cause no harm to the objectives of the policies in the plan.

---

[12] In *Scottish and Newcastle Breweries plc* v. *Secretary of State for the Environment* [1993] JPL 1055 Dillon LJ held that once the main planning argument (that the hotel could not be built outside the Green Belt) had been rejected there was no need to balance the small harm to the Green Belt against other planning arguments.

[13] [1993] JPL 739.

[14] [1994] JPL 427.

2.2 The effect of section 54A on the green belt policies

After some hesitancy it now seems established that the enactment of s.54A has affected the approach which planning authorities must take in deciding planning applications or appeals. The most accepted view would seem to be that there is a presumption in favour of the development plan in that the assumption is that the decision must be made according to the policies in the plan.[15] The presumption is therefore in favour of the plan itself and not for or against granting planning permission. In this regard it is interesting to note that whilst Roy Vandermeer QC sitting as a Deputy Judge has argued that the section should not be taken as providing a presumption in favour of refusing application not in conformity with the plan,[16] Sedley J has taken a diametrically opposite point of view. In a footnote to the *Teesside Development Corporation* decision,[17] he stated:

> Although not material to this case I record my doubts about the statement in the Department's guidance note PPG1, para 25 . . . that section 54A in effect 'introduces a presumption in favour of development proposals which are in accordance with the development plan'. The presumption introduced by section 54A seems to me to be a presumption in favour of the development plan itself, and so against non-conforming applications in general but not in favour of any particular proposal which happens to conform with it. (p.26)

My own view is that while Sedley J is correct to lay emphasis on the presumption being in favour of the development plan itself,[18] the consequence of this as to the particular planning application will depend on the relevant policies in the plan. These policies may be in favour or against the development. As the decision in *Sisson Cox Homes* v. *Secretary of State for the Environment*[19] illustrates, it will

[15] For discussions about the effect of s.54A, see Purdue, 'The impact of section 54A' [1994] JPL 399 and Herbert-Young, 'Reflections on section 54A and "Plan-led" decision-making' [1995] JPL 292. The view that there is a presumption in favour of the development plan has been confirmed by the House of Lords decision in *City of Edinburgh Council* v. *Secretary of State for Scotland* [1997] 1 WLR 1447.

[16] See *Bylander Waddell* v. *Secretary of State for the Environment* [1994] JPL 440.

[17] Ibid.

[18] The present version of PPG1 has been changed so that it simply refers to applications and appeals being determined in accordance with the plan; see para. 40.

[19] [1997] JPL 670. This decision concerned a policy in the development plan that development for housing should normally be permitted except in certain specified cases. It was held that where a proposed development did not come within any of the exceptions, this created a presumption in favour of the development but that this presumption could be defeated by other exceptions apart from those listed, if those other exceptions were material considerations. Presumably if the development had come within one of the exceptions, it could have been argued that the presumption went the other way in favour of refusing permission.

always depend on the wording of the policies. If the development-plan policies are in favour of granting permission, s.54A will create a presumption in favour of granting permission.

In the context of the Green Belt policies, the main effect of s.54A has been to move the emphasis away from PPG 2. This result was first made clear in *Houghton* v. *Secretary of State for the Environment and Bromley LBC*[20] where Malcolm Spence QC sitting as a Deputy Judge accepted that the *Pehrsson* approach had been altered in that: 'it was no longer the first consideration whether the development was appropriate because section 54A provided that the determination shall be made in accordance with the development plan unless material considerations indicate otherwise' (p.399).

In this case the inspector had misconstrued the policies in PPG 2 by holding that the laying out of a private tennis court was not an appropriate form of development in the Green Belt. The Deputy Judge held that this error had not affected the outcome as the development was contrary to the policies in the development plan on conservation areas and woodlands. He laid down that:

> because section 54A required first that the determination shall be made in accordance with the development plan unless material considerations indicated otherwise there were and would continue to be cases including the present case, where the proper appraisal of the development plan and other material considerations resulted in the determination of the application without the necessity to decide whether the development was appropriate or inappropriate. (pp.399–400)

Then in *Tandridge District Council* v. *Secretary of State for the Environment*[21] Gerald Moriarty QC similarly held that *Pehrsson* had been overtaken by and had to be applied subject to the provisions of s.54A. *Tandridge* concerned a proposal by a church to build new residential premises for its staff in the grounds of their church. The church was therefore arguing that this development came within para.13 of PPG 2 in its 1988 version, which exempted new buildings for institutions in extensive grounds from the general presumption against inappropriate development. The policies in the development plan in force at the time of the decision apparently laid down a slightly different criterion, in that such developments were not acceptable in their own right but instead 'may be appropriate or necessary'. The Deputy Judge interpreted the policies in the plan as requiring a test of strict necessity or essentiality and quashed the decision of the inspector (who had allowed the appeal) on the grounds that the inspector had misdirected

[20] [1996] JPL 396.
[21] [1997] JPL 132.

himself by not applying such a test. The Court of Appeal set aside the
Deputy Judge's decision on the grounds that he had been wrong to
introduce a test of essentiality.[22] Leggatt LJ (with whose judgment
Potter and Judge LJJ agreed) did not go into the question of the effect of
s.54A on the relationship between PPG 2 and the development plan, but
he did not contradict what the Deputy Judge had said about *Pehrsson*
having been overtaken by s.54A. Further it would seem clear from
Leggatt LJ's judgment that while PPG 2 provided a material consideration, the starting-point was the policies in the development plan.

Unfortunately neither judicial decision explains in any detail just how
Pehrsson has been overtaken by s.54A and what is the position, when
there is a conflict between the development-plan policies and government policies. Presumably in many cases the *Pehrsson* approach will
still apply if the development plan reproduces the policies set out in
PPG 2 about development in the Green Belt. Thus the first stage will
still be to decide whether the development is appropriate in the Green
Belt and, if not, whether there are any very special circumstances to
justify such inappropriate development. In this regard it is interesting to
note that in *Houghton* the policies in PPG 2 were reproduced in the
Unitary Plan and so the inspector had made the identical error of
construction with respect to the Green Belt policies in the plan. The
complication was that even if the development was appropriate to the
Green Belt, it was in conflict with other policies in the plan. In such
circumstances from *Pehrsson*, having determined that the development
was appropriate to the Green Belt, there would then have been a second
stage of deciding whether it would nevertheless cause such demonstrable harm to interests of acknowledged importance, that it ought to be
refused. The damage to the woodlands and the landscape could be
capable of amounting to such demonstrable harm. The main difference
in the post-s.54A world is that the first task of the decision-maker is to
decide what outcome would be in accordance with the policies in the
plan. Where there are other policies, apart from the Green Belt policies, in the development plan which are material to the proposed
development, the fact that the development is appropriate in the Green
Belt may not be conclusive. Thus in *Houghton* the Deputy Judge stated:

> Then in paragraph 16 he [the inspector] summed up to the effect that the
> development conflicted with the development plan in a variety of respects,
> omitting, deliberately it was suspected in the light of the *Pehrsson* proposi-
> tion, the mere fact that policy G2 [the Green Belt policy in the development
> plan] applied because the site was in the Green Belt. (p.399)

---

[22] [1997] JPL 646.

So the second stage of *Pehrsson* will not be necessary if the development plan makes clear that because of its conflict with other policies, the proposal should be refused even though it is otherwise appropriate to the Green Belt. The criticism which can be made of *Houghton* is that the inspector does not seem to have carried out that exercise since, because of his error, he treated the development as not being appropriate. Where the development plan incorporates the government's Green Belt policy *and* the development is found to be inappropriate, the development's conflict with other policies in the plan may justify dispensing with the second stage of considering whether there were very special circumstances to justify inappropriate development. The more difficult situation is where the development is considered to be appropriate to the Green Belt. In such a case, it is submitted that the decision-taker will have to decide whether the development, although appropriate in the Green Belt, is not in accordance with the development plan because it is in conflict with other development-plan policies.

Even where the development-plan policies are in conflict with government Green Belt policies, the plan is not conclusive as government policies can constitute material considerations which indicate otherwise. So in such a case there is a new second stage, which is different from *Pehrsson*. Having decided what is the outcome which is in accordance with the development plan, the decision-taker has then to decide whether government policies justify a different outcome. Direct conflicts will be rare as the department will try to ensure that the Green Belt policies in the development plans are in accordance with PPG 2. On the other hand local planning authorities may be able to argue that, as in *Tandridge*, there is nothing improper in having stricter Green Belt policies.

Where both development plan and government policies are being revised, it has already been pointed out that these drafts can be material considerations. In *Tandridge* the inspector's decision was made at a date when both the draft PPG 2 and the replacement structure plan were well advanced. Indeed the revised PPG 2 was finally published in the same form as the draft eleven days after the date of the decision and the replacement structure plan was formally adopted one month later. Leggatt LJ, however, accepted that:

> It is common ground that the Inspector was entitled to decide whether he would give any, and if so what, weight to the draft PPG 2, or indeed to the deposited replacement structure plan, even though that came into force a month or so after the Inspector's decision letter. (p.648)

Interestingly Leggatt went further and suggested that it would have been objectionable to have paid any attention to the draft PPG 2 as it differed from the development-plan policy. This would indicate that in so far as there is a hierarchy of policies, at the top there is the adopted development plan, next down are government policies, but draft policies (whether in the form of the development plan or government guidance) have little weight.

So, in conclusion, in the post-s.54A world there will be two distinct situations. They are:

(a) First, where the development plan adopts the same wording as government policies and there are no other development-plan policies in conflict. Here, the *Pehrsson* tests will still basically apply and the central questions will be whether the development is inappropriate and, if it is, whether there are any very special circumstances which justify granting permission.

(b) Second, where there is a conflict between the policies in the development plan and the government policies. Here, the primary question in law will be whether the development-plan policies favour refusing or granting permission and whether that presumption should be defeated because of the contrary material considerations. In practice, of course, the right of appeal will mean that the government policies will be likely to prevail, as the inspectors see themselves as standing in the shoes of the Secretary of State. This gets us back to *Pehrsson* in so far it explains the meaning of the government's Green Belt policies.

3 The Construction and Application of the Green Belt Policies

It is now trite law that a planning authority, whether it be a local planning authority or the Secretary of State, can err in law by misunderstanding or misconstruing a policy. This principle appears to have been first expressly laid down by Woolf J in *Gransden & Co.* v. *Secretary of State for the Environment,*[23] where he set out a series of propositions flowing from the fact that policy documents could amount to material considerations. The fourth of these propositions was that it was essential that the policy was properly understood by the determining body. Woolf J went on: 'If the body making the policy failed properly to understand the policy then the decision would be as defective as it would be if no regard had been paid to the policy' (p.521).

This approach was expressly endorsed at Court of Appeal level by Nolan LJ in *Horsham District Council* v. *Secretary of State for the*

---

[23] [1986] JPL 519.

Environment[24] and it has been repeatedly applied at High Court level. The difficulty in this apparently straightforward principle is in ascertaining what is an improper understanding and whether the meaning of a policy is a pure matter of law for the courts. It has already been seen with respect to the Green Belt policies that in *Pehrsson* the Court of Appeal clearly took it for granted that they had the right to lay down authoritively the overall approach to be taken. One result is that the words of Lord Donaldson took on a life of their own and these words were in turn made the subject of painstaking exegesis by both courts and commentators. This phenomenon is, of course, commonplace and it is standard for the words in a statute to become buried and almost forgotten under layers of case law. In reaction the court will sometimes refuse to define words and leave them to be given their 'ordinary' meaning.[25]

In the case of planning policies, however, there are particular dangers in the courts getting overly involved in their interpretation and application. Mr Lockhart Mummery QC sitting as a Deputy Judge in *Cooper* v. *Secretary of State for the Environment*[26] put the argument well when he stated:

> Planning policies were ... utterly distinct from statutes or contracts. They were not intended to provide a detailed framework governing the relation between individuals, or between public authorities and the individual. Rather, they were guidelines or principles – expressly open to review and amendment from time to time – intended to guide the decision-maker in the making of an essentially discretionary decision. For the most part, their understanding involved the assessment of ordinary words, often with an element of planning judgment (e.g. the concept of the 'adverse effect on the vitality and viability of town centres'). (pp.952–3)

On the other hand, it is important that policies are applied logically, fairly and consistently. Especially in the case of Green Belt policies the tangle of different documents can make the search for meaning difficult and the courts are supposed to be expert in ironing out such tangles and have long-standing concerns to prevent unfairness and abuse of power. The challenge is to be able to draw a line which stops at the right side of interference with planning judgements.

Before attempting to set out what this line is, it is important first to deal with two issues which can be particularly significant for the interpretation and implication of Green Belt policies. These issues are the

[24] [1992] JPL 334.

[25] The prime example is Lord Reid's statement about the meaning of insulting in *Cozens* v. *Brutus* [1973] AC 854.

[26] [1996] JPL 945.

distinction between the policies in the development plans and government policies and the distinction between the construction of a policy as opposed to the application of the policy to the particular facts.

3.1 Development-plan policies and government policies

It has been argued that, because the combination of s.70 and s.54A as a matter of law requires both regard to be had to the development-plan policies where relevant and for the application to be decided in accordance with those policies, the meaning of such policies is a pure matter of law for the courts. The argument may be based upon the distinction which Glidewell LJ made in *Bolton MBC* v. *Secretary of State for the Environment and Greater Manchester Waste Disposal Authority*[27] between matters which a decision-maker was obliged by statute to take into account and those where the obligation to take into account was to be implied from the nature of the decision and of the matter in question. Now this distinction (and the more difficult distinction between matters which the decision-maker is obliged to take into account and those matters where there is a discretion whether to consider the matters at all) can be important where there is a failure to take into account a particular policy, but it should not logically make any difference to the need for the decision-maker properly to understand whatever policy is being applied.

This would appear to be the line taken by the courts. In *ICP Developments Ltd* v. *Secretary of State for the Environment*[28] the argument was advanced that as the development plan had a special status under the 1990 Act, it was important that it should be construed with care. The Deputy Judge, Robin Purchas QC, however, held that the approach to construction should not differ because of its particular status as a result of s.54A of the 1990 Act. The same view was taken by Lockhart Mummery in *Cooper*[29] where he stated:

> Further, when similar policies relevant to a planning decision might appear both in the development plan and in the PPGs (for example as to Green Belts, countryside, retail etc.) it would be illogical for a different approach to be taken in the matter of construction as between the two policy sources. (p.953)

A similar issue arose in *R.* v. *Leominster District Council ex parte Patricia Pothecary*[30] where the Deputy Judge Malcolm Spence QC

[27] [1991] JPL 241.
[28] [1997] JPL 930.
[29] Ibid.
[30] [1997] JPL 835.

referred to the statement in the *Encyclopaedia of Planning* that whether
or not an application was in accordance with the development plan was
now a matter of law for the courts.[31] The Deputy Judge did not have to
decide this point as he held that the decision of the planning committee
that the development was in accordance with the plan was *Wednesbury*
unreasonable. The Court of Appeal overturned the Deputy Judge and
held that there were not sufficient grounds for holding the decision to
be perverse. In doing this none of their lordships commented expressly
on the extent to which the application of s.54A was a matter of law.
Nevertheless it is implicit in the approach taken by the Court of Appeal
that they will be reluctant to interfere with the planning authority's
view that a development is or is not in accordance with the policies.
Thus Schiemann LJ stated:

> However in many cases of which the present is an example each side of the
> argument will be able to cite different policies in the same or different plans
> in support of their conclusions. In many cases the relevant polices will
> contain within themselves value judgments upon which reasonable persons
> may differ.

The clear implication is that the decision as to whether an application is
in accordance with the development is not really a matter for the
courts.

3.2 Application as opposed to construction

Even where the courts are concerned with the application of the words
in a statute, they may hold that the application of those words in a
particular case is a matter of fact and degree for the decision-maker and
that the courts should only overturn that application if it is perverse. A
prime example is the definition of the development in the 1990 Act, the
application of which is a question of fact and degree for planning
authorities. There is therefore an even stronger argument that the application of policy is primarily a mixed question of planning judgment and
fact.

There would appear to be little direct authority on the point but in
the *ICP* case, it was argued by counsel for the applicant that the case of
Northavon DC v. *Secretary of State for the Environment*[32] was an
example of the application as opposed to the construction of Green Belt
policies. The issue in that case had been whether the application site
was an 'institution standing in extensive grounds'. Auld J had said that:

[31] Ibid at p.841.
[32] [1993] JPL 761.

The words spoke for themselves and were not readily susceptible to precise legal definition. Whether a proposed development met the description was in most cases likely to be a matter of fact or degree and planning judgment. He had said 'in most cases' because it was for the Court to say as matter of law whether the meaning given by the Secretary of State or one of his officers or inspectors to the expression when applying it was outside the ordinary and natural meaning of the words in their context (see Gransden . . .) The test to be applied by the Court was that it should only interfere where the decision-maker's interpretation was perverse in that he has given to the words in their context a meaning that they could not possibly have or restricted their meaning in a way that the breadth of their terms could not possibly justify. (p.763)

In *ICP* the Deputy Judge, Robin Purchas QC, had accepted that this test of Auld J's (basically the *Wednesbury* test) was to be applied not to the construction of a particular policy (which was a matter for the courts) but to the application of the policy to the facts. It will be seen that the distinction is probably not as simple as that and Auld J's test can have relevance to both the construction as well as the application of policy. It should also be noted that Auld J throughout referred to the decision-maker's *interpretation* of the words which suggests more than the mere application of policy. But putting this aside, the application of policy must be primarily a matter for the planning authority.

Returning to the fundamental question of the role of the courts in the construction of policy, Brooke LJ recently, in *R. v. Derbyshire County Council ex parte Woods*,[33] made the point that words may be capable of a range of meanings and that the responsibility of the court is to determine that range. It would therefore follow that in that sense and that sense alone it is a pure question of law. The important passage in his judgment (with which Sir John Balcombe and Butler-Sloss LJ agreed) is:

If there is a dispute about the meaning of the words included in a policy document which a planning authority is bound to take into account, it is of course for the court to determine as a matter of law, what the words are capable of meaning. If the decision-maker attaches a meaning to the words they are not capable of bearing, then it will have made an error of law, and it will have failed properly to understand the policy (see *Horsham DC* v. *Secretary of State for the Environment* 1 PLR 81 per Nolan LJ at page 88). If there is room for dispute about the breadth of the meaning the words may properly bear then there may in particular cases be material considerations of law which will deprive a word of one its possible shades of meaning in that case as a matter of law. (p.967)

[33] [1997] JPL 958.

The important corollary is that if the words are judged as properly capable of more than one meaning, the planning authority is given a flexibility and can adopt the meaning which it considers is most appropriate in the circumstances. This approach is similar to that taken by the Supreme Court of Canada as to the interpretations of legislation by certain decision-makers. The Supreme Court has declined to intervene unless the interpretation is patently unreasonable.[34] The justification for such 'judicial deference' is usually the special expertise of the decision-maker and the need to avoid overcomplicating the administration of the particular administrative scheme. In the case of the town and country planning system, the approach adopted by Brooke LJ would allow the courts to control the decision-makers without interfering with matters of planning judgment.

Brooke LJ's judgment also helps to explain some of the previous judicial decisions. First, Brooke LJ expressly affirmed that his statement of the law was the underlying principle behind Auld J's statement of the law in *Northavon*. This would indicate that while *Northavon* was primarily about the application of the words to particular facts, Auld J was also allowing the decision-maker some latitude as to the interpretation or construction of the policies where the words are capable of a range of meanings. Secondly in *HMJ Caters Ltd* v. *Secretary of State for the Environment*[35] Lionel Read QC, sitting as Deputy Judge, while accepting that the meaning and effect of the particular development-plan policy at issue was purely a matter of legal construction, doubted whether the meaning and effect of the shopping policy as a whole was a pure question of law. These doubts can again be understood once it is accepted that the courts, having made an initial construction of the policy, can give the decision-maker a choice as to the most appropriate meaning.

The extent to which words are capable of giving rise to different meanings will vary. Brooke LJ gave, as an example of the way courts can restrict the range of possible meanings of words by imposing on them a specific construction, the case of *R.* v. *Radio Authority ex parte Bull*.[36] In this case Lord Woolf MR had to construe s.92(2)(a) of the Broadcasting Act 1990 which referred to 'a body whose objects are wholly or mainly of a political nature'. Lord Woolf MR, having taken into account that the statute was restricting freedom of communication, held that 'mainly' should be construed in a way which limited the restriction to bodies whose objects were at least 75 per cent political. A

---

[34] See in particular *Canadian Union of Public Employees* v. *New Brunswick Liquor Corporation* [1979] 2 SCR (NB).
[35] [1993] JPL 337.
[36] [1997] 2 All ER 561.

similar example of the construction of the words in a planning policy is the case of *Clowes Developments Ltd* v. *Secretary of State for the Environment*.[37] This case involved the construction and application of PPG 24 and turned on whether the phrase 'several times' could cover a situation when an event occurred 'more than once, i.e. two or more times'. His Honour Judge Rich held: 'The natural meaning of "several" is in my judgment, at least more than two although less than whatever one might mean by "many".' In such cases the initial 'construction' of the court limits the scope of the decision-maker, but more often planning policies will be written in a way that allows flexibility.

In the judgments quoted there have been references to the *construction* and the *interpretation* of policies, to the *meaning* and *effect* of policies and finally to the *application* of policies. This confusion of terminology stems from the fact that in practice it is hard to make clear-cut distinctions even between construction and application, as the two tend to get mixed up. J. A. Corry some years ago argued that the distinction between determining the meaning of the statute and applying that meaning to a particular set of facts was unhelpful. He pointed out that:

> no judge ever begins the process of judging until he knows the facts upon which he is to decide. Then he begins to think of the statute in relation to those facts and they inevitably colour his interpretation. If he says the meaning of the statute is clear, it is because it speaks plainly about his facts. In considering his decision, he goes back and forth from facts to statute and from statute to facts, and the processes of interpretation and application are telescoped together in a manner which defies separation.[38]

Planning authorities and the courts must both go through a similar process when faced with the question of whether a particular development is or is not appropriate in the Green Belt. Even if the planning authority does not initially attempt to define what the words in the policy mean, the actual decision infers a particular meaning.

Lord Diplock has similarly denied that the distinction is useful. In *Re Racal Communications Ltd*[39] he criticized the approach of the majority of the Court of Appeal in *Pearlman* v. *Harrow School*[40] who had found that a County Court had erred in law in holding that the installation of a central heating system was a 'structural alteration, extension or addition'. Lord Diplock stated:

[37] Unreported, 18 October 1996.
[38] See Corry, 'Administrative law and the interpretation of statutes', (1936) 1, *University of Toronto Law Journal*, 286 at p.290.
[39] [1981] AC 374.
[40] [1979] QB 56.

If the meaning of ordinary words when used in a statute becomes a question of law, here was a typical question of mixed law fact and degree which only a scholiast would think it appropriate to dissect into two separate questions, one for the decision by the superior court, viz. the meaning of those words – a question which must entail considerations of degree; and the other for decision by the County Court, viz. the application of the words to the particular installation – a question which also entails considerations of degree. The County Court Judge had not ventured upon any definition of the words 'structural alteration, extension or addition'. So there was really no material on which to hold that he had got the meaning wrong rather than its application to the facts. Nevertheless the majority of the Court of Appeal in *Pearlman* held that Parliament had indeed intended that such a dissection should be made and since they would not have come to the same conclusion themselves on the facts of the case they inferred that the judge's error was one of interpretation of the words 'structural alteration extension or addition'.

Yet, as Lord Diplock appeared to admit, the more that the decision-maker does attempt to define the words, the more vulnerable that decision is to review by the superior courts. In the case of a statute this is because the courts consider that the interpretation of legislation is particularly within their competence. Even in the case of Green Belt policies, where the courts have no claim to special competence, they can provide a useful function in explaining the meaning of those policies at a level of abstraction or generality that extends beyond the facts of the particular case. Therefore the most difficult issue, as always, is judging when it is appropriate for the courts to overturn the interpretation of the planning authority. In the recent decision of *Virgin Cinema Properties Ltd* v. *Secretary of State for the Environment*[41] George Bartlett QC sitting as a Deputy Judge argued that the court should only intervene if the interpretation was *Wednesbury* unreasonable. The Deputy Judge unequivocally stated:

> Since a planning policy does not confer rights and duties that are legally enforceable I cannot see that it could ever be a matter for the court to determine its meaning as a matter of law for the purpose of deciding an issue arising from the making of a planning application . . . Any conclusion that is formed by the decision-maker as part of that decision can, in my judgment, be challenged only on *Wednesbury* grounds unless it is a conclusion of law. A conclusion on the meaning to be attached to a statute or a statutory instrument or a planning permission (which confers a legal privilege) is a conclusion of law, and a court can accordingly determine whether the conclusion is correct. A conclusion on the meaning of a planning policy, on the other hand, is a matter for the decision-maker in the case. On the review

[41] [1998] PLCR 1.

the role of the court, in my judgment, is to say whether the decision-maker has attributed to the policy a meaning which he could not reasonably have attributed to it or, in forming his conclusion, has taken into account irrelevant matters or disregarded matters that were relevant. The court thus determines the ambit of reasonableness, which is matter of law. (pp.7–8)

Although the Deputy Judge does not refer to Brooke LJ's judgment in the *Derbyshire* decision, the approach is very similar. The crucial difference lies in George Bartlett's reference to *Wednesbury*. The *Wednesbury* test, with its connotations of the totally unreasonable decision-maker, is perhaps inappropriate in this context, and it is significant that the Deputy Judge simply refers to the meaning being reasonable. Further he later makes the point that where the point of interpretation is simply the meaning of ordinary words, there may be only one reasonable meaning.

Overall it is the approach set out by Brooke LJ that does seem to strike the right balance between what Beatson has described as 'judicial control and administrative autonomy'.[42]

4 Conclusions

The upgrading of the status of the development plan does mean that at least in theory Green Belt policies (unless they are faithfully reproduced in the relevant development plan) could be undermined by conflicting policies in the development plan. In practice this is unlikely because s.54A does still allow flexibility. It would be possible to give the Green Belt its own statutory base as with listed buildings and conservation areas. Thus it could be made a requirement, in determining applications to development in a designated Green Belt, that very special attention be given to the need for such developments to be appropriate. In the case of listed buildings it has been accepted that s.54A does not override s.66(1) of the Planning (Listed Buildings and Conservation Areas) Act 1990 and that the need to have 'special regard to the desirability of preserving' a listed building, could result in a different outcome from that indicated by the development plan.[43] What is not clear is the extent to which the term 'special regard' means that the need to preserve the listed building should in law be given an added weight.[44] Indeed it can be argued that a specific statutory recognition of the importance of the Green Belt could just lead to further complications about the precise

[42] See Beatson, 'The scope of judicial review for error of law', (1984) 4 *Oxford Journal of Legal Studies*, 22.

[43] See *Heatherington (UK) Ltd* v. *Secretary of State for the Environment* [1995] JPL 228.

[44] See ministerial decision following the Heatherington decision; [1996] JPL 615.

interrelationship of s.54A and other statutory provisions. It is more important that central government and the local planning authorities try to ensure that there is consistency and correlation of both the different strands of policy within the development plan itself and of those policies to the Green Belt policies set out in PPG 2.

As to the role of the courts, in *MJT Securities Ltd* v. *Secretary of State for the Environment*[44] Brooke J (as he then was) said that he agreed with this commentator's view that the need for reasons to be adequate and intelligible had imposed a check on the quality of decision-making. It is an important aspect of accountability that both local planning authorities and inspectors know that their decisions on the Green Belt may end up being carefully examined in the High Court. The inevitable danger is that the courts can overreach themselves. The *Pehrsson* decision is perhaps an example where the Court of Appeal went too far in imposing a set of rules as to how the Green Belt policies had to be applied. However, there are now welcome signs that the judiciary are coming to accept that both the construction and the application of the Green Belt policies are not questions of pure law and their power to impose their own view of the meaning is strictly limited.

3

Rural Development: Negotiating Control

JEREMY ROWAN-ROBINSON AND ANNE-MICHELLE SLATER

1 Introduction

The White Paper *This Common Inheritance*[1] and the European Union Fifth Action Programme on the Environment *Towards Sustainability*[2] both emphasize that responsibility for the environment is shared. 'It is not a duty for Government alone', states the White Paper (para.1.38). 'It is an obligation on us all.' With the notion of 'shared responsibility' in mind, both documents advocate broadening the range of instruments available for implementing environmental policy. The Fifth Action Programme, in particular, argues that implicit in this notion is the need for a more consensual and co-operative approach to regulating behaviour: 'Whereas previous environmental measures tended to be prescriptive in character with an emphasis on the "thou shalt not" approach, the new strategy leans more towards a "let's work together" approach.'

This chapter assesses the contribution of one such instrument, planning agreements, in promoting shared responsibility for the management of the countryside. Although we make reference to the law in Scotland, much of the general discussion about practice is equally relevant to England and Wales.

Agreements would seem, almost by definition, to accord well with the search for a more consensual and co-operative approach to regulation. The key feature of an agreement is that people choose whether or

---

[1] Cm. 1200 (HMSO, 1990).
[2] COM (92) 23, 1992.

not to accept regulation of their behaviour. The assumption is that when arrangements are entered into voluntarily and offer some return for the restrictions imposed, there should be more willing and effective compliance with the agreed restrictions than if they had been imposed through a conventional 'command and control' system.

There is nothing very new about the use of agreements to regulate the management of the countryside. The use of land for agriculture and forestry has long been free of formal regulation. Unlike development, such activities have remained part of the value of the land to the owner. Landowners have the 'right' to conduct these activities which, at least historically, were perceived as being environmentally benign. Successive administrations have relied on the voluntary approach to change behaviour in the public interest on the premise that a particular approach to land management requires the continuing commitment of those on the ground, and this is best achieved by obtaining their willing co-operation. In such cases the landowner is in a strong bargaining position.[3] The negotiation between the landowner and the state is characterized by freedom of contract, and the cost of regulation will be borne by the state, generally through a compensation payment. The payment is justified theoretically, and somewhat tenuously, on the ground that the landowner will have paid a price for the land that reflects the right to carry on the activity. If that activity is now to be controlled, the consequent loss in the existing use value of the land should be compensated.[4] Agreements for national nature reserves under s.16 of the National Parks and Access to the Countryside Act 1949, management agreements under s.49A of the Countryside (Scotland) Act 1967, SSSI agreements under s.15 of the Countryside Act 1968 and 'environmentally sensitive area' agreements under s.18 of the Agriculture Act 1986 all provide examples of a consensual and co-operative approach to regulating the management of the countryside.

Planning agreements differ from the sort of approach to the management of the countryside that we have just described. They are almost always concerned with a proposal for the development of land. Development is subject to formal regulation, and the regime of control is set out in part III of the Town and Country Planning (Scotland) Act 1997. A grant of planning permission is required before development can be carried out (1997 Act, s.28(1)). Amongst other provisions in part III, s.75 provides that a planning authority may enter into agree-

---

[3] A. Ross and J. Rowan-Robinson, *The Impact of Voluntary Agreements on Access to Justice in Environmental Protection* (W. G. Hart Legal Workshop, 1997); *Access to Environmental Justice* (School for Advanced Legal Studies, London, July 1997).

[4] W. Waldegrave, *Operation and Effectiveness of Part II of the Wildlife and Countryside Act*, First Report of the Environment Committee of the House of Commons, 1985, para.14.

ment with a person having an interest in land with a view to restricting or regulating the development or use of land. Research shows that such agreements are almost always triggered by an application for planning permission.[5] Planning agreements are employed, not to bring under control a new activity, but to run alongside and supplement a conventional command-and-control regime. They are negotiated, not as a substitute for, but in the shadow of conventional regulation and, like the planning system as a whole, they provide a vehicle for managing conflict between different interests.[6]

Although these agreements, like the others we have referred to, introduce a consensual and co-operative element into decision-making, the bargaining strength of the parties is differently distributed. The applicant is seeking a permit to carry on the activity and the grant of the permit will be linked to the prior completion of the agreement. The state is, therefore, in the stronger bargaining position and the cost of regulation is borne by the applicant.[7]

Research shows agreements being used for a wide range of purposes.[8] Although the focus has been very much on urban development, this has not been exclusively so. Agreements have been used, for example, to ensure the appropriate management and eventual restoration of mineral workings, to restrict the occupancy of new houses in the countryside to those able to demonstrate an essential local need, to regulate the sort of goods sold in farm shops, to impose a limit on the period of occupation of chalets and static caravans, to tie short-based processing facilities to offshore fish farms, to provide for public access and to secure the allocation of land as a country park. The Countryside Commission has been actively encouraging the use of planning agreements to enhance the beauty of the countryside and to increase the opportunities for its enjoyment.[9]

The use of planning agreements over the years, and particularly since the mid-1970s, has generated considerable criticism. Much of this has been directed at the pursuit of what is generally referred to as 'planning gain'. The term gives rise to definitional problems, but what most people seem to have in mind is some sort of benefit to the community which was not part of the original proposal by the developer, and was

---

[5] J. Rowan-Robinson and R. Durman, *Section 50 Agreement: Final Report* (Scottish Office, 1992); Grimley J. R. Eve in association with Thames Polytechnic and Alsop Wilkinson, *The Use of Planning Agreements* (HMSO, 1992).

[6] P. Healey, M. Purdue and F. Ennis, *Negotiating Development* (London: E. & F. N. Spon), 1995, p.6.

[7] A. Ross and J. Rowan-Robinson, above n.3.

[8] M. Elson, *Negotiating the Future: Planning Gain in the 1990s* (ARC Ltd, 1990); Rowan-Robinson and Durman, and Grimley J. R. Eve et al., above n.5.

[9] Countryside Commission, 'Countryside planning statement', CCP 440, 1993.

therefore negotiated, and is not of itself of any commercial advantage to the developer. Critics have been concerned about the apparent sale of planning permissions, with the levying of unauthorized development charges, with the trading of established planning policy for financial benefits, with the introduction of additional delay into the process and with the circumvention of the disciplines of public scrutiny and external review.[10]

More recently, the negotiation of planning decisions has acquired wider acceptance. This may partly reflect some change of emphasis by the government as regards the role of development control generally. Attention is focusing less on the system as a 'burden' on business and more on its role in adding value to the environment.[11] This wider acceptance of planning agreements also owes something to new legislation on 'planning obligations' in England and Wales, to some judicial clarification of the legitimate scope of agreements and to guidance on the use of agreements (and unilateral obligations in England and Wales) from the Department of the Environment, the Welsh Office and the Scottish Office. Furthermore, there has been a gradual change in the relationship between the state and the market in the development process which has resulted in a reduction in the public sector's development and infrastructure role and increasing pressure to seek private-sector resources for community facilities.[12] Planning agreements have provided a vehicle for achieving this redistribution of cost.

Our purpose in this chapter is to make some assessment of the role of planning agreements in managing conflict between different interests. More generally, our concern is with the role of agreements in the management of the countryside and in promoting shared responsibility for the environment. The assessment draws on earlier literature on agreements and will be informed by two case studies in which one of the authors has been involved. The case studies have been selected because the agreements in question are directed at managing potentially serious countryside conflicts and at conserving or enhancing the environment.

The first case study examines the 'lowland crofting' scheme initiated by the former West Lothian District Council (now West Lothian Council). The scheme departs from conventional planning policy which seeks to restrict development in the countryside to that which satisfies

---

[10] See, for example from an extensive literature, Sir Desmond Heap and A. J. Ward, 'Planning bargaining – the pros and the cons: or, how much can the system stand', [1980] JPL 631; Report of the Property Advisory Group, *Planning Gain* (1981).

[11] Elson, above n.8; Healey, Purdue and Ennis, above n.6, p.37.

[12] P. Healey, M. Purdue and F. Ennis, 'Rationales for planning gain', *Policy Studies*, 13(2), p.18.

an essential local need. The lowland crofting scheme aims to attract residential development with workspace into an area of degraded landscape in the central belt of Scotland while at the same time bringing about landscape, conservation or public access improvements. The second case study focuses on the way in which the negotiation of an agreement by Highland Regional Council (now Highland Council) has enabled planning permission to be granted for a major development – the construction of a funicular or cable railway on Cairngorm – while ensuring the continued integrity of a nearby site of outstanding nature conservation importance.

The criticisms referred to above offer a focus for our assessment of the role of agreements. In particular, we will be looking at what benefits agreements offer which cannot be obtained through the normal exercise of development control powers, at the question of trading established policy for planning gains, and at the extent to which the disciplines of scrutiny and external review are being circumvented. The case studies are now considered in turn.

2 Lowland Crofting

2.1 The origins and development of the policy

'Lowland crofting', observe Rankin and Hartley, 'is a pioneering planning idea that is creating new woodlands, low density housing, businesses and rationalised farms in the bleak landscapes of Central Scotland.'[13] Its origins lie in the drive to improve the landscape of Scotland's central belt. In 1978 the Central Scotland Woodlands Initiative was established to improve the landscape between Edinburgh and Glasgow by creating the central Scotland forest. Much of the area was characterized by industrial dereliction and a degraded physical environment with a very low level of woodland cover. The overall aim was the improvement of the landscape and extensive tree planting. The Central Scotland Countryside Trust, a private charitable company, was set up to achieve the aim. Although the goal was clear, implementation was slow.

During the 1980s, West Lothian District Council, responsible for an area located in the central belt between Edinburgh and Glasgow, was exploring ways of attracting inward investment. It had concluded that it could not compete on economic or 'quality of life' terms with other locations because of the industrial dereliction and poor-quality landscape which characterized parts of West Lothian. The prospect of

[13] R. Rankin and J. Hartley, 'Lowland crofting', *Scottish Planning and Environmental Law* (No. 65, 1998).

linking woodland planting to new residential development seemed worthy of consideration to both the authority and the Trust. However, the Council was aware of the planning risks inherent in opening the door to uncontrolled development in the countryside. Accordingly, a planning advisory group was convened to look at the implications. The link with the Central Scotland Woodlands Initiative ensured representation on the group, not only from the District Council, but from the Scottish Office, the Countryside Commission for Scotland, the Scottish Development Agency and Lothian Regional Council.

One of the first steps was to identify an area in the west of the district for a pilot study. An area was selected because of its combination of poor-quality agricultural land and degraded landscape. The advisory group concluded that within this area farm restructuring incorporating low-density residential and workspace development linked to woodland planting could combine the benefits of landscape improvement and economic development without jeopardizing conventional planning policy which seeks to restrict development in the countryside to that which meets an essential local need. The District Council incorporated this policy of selective development in the countryside, which became known as the 'Lowland Crofting' policy,[14] into the Calders Area Local Plan (adopted 1995) and the Finalized Bathgate Area Local Plan adopted August 1998. The policy precisely defines the area eligible for farm restructuring and clearly sets out the key elements of lowland crofting. These include confining schemes to whole farms or other large areas, restricting residential density to ten houses per fifty hectares, avoiding suburbanization and ribbon development, supporting small businesses and requiring a minimum of 30 per cent of each farm to be planted as woodland. No objections to the policy were received during the public consultation process. The policy has since received support, on a trial basis, in the Lothian Region Structure Plan approved by the Secretary of State on 4 July 1997.

The intention was that the lowland crofting policy would operate through the granting of a single outline planning permission for the restructuring of an existing farm within the identified area. The restructuring would involve three land uses comprising low-density housing, where possible with workshops, woodland planting paid for out of the release of the land for housing, and agriculture. Farming would continue on the best of the agricultural land. Public access and nature conservation objectives would also be incorporated in suitable cases. These uses would be set out in a management plan. Each use would extend to approximately one-third of the area of the farm. The

[14] The term 'lowland crofting' was borrowed from the small-scale pluri-activity that characterizes rural development in the crofting counties of Scotland.

minimum plot size for the houses would be one hectare. Practical guidance for landowners on the operation of the lowland crofting policy was provided by the council in the *Lowland Crofting Handbook*. Early soundings were conducted amongst landowners in the area to test the response and these indicated a reasonable measure of interest in the scheme.

The Council recognized that lowland crofting could lead to uncontrolled development in the countryside and establish an undesirable precedent unless it was carefully managed. The key to implementation was to be a planning agreement under what was then s.50 of the Town and Country Planning (Scotland) Act 1972. S.50 enabled the planning authority to enter into an agreement with a person interested in land for the purpose of restricting or regulating the development or use of the land. This provision (now s.75 of the 1997 Act) corresponded to the old form of s.106 of the Town and Country Planning Act for England and Wales, although there were differences in the underlying common law background. A model agreement was drafted and reviewed by the advisory group to illustrate the way in which the various elements of the scheme could be effectively secured, and reference to the role of the agreement was incorporated into the local plan. The plan draws attention to the principal matters to be covered by an agreement.

The Council's concern to distinguish their approach to development in the lowland crofting area from development in other parts of the countryside was given early support in an appeal decision in 1992.[15] An appeal against a refusal of permission for a new house in the countryside cited the lowland crofting scheme in its favour. The appeal site had formerly been part of one of the farms approved for lowland crofting. None the less, the reporter in his decision clearly differentiated between the 'package' of housing, woodland and agriculture required for lowland crofting compared with unrestricted development in the countryside.

Progress with implementation of the policy has been encouraging. Five sites in the lowland crofting area were brought forward for development as a trial run during the first half of the 1990s, two of them by New Lives and New Landscapes, a development company set up specifically to undertake lowland crofting development. The diagrams show the before and after position with one of the sites. Planning permissions have been granted for the five sites covering some 395 hectares of farmland. Fifty-five houses linked to workshops have been built and others are in course of construction. Businesses being carried on in the workshops range from local tradesmen such as joiners and electricians to a livery and horse-blanket manufacturer. Many croft

[15] Decision letter dated 25 August 1992, reference PPA/LD/245.

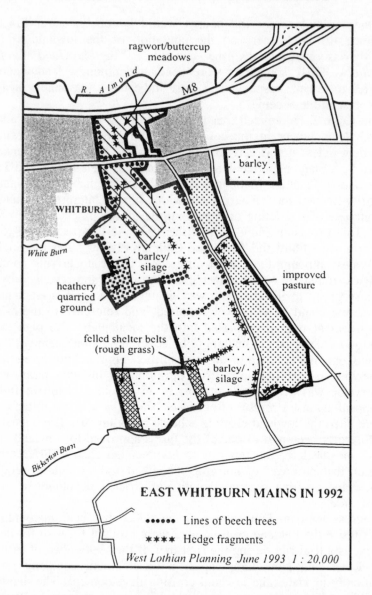

ragwort/buttercup
meadows

R. Almond

M8

barley

WHITBURN

White Burn

barley/
silage

improved
pasture

heathery
quarried
ground

felled shelter belts
(rough grass)

barley/
silage

Bickerton Burn

EAST WHITBURN MAINS IN 1992

●●●●●● Lines of beech trees

✳✳✳✳ Hedge fragments

West Lothian Planning June 1993 1 : 20,000

owners use their homes as an office base but, apart from a basket manufacturer who intends to use the willow grown on the croft, few land-based businesses have been established to date. One hundred and twenty-three hectares of woodland have been planted, twenty-five hectares of nature conservation interest have been safeguarded and forty-three kilometres of public paths and bridleways have been laid out. The best of the agricultural land on the sites continues to be farmed traditionally and is protected under the scheme from other land

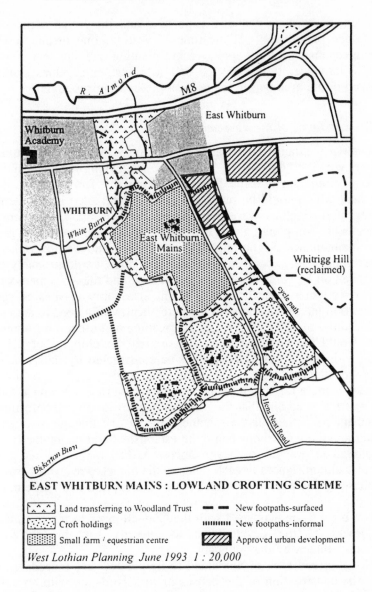

EAST WHITBURN MAINS : LOWLAND CROFTING SCHEME

Land transferring to Woodland Trust	New footpaths-surfaced
Croft holdings	New footpaths-informal
Small farm / equestrian centre	Approved urban development

West Lothian Planning June 1993 1 : 20,000

uses. Overall, there is general agreement that the policy is achieving substantial environmental improvements.[16] As Cooper observes, 'lowland crofting is an effective way of generating environmental

[16] See, for example, Rankin and Hartley, above n.13; A. Cooper, 'Lowland crofting: positive planning in a degraded rural environment', unpublished honours dissertation for the degree of Bachelor of Land Economy, Department of Land Economy, Aberdeen University, 1995; D. Jarman, 'Lowland crofting', unpublished paper presented to the Royal Town Planning Institute Conference, Newcastle, 1992.

improvement because it adopts a positive and integrated approach to countryside planning.'[17] At the time of writing, one further lowland crofting scheme has been approved but planting and site servicing has yet to commence. It is expected that four further schemes could be approved in the area before the present policy requires review.

2.2 The substance of the agreement

The District Council were clear from the outset that implementation of the policy would depend on a suitably framed agreement, and the advisory group spent some time discussing the format of a model agreement which could be made available to interested landowners. A number of difficulties were anticipated. First of all, there were the arrangements for planting the woodland on the one hand and for its future maintenance on the other. The former would be undertaken by the developer, the expectation was that the latter would probably have to be taken on by some other person or body, and the agreement would need to recognize this. The same might also apply to sites of nature conservation interest. Secondly, the agreement would need to anticipate that the initial planting, servicing, landscaping and other environmental works would be carried out by the original developer, but that the houses with linked businesses would be constructed by individuals on their own allocated plots. The agreement would need to secure the necessary coherence by ensuring that an appropriate phasing arrangement was followed and that the different parties involved conformed to the management plan for the scheme. Thirdly, the linkage between the housing and the workshops had to be established and maintained.

Although in practice each agreement has had to be tailored to the particular circumstances of each scheme, the model agreement contained the following key provisions which have been applied to all schemes:

(a) a bond to be deposited with the Council prior to the commence-ment of the development as security for the obligations undertaken by the applicant;

(b) the agreed area of woodland to be planted and fenced prior to the construction of the houses or in accordance with an agreed phasing plan;

(c) agreed public paths to be provided and agreed nature conserva-tion areas to be fenced off prior to the construction of the houses;

(d) access roads to be laid out prior to the construction of the houses;

[17] Ibid.

(e) the particulars of sale for each croft holding to be subject to the prior approval of the head of planning of the Council;

(f) an undertaking that a condition would be imposed on the title of each croft holding to secure the future maintenance of facilities to be shared with other croft holdings;

(g) no house to be occupied until adequate arrangements made for sewage treatment;

(h) restriction on further subdivision;

(i) ensuring that business carried on in the workshop will not constitute a nuisance to neighbours;

(j) a woodland management plan to be prepared and implemented to secure the future management of the woodland, including, where appropriate, arrangements for disposing of the woodland to some third party to undertake the management. All schemes to date have attracted Forestry Authority grants and the woodland is regulated by their requirements for a ten-year period. At one site the area to be planted as woodland was transferred to the Scottish Woodlands Trust. At another, the farmer undertook the structural planting; responsibility for planting and maintaining woodland within the individual crofts rested with the croft owners;

(k) a wildlife and habitat management agreement to be prepared and implemented to secure the future management of such areas, where appropriate. Such an arrangement has only been considered appropriate at one site – an area of raised bog. Negotiations are in progress with the Scottish Wildlife Trust with regard to the future management of the site. If these are unsuccessful, the local authority will acquire and manage the site;

(l) provision for public access to the paths in appropriate cases coupled with arrangements for the maintenance of the paths.

An agreement dealing with these matters has been signed by the landowner for each farm. In this way the Council has been able to maintain close control over the schemes.

The use of planning agreements to implement the lowland crofting policy is evaluated after we have described the position with the Cairngorm funicular.

3 The Cairngorm Funicular

3.1 The application

In August 1994 a planning application was submitted by the Cairngorm Chairlift Co. Ltd, as lessees of the Cairngorm ski area, to what was then Highland Regional Council to replace the main chairlift with a funicular railway. Specifically, the application sought planning permission for the construction of a funicular railway from the car park at Coire Cas to the Ptarmigan Restaurant near the summit of Cairngorm, the removal of the existing two-stage chairlift and the chairlift stations, the alteration and extension of existing buildings to incorporate new funicular stations, catering and exhibition facilities, administration offices and workshops and other ancillary works. The application was accompanied by an environmental statement as required by the Environmental Assessment (Scotland) Regulations 1988.

The arguments advanced in support of the application were that the existing chairlift was vulnerable to closure because of wind, it offered no weather protection to passengers, it had insufficient capacity in the winter, it was labour-intensive as regards operation and management, it suffered from obsolescence (it had been in operation since 1961) with consequent problems in obtaining spares and it was poorly located in relation to the car park. The objective of the proposed development was to provide a more modern and reliable uplift facility for skiers. Other options, including a modern detachable chairlift system and a single or double monocable gondola system, had been considered but discarded in favour of a funicular on grounds of capital and operating costs, passenger accessibility and comfort and performance in strong winds.

The intention was that the funicular, like the main chairlift, would be open all the year round with summer usage necessary to make it commercially viable. It was estimated that with the funicular the number of summer visitors might rise from the present figure of about 60,000 to around 225,000.

In response to consultation, Scottish Natural Heritage (SNH), with some support from two neighbouring planning authorities, expressed major reservations about the proposal. SNH was established in 1991 and combines the functions formerly discharged by the Nature Conservancy Council for Scotland and the Countryside Commission for Scotland. Amongst other functions, it is responsible for the conservation and enhancement of the natural heritage of Scotland (Natural Heritage (Scotland) Act 1991, s.1). SNH's principal objection centred on the adverse effect that the increased visitor numbers in the summit area of Cairngorm and on the adjoining Cairngorm/Ben Macdhui plateau might have on an area of outstanding ecological importance.

A large area of land immediately adjoining and to the west of the ski area and running south from the summit of Cairngorm, and including the plateau and the Northern Corries, is the subject of multiple conservation designations. The Northern Corries are a site of special scientific interest, the plateau forms part of a national nature reserve owned by the Royal Society for the Protection of Birds (RSPB). The SSSI and much of the nature reserve are included in a proposed (now designated) Special Protection Area for Birds under the Birds Directive (EC/79.409) and part of that area has also been proposed as a Special Area of Conservation under the Habitats Directive (EC/02/43) (together referred to in this chapter as the 'European sites'). Finally, the government have proposed that the Cairngorms should be nominated as a World Heritage Site of National Importance. The principal designations and their relationship to the proposed development are shown on the plan.

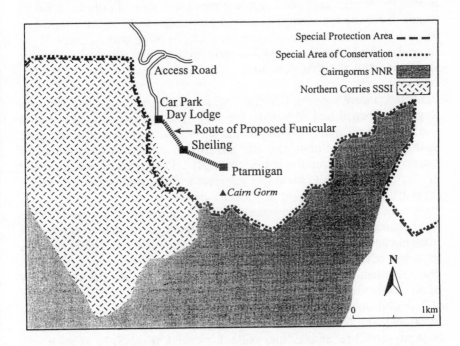

Of the designations, the proposed European sites posed the greatest difficulty in determining the application. The Habitats Directive has been given effect through the Conservation (Natural Habitats Etc.) Regulations 1994. Where a project is likely to have a significant effect on a European site, a planning authority is required to make an appropriate assessment of the implications for the site having regard to its conservation objectives. Amongst other things, the authority must consult with SNH (in Scotland) and take account of their representations. The authority, having regard to the outcome of the assessment, may only grant permission if the project will not adversely affect the integrity of the site (reg.48). Although the two proposed European sites on Cairngorm had not, at that time, been formally designated, the government stated that proposed sites should be treated as though they were designated (SOEnvD Circular 6/1995). Not surprisingly, given the large increase in the number of summer visitors which the funicular is expected to bring to the summit area of Cairngorm, the question of the effect of the proposal on the integrity of these sites was at the heart of SNH's concern.

In an attempt to deal with the concern about the threat to the European sites, the chairlift company lodged a draft visitor-management plan with the planning authority in January 1996. Amongst other proposals, it was suggested that summer users should only be allowed to exit from the top station to take a ranger-led walk to the summit or to walk down the mountain to the car park. In other words, users of the funicular would not be allowed to stray into the European sites. As we shall see (below), this concession was insufficient to resolve SNH's concerns.

In the meantime, in addition to the statutory consultations, the Regional Council had advertised the lodging of the planning application and the accompanying environmental statement. Subsequently, the draft visitor-management plan was also advertised. The proposal provoked a massive response from the public. In total, 1,114 letters of objection and 722 letters of support (some in cyclostyle format) were received. Those supporting the application tended to be concentrated locally in the Aviemore area and focused largely on the benefits of the proposal to the local economy. The objectors were distributed more widely through both Scotland and England, with few from the Aviemore area. Their concerns included adverse ecological and visual impact, loss of wildness, the draconian nature of the proposed visitor management and the availability of alternative solutions to the need for improved uplift facilities.

The objectors included a number of NGOs (non governmental organizations): the National Trust for Scotland, the Ramblers' Association, Scottish Wildlife and Countryside Link and the RSPB. The RSPB objection was particularly significant given its ownership of much of the plateau and its influence through informal access to the scientific community of SNH. In a lengthy letter of objection submitted in February 1996, the RSPB drew attention to the ecological importance of the Cairngorms, the possible impact of the development on the ecology, and the inadequacies in the proposed mitigation measures, especially the draft visitor-management plan.

3.2 Heads of agreement

Because of the stringent requirements of the Habitats Regulations (above), the overlapping jurisdictions of the planning authority and

SNH and the need to demonstrate careful, continuing and flexible regulation of the development should planning permission be granted, the Regional Council was in no doubt from the beginning that normal development-control powers would need to be supplemented by an agreement in this case.

The chairlift company, as applicants and as lessees of the ski area, and Highlands and Islands Enterprise, as owners of the ski area, and the heritable creditor with a security over part of the ski area, would need to be joined to consent to the terms. This could all be achieved through an agreement with the Council under what was then s.50 of the Town and Country Planning (Scotland) Act 1972.

More difficult was the position of SNH who, in view of their duties under the Natural Heritage (Scotland) Act 1991 and their position under the Habitats Regulations, would need to be given an executive role in any agreement, but who could not be joined under s.50 of the 1972 Act as they were neither the planning authority nor a person having an interest in the land. This difficulty was overcome by joining SNH as a party to the agreement under s.49A of the Countryside (Scotland) Act 1967. Section 49A enables SNH to enter into a management agreement with any person having an interest in land so as to secure the conservation and enhancement of the natural heritage of Scotland.

Consideration was also given to the involvement of those with an interest in the land comprised in the European sites, in particular the RSPB, as it was the consequences of the development for these sites which were the focus of concern. However, it was evident that the solution to the concern (assuming a solution could be found) lay in management of activity in the ski area. The RSPB was not, therefore, joined as a party but it was invited to comment on the heads of agreement, an opportunity which it accepted.[18]

Having determined the parties, the Council drafted heads of agreement for consideration. Notwithstanding considerable negotiation over these, SNH remained unconvinced that the safeguards envisaged would ensure the integrity of the European sites, and they maintained their objection to the proposal. That was the position on 4 March 1996 when the application eventually came before the planning committee for a decision.

Given the volume of representations, the Council convened a special meeting of the committee and this was held in Aviemore rather than Inverness. Perhaps not surprisingly, strong local support for the proposal was evident during the day. The planning officer's report,

[18] Letter of 12 February 1996 from the RSPB to the Director of Planning of Highland Regional Council.

which was made available to objectors, ran to 125 pages. It summarized the arguments for and against the proposal, explained relevant planning policy, listed the supporters and objectors, included copies of key correspondence with SNH and the RSPB, provided an extract from the draft visitor-management plan, set out the heads of agreement as amended during negotiations, and indicated that, while in his view the proposal was acceptable subject to conditions and completion of the agreement, a decision should be postponed pending further negotiations with SNH. During the morning, the committee provided an opportunity for the applicants and objectors to make representations. In the afternoon, the committee discussed the application and the representations and concluded unanimously that they were minded to grant conditional permission but that a final decision would be postponed to allow further negotiations with SNH in an effort to resolve their objection.

In the light of SNH's continued objection, the chairlift company subsequently proposed two radical changes to the draft visitor-management plan, changes which had been canvassed earlier as a possible fall-back position if the plan proved inadequate. First of all, the company now proposed to operate a closed system at the top station. In other words, summer users of the funicular would be unable to leave the top station to walk to the summit or to walk back down the mountain. They would be able to visit the viewing area, the interpretative facility and the restaurant, and would then return on the funicular. Secondly, the company proposed to institute a charging regime for visitors using the ski-area car park. The intention would be to discourage extensive use of the car park by summer visitors other than for accessing the funicular. The Council, for their part, undertook to pursue the making of a clearway order to prevent parking on the access road to the car park. The draft heads of agreement were further revised to reflect these changes.

These changes satisfied SNH that the requirements of the Habitats Directive and the regulations could be met and they indicated to the Council that they were minded to withdraw their objection subject to completion of the agreement and to revisions to the visitor-management plan (letter, 10 May 1996).

3.3 The substance of the agreement

Between May 1996 and March 1997 negotiations continued between the parties to settle the detailed provisions of the agreement. These included the following matters:

(a) an undertaking by the planning authority to issue planning permission following execution of the agreement;

(b) the applicants to meet the cost of a base-line survey which would provide a record of the existing condition of the area and to undertake prior to commencement of development that part of the survey affecting the ski area;

(c) the applicants to submit for final approval of the Council and SNH a visitor-management plan, the plan to be submitted within nine months of commencement of the development, to be approved before the funicular can be brought into public use and thereafter to be implemented; amongst other things, the plan is to deal with the detailed arrangements for monitoring the impact of the development; a breach of the terms of the plan to be treated as a breach of the terms of the agreement;

(d) prior to commencement of development, the applicants to submit for the approval of the Council and SNH a scheme for implementing the development having particular regard to such matters as reinstatement of land and monitoring of the effects; the applicants to implement the scheme as approved;

(e) provision for the preparation by an expert at the applicants' expense of an annual report on the impact of non-skiing visitors;

(f) provision for the Council and SNH to stipulate changes to the management regime if monitoring or the annual report shows this to be necessary and for the applicants to request a review of the regime, the changes to be incorporated into and to become part of the visitor-management plan and to be carried out at the applicants' expense;

(g) arrangements for safeguarding the environment in the event of temporary or permanent discontinuance of the operation of the funicular, including arrangements for removal and reinstatement;

(h) enforcement arrangements in the event of default including the provision of a bond, the taking of direct action and suspension of the operation of the funicular;

(i) arrangements between the Council and SNH with regard to decision-making including allowing SNH the final say where a matter is likely to affect the integrity of a European site;

(j) arrangements for ensuring that any new operator of the funicular is subject to the terms of the agreement.

The agreement was finally completed and lodged for recording in the Register of Sasines, and planning permission was granted on 27 March 1997. On 28 May 1997 the World Wildlife Fund (UK) and the RSPB unsuccessfully petitioned for judicial review, *inter alia*, of the decision to grant planning permission for the construction of the funicular railway on Cairngorm.

4 Evaluation

Loughlin[19] drew a distinction between the 'architectural/engineering' model of agreements in which the focus is on the orderly arrangement of physical resources, the 'social cost' model in which agreements are used to internalize certain costs which would otherwise be borne by the public at large, and the 'social needs' model in which agreements are used up to a point to secure some redistribution of resources. This analytical framework was developed by Healey et al.[20] Healey identified three groups of 'rationales' for the use of agreements. First of all, agreements may be concerned with the implementation of planned development. In such cases, developers are encouraged to contribute to the provision of planned infrastructure to enable their development scheme to continue. Secondly, agreements are employed to address the social costs of development. The focus is on accommodating the development within a wider area. Thirdly, agreements are used to secure a cross-subsidy to the community out of the developer's profits. The grant of planning permission releases development value for the benefit of the developer. The agreement ensures that some of the benefit is returned to the community – a sort of local betterment tax.

The use of agreements to implement the lowland crofting policy would seem to be a manifestation of all three rationales with an emphasis on the second and third. The agreements are concerned with securing the necessary infrastructure in order that the development can proceed, with accommodating the development within its wider area, and with securing a cross-subsidy for the benefit of the community. The predominant purpose of the agreements, however, is to secure the cross-subsidy: the establishment of woodland and the provision of public access and sites of nature conservation interest. The development value unlocked by the release of the land for lowland crofting enables the planting of the woodland to be achieved. The courts have countenanced an arrangement whereby the profits from a development are used to enable another desirable (in planning terms) activity to proceed.[21] The agreement for the Cairngorm funicular, on the other hand, is primarily concerned with the second rationale. The focus is heavily on internalizing the social costs of the development – in this case ensuring that the development does not adversely affect the integrity of the European sites.

Earlier in this chapter we identified a number of criticisms of

---

[19] M. Loughlin, 'Planning gain: law, policy and practice', (1981) *Oxford Journal of Legal Studies*, 1(1), p.61.

[20] Healey, Purdue and Ennis, above n.6, chs 1 and 6.

[21] *Brighton Borough Council* v. *Secretary of State for the Environment* [1973] JPL

agreements which would provide a focus for our evaluation of their role. These are now considered in turn.

4.1 The benefits of using an agreement

A planning agreement enables the planning authority to exert continuing control through the life of a development. Although in law there would seem to be nothing to prevent planning authorities from attaching conditions which impose continuing obligations on the applicant with regard to the future management of a development, in practice such control may need to be flexible. Although a certain amount of flexibility can be achieved through the use of *Grampian* conditions,[22] planning authorities sometimes require greater precision than negatively worded conditions can offer. With both case studies, the planning authorities were evidently concerned as much with the future management of the developments as with their initial construction. Satisfactory arrangements for the continuing management of the woodlands, for example, is clearly an important factor in permitting lowland crofting, but such arrangements may take different forms and the planning authority may need to respond flexibly. This flexibility is more easily achieved in an agreement than in a condition.[23]

The funicular agreement goes further. Although, as explained above, continuing control of development is possible, the development-control process operates essentially as a once-and-for-all response to an application for planning permission. In other words, unlike more modern regimes of control, there is no opportunity to review and alter control arrangements in the light of experience with the development, except through an order procedure coupled with the payment of compensation. The funicular agreement enables Highland Council and SNH to alter control arrangements without compensation should monitoring show that this is required to continue to safeguard the nature conservation interest of the European sites. The agreement extends the Council's development control powers in a way that could not be achieved through conditions.

173; *Northumberland County Council* v. *Secretary of State for the Environment* [1989] JPL 700; *R.* v. *Westminster City Council ex parte Monahan* [1990] 1 QB 87; *Wansdyke District Council* v. *Secretary of State for the Environment* [1992] JPL 1168.

[22] A *Grampian* condition takes its name from the decision in *Grampian Regional Council* v. *Aberdeen District Council* [1984] SLT 197. Such a condition is negatively worded and makes the commencement or occupation of a development contingent on the happening of a specified event.

[23] A number of studies have noted this as an important reason for the use of agreements: Rowan-Robinson and Durman, above n.5; Grimley J. R. Eve in association with Thames Polytechnic and Alsop Wilkinson, above n.5; Healey, Purdue and Ennis, above n.6.

A further advantage is evident with lowland crofting. The agreement secures community benefits in the form of the planting of woodland and, in appropriate cases, the provision of public access and of nature conservation sites. These benefits are required as compensation for permitting development in the countryside and are in line with the trend observed by Purdue et al. towards using agreements increasingly to alleviate or compensate for a wide range of social, economic and environmental impacts.[24] The use of agreements in this way would seem to be in line with the thinking of the Countryside Commission.[25] The Commission have expressed the opinion that there is scope through the use of agreements to achieve more benefits for the countryside when development has to take place in rural areas. The statement encourages planning authorities to think how to compensate for the impacts of development in the countryside. Although serving a planning purpose, it is questionable how far the requirements referred to above would, in terms of the legal tests for conditions, be regarded as fairly and reasonably related to the development and whether it would be seen as reasonable. Here, too, the agreement enables West Lothian Council to extend its development control powers.

The agreements also benefited applicants and planning authorities by removing an obstacle to the grant of planning permission. There is no doubt that both sides saw clear advantages in negotiation. Members of the Highland Council planning committee were persuaded of the economic benefits to the local area which would follow from the construction of the funicular and were anxious to secure these benefits, provided this could be done in a way which did not adversely affect the integrity of the European sites. The agreement gave the Council and SNH confidence that the necessary degree of control could be exerted. West Lothian Council were willing to allow housing development in the lowland crofting area provided they could be sure it would bring about an improvement in the landscape and attract inward investment while not jeopardizing other planning policies. The agreement provided the advisory group and the Council with the necessary assurance that the compensatory benefits would follow. West Lothian's experience with lowland crofting is stimulating considerable interest among other local authorities.[26] In both cases, planning permissions could not have been granted in the absence of the agreements.

In both case studies, the applicants were obviously anxious to secure a grant of planning permission and this was an important motivator. It

[24] M. Purdue, P. Healey and F. Ennis, 'Planning gain and the grant of planning permission: is the United States "test of the rational nexus" the appropriate solution?' [1992] JPL 1012.

[25] Countryside Commission, 'Countryside planning statement', CCP 440, 1993.

[26] Rankin and Hartley, above n.13.

is unlikely that they welcomed the additional control secured by agreement; on the other hand, it is probable that the applicants also saw some benefit in being able to tailor regulation to their particular circumstances, a benefit that is not often available with conditions. Conditions, for the most part, are simply imposed rather than negotiated.

4.2 Planning policy and planning agreements

We referred earlier to the criticism that the negotiation of planning gains may lead planning authorities to abandon or compromise established planning policy. One of the concerns about lowland crofting was that it might be seen as abandoning conventional restrictive policy on development in the countryside in return for privately funded woodland and other benefits. To answer this criticism, the planning authority were careful to confine the scheme to an identified area of degraded landscape and poor-quality agricultural land. This strategy was supported in an appeal decision at an early stage in the implementation of the scheme when the reporter rejected an argument for a similar relaxation on land outwith, but with a common boundary to, the identified area.[27]

In SODD (Scottish Office Development Department) Circular 12/1996, *Planning Agreements*, the Secretary of State encourages planning authorities to give guidance in their development plans on the particular circumstances in which planning authorities will seek to use agreements (para.14).[28] Such guidance should enable developers to anticipate the financial implications for their development projects, including the consequences for land values. The minister goes on to suggest that such policies should be as precise as possible because general statements of intent are unhelpful. The lowland crofting scheme is unusual both in the degree of precision to be found in the local plan and in the fact that the policy preceded practice. Healey et al. note that generally it is only when established practices become settled that policies are set out in development plans.[29]

The agreement for the Cairngorm funicular is a response to a one-off planning application and is directed at anticipating and alleviating the social costs of the development. The development plan cannot usually provide any forewarning about the use of agreements in such cases, although general statements about the distribution of the cost of infrastructure are becoming commonplace in structure plans.

[27] Decision letter dated 25 August 1992, reference PPA/LD/245.

[28] See, too, on the role of development plans Rowan-Robinson and Durman, above n.5; Grimley J. R. Eve in association with Thames Polytechnic and Alsop Wilkinson, above n.5; Elson, above n.8; and Healey, Purdue and Ennis, above n.6.

[29] Ibid., p.176.

4.3 The procedural implications of negotiating development control

One of the criticisms directed at the negotiation of planning agreements is that an important factor in the decision-making process on a development may circumvent the normal processes of publicity and representation. Some fifteen years ago, the Law Society recommended that 'no less publicity and opportunity for consultation should be accorded to a proposal for development which involves the making of a planning gain than is required for the application itself'.[30] Although criticisms such as this were considered by the government during the passage through Parliament of the Planning and Compensation Act 1991, there has been no legislation. Official advice from the Department of the Environment, however, goes some way towards meeting the point. Circular 1/97 acknowledges that 'there is an obvious and legitimate interest in planning obligations; the process of negotiating planning obligations should therefore be conducted as openly, fairly and reasonably as possible' (Annex B, para.B19). Planning obligations and related correspondence, continues the circular, should, as a minimum, be listed as background papers to the planning committee report on the development in question. That practice remains a long way short of advice is evident from the recent criticism of the position by the Nolan Committee on Standards in Public Life in its report on local government.[31] The report recommends that negotiations for planning obligations should be more open and that the agreed heads of terms should be reported to the planning committee. The government's response falls some way short of this. Legislation is proposed which will require information about completed agreements to be included in planning registers.

Healey et al. argue that negotiated control needs to be pursued in a way which is justifiable, systematic, open and accountable.[32] 'The challenge for authorities was to find ways of demonstrating to all interested parties that negotiated agreements were reasonable and in line with planning policy, while maintaining the flexibility to negotiate a mutually satisfactory agreement.' Our view is that in both case studies the process followed went a long way towards meeting this challenge. The lowland crofting agreements have the backing of an adopted local plan policy. As the SODD circular points out, 'by including policies in

[30] The Law Society, 'Planning gain: the Law Society's observations' [1982] JPL 346.

[31] *Standards in Public Life: Standards of Conduct in Local Government in England, Scotland and Wales*, Third report of the Committee on Standards in Public Life (HMSO, 1997).

[32] P. Healey, M. Purdue and F. Ennis, *Gains from Planning? Dealing with the Impacts of Development* (Joseph Rowntree Foundation, 1993). See, too, Elson, above n.8.

the development plans on the circumstances in which planning agreements would be sought there is an opportunity for the local community and the development industry to comment.' The funicular agreement lacks the benefit of development plan support but the case study demonstrates that the planning authority went to considerable lengths to inform the public about the heads of agreement. The RSPB, one of the principal objectors, took the opportunity to comment on the heads of agreement. Furthermore, there was a short presentation about the heads of agreement at the planning committee meeting held in public at Aviemore on 4 March 1996. The details of the obligations and the legal drafting were inevitably a matter of private negotiation between the parties, but the agreement in its final form was lodged in the Register of Sasines and is available for public inspection. Some of those objecting to the funicular were critical because no information was released about the outcome of the negotiations over the agreement and the visitor-management plan and there was, therefore, no opportunity to comment at this final stage in the decision-making process. Some form of final report to the planning committee on the outcome of negotiations should be possible with controversial proposals and would help to promote transparency and confidence in the process. Overall, however, we think the processes of publicity and representation were adequately safeguarded in these cases.

5 Conclusion

At the beginning of this chapter we referred to agreements as an example of a more consensual and co-operative approach to regulation. Although negotiated in the shadow of conventional regulation, the two case studies illustrate the way in which planning authorities and developers can come together to resolve significant environmental conflicts in the development and management of the countryside. In both cases, the agreements enabled the parties to overcome what would otherwise have been insuperable obstacles to development and in a way which enabled them to achieve their own objectives. We cannot generalize on the basis of two case studies; but they are, none the less, indicative of what the EU Fifth Action Programme on the Environment refers to as a 'let's work together approach' to resolving environmental problems.

These agreements were concluded against the background of a changing climate of opinion by the executive and the judiciary about the legitimacy of negotiating control. The change has been gradual but there is now recognition of the benefits, both public and private, that negotiation can bring. Planning agreements are no longer characterized as dubious back-room deals. There is also recognition that the proper scope of negotiation can extend beyond the 'implementation of planned development' rationale referred to by Healey et al. to tackle the 'social costs' of development and, up to a point, to condone cross-subsidy where it compensates for social costs.[33] Subject to proper safeguards, the potential role for agreements in resolving countryside development conflicts is considerable.

---

[33] There is even some support for Loughlin's 'social needs' model, above n.19, providing there is at least a tenuous link between the community benefit and the proposed development – see *Tesco Stores Ltd* v. *Secretary of State for the Environment* [1995] JPL 581, although a community-benefits approach is being resisted as a matter of policy by the Department of the Environment and the Scottish Office Development Department.

4

Sustaining Biodiversity: The Contribution of the Planning System in Controlling Development

WENDY LE-LAS

1 Introduction

In June 1992 around 150 heads of states or governments attended the United Nations Conference on Environment and Development, in Rio de Janeiro, colloquially known as the 'Earth Summit'. If nothing else, such a gathering showed that the conflict between the environment and economic development had assumed a high priority in the political agenda. Amongst the important documents emanating from the Earth Summit was the Biodiversity Convention signed by over 150 countries, including the United Kingdom.[1]

Many species threatened with global extinction are found within our shores. Our woods, waters and open spaces provide habitats for an abundant variety of wildlife. There are dozens of species which are found in the UK and nowhere else in the world. Other species may not be confined to the UK but occur here in internationally significant numbers: it is incumbent upon us to ensure their survival.[2] Dozens of UK species are listed as threatened with extinction by the International Union for the Conservation of Nature.[3]

Having signed the Biodiversity Convention, the British government set up the Biodiversity Steering Group, comprised of the great and the

[1] *Biodiversity: The UK Action Plan* (HMSO, 1994) paras.1.3–1.4.
[2] *Biodiversity Challenge: An Agenda for Conservation in the UK* (RSPB/WWF) pp.1, 2.
[3] Ibid.

good in the world of nature conservation. Their report provided action plans for 116 of the most seriously threatened species and fourteen of the most endangered habitats in Britain. These are set within the context of the pressures on the thirty-seven habitat types to be found in this country.[4] It was not ever thus: flora and fauna now on the verge of extinction were once considered common.

To judge from the report, there would appear to be three main culprits which have led to this sorry state of affairs: urbanization in all its guises; water abstraction, water pollution and air pollution; and modern agricultural and forestry techniques. Urbanization, pollution and abstraction are a threat to a third of the species, whereas farming and forestry adversely affect 60 per cent. With regard to the endangered habitats, urbanization, water abstraction, water and air pollution adversely affect half of them, whereas and farming and forestry affect 70 per cent. From this superficial glance at the causes of damage to wildlife, it would appear that modern farming practices have had a more detrimental effect than urbanization, but for those who care about the natural world, this should not be a reason for complacency.

The main body of this chapter is based on practical experience of the relationship between nature conservation and development-control procedures, including enforcement. The concluding section shows that although the status quo could be improved by specific changes to planning law and procedure, the implementation of the Biodiversity Convention would transform the culture in which decisions are taken to the long-term advantage of the natural world.

2 Boundaries of the Planning System

It should be explained at the outset that the scope of the planning system defies rationality; it is a matter of convention born of historical accident. It will be shown that many of the activities which are damaging to wildlife do not fall within its sphere of influence.

The British planning system, under the 1990 Town and Country Planning Act (TCPA), is based on local government. As local authority boundaries do not extend beyond the low-water mark, development beyond the latter is the responsibility of the Crown rather than the planners. Agriculture and forestry, in terms of the use of land and existing buildings, are specifically excluded from being defined as 'development' under s.55 of the 1990 TCPA. The reason why agriculture, and indeed afforestation, was not brought within the curtilage of the 1947 TCPA, and subsequent Acts, was that it was assumed that there would be no conflict between productivity and the environment.[5]

[4] *BIODIVERSITY: The UK Steering Group Report* (HMSO, 1995), vol.2, Annex G.
[5] Marion Shoard, *The Theft of the Countryside* (Temple Smith, 1980), 101.

The control of pollution from existing premises is the responsibility of the Environment Agency, and it is only when there is to be an intensification of an existing use, or a new operational development is proposed, that a planning application becomes necessary. Trunk roads and motorways are outwith the planning system altogether: they are the responsibility of the Highways Agency, and the procedures are based on the Highways Acts. Energy installations, such as power stations, power lines and pipelines, come under the Electricity Acts and Pipeline Acts respectively, and thus fall outside the boundaries of the planning system.

3 Bias towards Development

Having explored the boundaries of the planning system, it is necessary to look at the ethos under which the system works. Only then can one appreciate the strength of the forces working against biodiversity: it is no wonder that a third of the species and half of the habitats listed by the Biodiversity Steering Group have been adversely affected by urbanization and its resultant pollution.

Alder[6] has pointed out that the British legal system is firmly anthropocentric: nature is seen as a resource to be exploited by man to furnish his requirements in the short term, rather than with any view to the needs of posterity. The law is geared to the protection of private property rights and the free flow of market capitalism. The roots of planning law lie in nineteenth-century public-health legislation: property owners in the burgeoning towns and cities were amongst the few who were enfranchised, and would not have supported legislation had it been thought to inhibit their legitimate right, as they saw it, to do what they liked with their own. The appeal system was created to safeguard such liberties.[7]

The famous phrase 'presumption in favour of development' originates in a 1923 circular from the Ministry of Health. It disappeared in the 1992 version of PPG 1, but the sentiment is firmly entrenched in the system.[8] Although there has been a change in government since this PPG was issued it is inconceivable that any government could get elected which posed a threat to such a fundamental tenet of British society.

The bias in favour of development is most obviously demonstrated by

---

[6] John Alder, 'Legal values and environmental values', in Christopher Rodgers (ed.), *Nature Conservation and Countryside Law* (University of Wales Press, 1996), 20–31.

[7] W. G. Le-Las, *Playing the Public Inquiry Game: An Objector's Guide* (Viridis, 1987), section I, 1–4.

[8] PPG 1, 1997, para.36.

the lack of third-party rights to appeal against the granting of a planning permission.[9] However, there are many, more subtle ways in which the planning system has been shaped to facilitate development. Ever since the advent of development plans in 1947, there have been anxieties about keeping them up to date so as not to inhibit new proposals. The speeding-up of the appeals system began in 1962, with the introduction of written representations, and the pressure on expediting appeals has continued until the present day. However, the idea that planning should be the servant of economic development was given considerable impetus by the 1985 White Paper, characteristically entitled 'Lifting the burden'.[10] Accordingly, the last ten years have witnessed:

(a) the introduction into planning legislation of modern develop-
      ment such as agribusiness and electronic communications: this
      means that development is not delayed by outmoded language;
(b) the expansion of permitted-development rights;
(c) the de minimis approach to the use of discretionary powers such
      as the requirement for Schedule 2 EAs (Environmental
      Assessments);
(d) the sheer difficulty of getting cases called in by the Secretary of
      State,[11] even if they are departures from the development plan,
      local authority schemes, or if the application is accompanied by
      an Environmental Statement (ES) which deserves the scrutiny of
      an inquiry;
(e) the advent of nature conservation and pollution watchdogs
      whose advice is tailored to the pro-development culture, and
      whose resources are too inadequate to enable them to query the
      developer's data or intentions;[12]
(f) financial stringency towards local authorities, which depletes
      their ability to fight applications in terms of basic data and
      officer time to appear at inquiries. This is compounded by the
      threat of costs[13] being awarded to the developer on appeal.

[9] In the Isle of Man up to a third of all appeals are lodged by third parties, and 16 per cent are won (compared with only double that percentage won by appellants). Le-Las, Understanding the Development Jigsaw: A User's Guide to Procedures (Buccaneer Books, 1997), 219. In Eire, too, over a third of appeals are against grants of planning permission: 29 per cent were refused permission and in 65 per cent conditions were revised. See Yvonne Scannell, 'Public participation rights in Irish environmental law', in Sustaining Environmental Law: Conference Proceedings, 9, 10 October 1998, Imperial College, London.
[10] Cmnd. 9571.
[11] Fewer than a hundred applications are called in per year under s.77 of the 1990 TCPA, out of about half a million applications per year.
[12] WWF, A Muzzled Watchdog? Is English Nature Protecting Wildlife? (WWF, November 1997).

There are occasions when these factors will militate against the proper consideration of biodiversity issues in the face of pressure for development. The natural world in general, as opposed to sites of SSSI rank and above, is affected by the expansion in the number of categories of permitted development. The minimization of the number of Schedule 2 EAs means that LPAs have to work out the potential impact on 'flora, fauna, soil, air and water'. This may be less than adequate because of lack of resources. A similar effect may occur if an application, which is accompanied by an ES, is not subject to an inquiry: an ES may be economical with the truth over biodiversity issues; if the LPA is either 'the developer' or favourably inclined towards a proposal, it may not be receptive to arguments about the adverse effects on the natural world.

These effects may be compounded by the attitude of the statutory watchdogs, i.e. the Environment Agency and English Nature. They are expected to facilitate development:[14] it is only in exceptional cases that they are permitted to say 'No'. If their resources are slim, then there is a tendency to skimp on the research work necessary to back up a refusal. How can this affect biodiversity? Suppose a waste dump is proposed on a site upstream from an SSSI, and the Environment Agency takes the view that no risk assessment is required because it would be expensive, rather than because they are certain that the leachate will not enter the groundwater system. English Nature is thereby prevented from objecting on grounds of water pollution. This in turn may have other knock-on effects, for example, if, at the same time as the application is being considered, the boundaries of a Special Landscape Area are being debated via the local plan process, it is hard for the LPA to argue that the site in question is a valued 'green corridor' as English Nature appear to have no objection to the proposed development. Alternatively, or in addition, the statutory agencies may be less than enthusiastic about applying the powers available to them to mitigate the effects of a proposed development, e.g. English Nature not being prepared to enter into a management agreement with a developer with a potentially damaging proposal on an adjacent site, by using their powers under the 1968 Countryside Act, s.15.

If these watchdogs do not bark loud enough, or at all, then the LPAs and other government agencies are obliged to accept that there is no problem, even if they have professional misgivings on the issue. Only

[13] DoE Circular 8/93 on the award of costs in planning and other proceedings. It will be apparent that there are more pitfalls for LPAs than appellants. For commentary on how this works in practice see W. G. Le-Las, *Understanding the Development Jigsaw*, 86, 88, 89.

[14] See PPG 9, *Nature Conservation* and PPG 23, *Planning and Pollution Control*, *passim*.

third parties are in a position to query the wisdom of these statutory agencies, but of course that depends on the expertise at their disposal, and their ability to enter the site to ascertain the facts.

4 Biodiversity and Development Control

4.1 Defining 'development'

Since the passing of the 1947 TCPA, it has been necessary to apply for planning permission to develop land. In practice, development is divided into two categories: 'operations' and 'change of use'. According to s.55 of the 1990 TCPA: 'development means the carrying out of building, engineering, mining or other operations in, on, over, or under land, or the making of any material change of use of any buildings or other land.' Most of the works classified as operations have the potential to affect biodiversity.[15] What about change of use? Any change has to be 'material', i.e. substantial, and it can include an intensification of the same use. It may be less frequent than with operations, but there are occasions when biodiversity can be put at risk by a change of use, e.g. increased noise caused by more intensive use of an airfield.

Given that everything is caught within the boundaries of the planning system and within the definition of 'development', the burden on the authorities would be excessive were it not for 'permitted development', i.e. a class of actions for which planning permission is deemed to be granted. These are set out in detail in the General Permitted Development Order 1995 (GPDO), Article 3, Schedule 2. The activities which might have a particular impact on biodiversity include those of farmers, foresters, land drainage authorities, the Environment Agency, statutory undertakers, sewerage undertakers, aviation authorities, minerals operators, and educational institutions. Permitted development rights can be withdrawn or limited by four things: the need for an environmental assessment (EA) of the project; Article 4 Directions; planning conditions; and the proximity of a Special Protection Area (SPA) or a Special Area of Conservation (SAC). Clearly the last two categories are relevant to biodiversity, but so might the others be, depending on the circumstances.

4.2 Environmental assessment

The most recent EC directive on the subject is 97/11/EC, amending 85/337/EEC. It has both expanded the number of subjects, and refined the existing categories requiring EA. In Britain some 70 per cent of

---

[15] Le-Las, *Understanding the Development Jigsaw*, 48, 49.

EAs fall within the planning system. From the point of view of bio-diversity, whether the EA falls within or outside the planning system is perhaps less important than whether it is mandatory, discretionary or outside the framework altogether. In order to minimize the burden on developers, whether in the private or public sectors, thresholds have been set for Annex II projects: only if a scheme is of a certain size, character or location is an EA required. Currently there is great debate about how to set thresholds which minimize costs, whilst safeguarding sensitive sites.[16]

Government advises that a potentially significant impact on the character of an SSSI should be enough to trigger an EA for an Annex II project.[17] This is even more likely if the development is in or close to an SPA or SAC.[18] This is fine for designated sites of SSSI rank or above, especially given that Circulars 15/88 and 7/94 are riddled with exemptions designed to minimize cost to business and expedite development. However, flora and fauna existing on the 92 per cent[19] of England and Wales beyond their boundaries is subject to the *de minimis* approach to EA.

Scrutinizing information furnished by the applicant is the vital first stage in assessing the impact of a proposal. The EA process provides for both consultation with key parties, such as statutory consultees, and much more information than would be provided by an ordinary planning application.[20] None the less, when an ES is required, a different set of problems can arise. Consultants paid by a developer are likely to produce a glossy document, designed to sell the idea to the LPA. Furthermore it may be 'economical with the truth'. Too often, LPAs are desperate for employment and are eager to believe the promises of a developer, whatever the adverse effects on the environment, including biodiversity. Unless the scheme is called in by the Secretary of State, and he may have similar reasons for not doing so, there will be no rigorous testing of the evidence by the opposition before an independent inspector.

[16] However, the Dutch Dykes case which went before the European Court of Justice in October 1996, emphasized the primary need to ascertain the significance of the impact, by the appropriate authority, rather than assuming that everything that falls below a certain threshold, or outside a given procedure, will have no significant impact on the environment. [1996] ECR I–5403.

[17] DoE Circular 15/88, *Environmental Assessment*, para.24.

[18] PPG 9, *Nature Conservation*, paras.38, 39.

[19] Of the combined area of England and Wales 7.78 per cent is designated as SSSI.

[20] *Berkeley* v. *Secretary of State for the Environment and Fulham Football Club* (Court of Appeal, Civil Division, 12 February 1998) confuses the substance with the process of EA, i.e. because volumes of information were available it was assumed that this was the equivalent of an ES. The procedural side of EA, which is important to participants, was discounted.

4.3 Development plans

As has been shown, biodiversity is on the receiving end of a planning system geared to facilitating development at the speed required by the economy of the day. When a planning application is lodged, by what criteria is it determined? In the 1991 Planning and Compensation Act there appeared this crucial provision: 'Where, in making a determination under the Planning Acts, regard is to be had to the development plan, the determination shall be made in accordance with the development plan unless material considerations indicate otherwise.'[21] The *development plan* is a generic term which covers structure plans, local plans and UDPs (unitary development plans).[22] The recent review of local government has resulted in an incredibly complex system outside the metropolitan counties in England, with every conceivable, and some inconceivable permutations and combinations of structure plans, local plans and UDPs.[23] In the Principality, the Local Government (Wales) Act 1994 requires each new unitary council to prepare a UDP in due course.

How does the development-plan system take on board the complexities of the natural world? In order to be digestible by the planning system, flora and fauna have to be quantified and labelled. If there are significant numbers in one place then the site might receive a designation. The latter range from sites of international importance, such as Ramsar Sites, SPAs and SACs, to sites of national significance, such as NNRs and SSSIs, to sites of regional or local prominence, such as LNRs, non-statutory nature reserves etc.[24] The significance of the hierarchy of site designations in development plans is apparent from PPG 9, paras.22, 23, 25. None the less: 'Local planning authorities should have regard to the relative significance of international, national, local and informal designations in considering the weight to be attached to nature conservation value, and *take care to avoid unnecessary constraints on development*' (PPG 9, para.18, emphasis added).

Whilst the shortcomings of the SSSI regime are well known to nature conservation professionals and ecologically minded lawyers, many planners and the general public would be amazed that their protection is virtually voluntary, such are the shortcomings of the 1981 Wildlife and Countryside Act.[25] They regard SSSIs as somehow 'important', even if

[21] Planning and Compensation Act 1991, s.26 inserted into TCPA 1990 as s.54A.
[22] PPG 12, para.3.2.
[23] Le-Las, *Understanding the Development Jigsaw*, 12, 13 and Appendix X.
[24] PPG 9, *Nature Conservation*, 5.
[25] S. Ball, 'Reforming the law of habitat protection', in Rodgers, *Nature Conservation, passim*. See also W. G. Le-Las, 'The significance of the Habitats Directive for the British planning system', in *The Implementation of the EC Habitats Directive in Member States*, ed. C. Backes, M. van Rijswick and L. Warren (forthcoming, Kluwer International, 1999).

they do not understand the scientific basis of the designation. This is reflected in the treatment of SSSIs, of all denominations, in development plans: by and large damaging development is diverted away from them.

None the less, problems can arise with linear development like roads, railways and pipelines, which are wont to avoid buildings because of the economic and social disruption involved, not to mention the payment of compensation commensurate with development-land rates. Linear developments seem to have a predilection for going through SSSIs, of all ranks, because those protesting have relatively little economic or political clout. Difficulties may also arise with proposals destined for a particular site because of its proximity to existing commercial development, e.g. Lappel Bank SPA to the port of Sheerness.

Unfortunately Article 6.4 of the Habitats Directive allows Member States to go ahead with schemes in *Natura 2000* sites[26] which despite their negative impact on a site: 'must nevertheless be carried out for imperative reasons of overrriding public interest, including those of a social or economic nature'. Where a priority species or habitat is involved, there is a little more but not complete protection: the proposal can only go ahead if the reasons relate to public health, public safety, beneficial consequences to the environment, or other reasons, which the EC considers to be imperative reasons of overriding public interest. Obviously the EC will be subject to lobbying by Member States and large corporate interests.

During the development-plan process there may be problems with regard to consulting English Nature and the Countryside Council for Wales. If, as a result of protests, a proposal is shifted to another location near a site of SSSI rank or above, the LPA may omit notifying the statutory nature conservation body. If they are consulted then the lack of resources, alluded to earlier, may mean that they do not realize how potentially damaging this proposed neighbour could be.

It is important to remember that the viability of these sites is very dependent on the interaction with flora and fauna existing in the wider world. What about habitats and species which do not make it into the charmed circle of designated sites, or their consultation areas?

The Habitats Directive requires Member States to endeavour to encourage the management of features of the landscape which are of major importance for wild flora and fauna . . . These features are those which, because of their linear and continuous structure, or their function as stepping stones, are essential for migration, dispersal and genetic exchange. (PPG 9, para.16)

[26] Defined in Article 3(1) of the Habitats Directive as SPAs and SACs.

Development plans which have come on stream since the advent of the Conservation (Natural Habitats etc.) Regulations 1994, are likely to contain policies reflecting the spirit of Article 10 of the Habitats Directive. However, LPAs overzealous to protect the natural environment will be brought back into line by the Planning Inspectorate: policies must not exceed the guidance given in circulars and PPGs.[27] Nevertheless, with regard to applications for outline permission, they are allowed to ask for site appraisals, which include the nature conservation interest, under Article 3(2) of the 1995 General Development Procedure Order.

4.4 Material considerations

When determining a planning application, the development plan clearly plays a key role, but the other half of the equation concerns material considerations, which have been defined as any issue which relates to the use of land.[28] Biodiversity is clearly capable of being treated as a material consideration if the proposed development is not destined for a designated site safeguarded in the development plan. To acquire the requisite weight the flora and/or fauna have to be classified and counted by a reputable person or body. To assert that the site contains a bird protected by the Habitats Directive, without evidence of numbers recorded by, say, the RSPB, is useless. Unfortunately habitats and species only get onto lists when they are endangered: if they are still plentiful, or at least numbers have not reached critical levels, then they are seen as expendable. Thus, in practice, biodiversity will only graduate to becoming a material consideration, if it is on the danger list.

4.5 Weighing the evidence

The latest version of PPG 1 spells out how decisions should be reached on planning applications.[29] First of all there is the matter of whether the proposal accords with the development plan(s) of whatever denomination, and how up-to-date it is. As we have seen, the development plan process is wont to exclude development from sites designated for nature conservation. That said, large schemes and linear proposals may well come into conflict with such sites or land adjacent to them. It is rare for such proposals not to feature in a development plan because major schemes have a long gestation period: the arguments for and against, including impact on biodiversity, will have been

[27] See, for example, the inspector's report on the Canterbury District Local Plan 1997.
[28] L. J. Cook, *Stringer* v. *Ministry of Housing and Local Government 1971*.
[29] PPG 1, 1997, *General Policy and Principles*, paras.40, 48.

thrashed out during the development-plan process. Given the importance of s.54A, it is essential that biodiversity gets the best possible deal
in the development plan.

However, in the real world it is rare for there not to be a relevant
plan grinding its way through the process, en route to adoption. Plans
which are emerging now are more likely to reflect the thinking of, say,
the Habitats Directive. None the less, as has been shown, even the
most prestigious European designations do not impose a moratorium on
development.

In addition to the protection of designated sites in the development
plan, biodiversity may also figure as a material consideration, probably
competing with other material considerations working against its interests. If a proposal does not accord with the development plan, then it is
a matter of the balance of material considerations. Biodiversity lacks a
political constituency with sufficient economic clout to enable it to win
a planning battle outright. To stand any chance of staving off development pressures, those concerned have to find more powerful allies.

Planning disputes can be likened to a game in which the 'counters'
are fragments of government or EU policy. Each side aims to prove
that their case exemplifies official policy on this issue, unlike that of
the opposition whose stance is bound to cause demonstrable harm to
interests of acknowledged importance. The adjudicator, be it the LPA
or the Secretary of State, will decide in favour of the party whose case,
as a whole, most nearly approximates to government policy. Given that
the natural world is on the receiving end of decisions to develop, the
focus of the dispute will be the proposal in question rather than nature
conservation: those concerned with the latter will usually find themselves fighting a rearguard action. In practice, therefore, any
designation lower than an SSSI is worth little because it will pale into
insignificance against the supposed social and economic benefits of the
proposal. It is open season on biodiversity existing on the 92 per cent
of land outside designated sites.

How this works in practice can be seen from the following extract
from an inspector's report, concerning an appeal against a refusal to
build housing on some vacant land which local people feared would
displace a colony of swifts:

The Structure Plan advocates the full use of vacant or underutilised land in
built up areas, and housing policy 5 requires development to be carried out
at as high a density as is compatible with the type of dwelling being
provided and the constraints on the site . . . Given the lack of scientific data
on the flight and behaviour of the swifts, I accept that it is not possible to
predict with certainty the effect of the proposal on the colony . . . The
suggested planning condition preventing the construction work on the

proposed house during the breeding season, would minimise damage ...
Given the low conservation status of the swifts and the need to make beneficial use of the vacant plot, I consider that even if the proposal were certain
to lead to the displacement of the swift colony, the weight I could attach to
the matter would not be sufficient to justify dismissing the appeal.[30]

Another example is a proposed development on some land frequented
by birds protected by the Habitats Directive:

The site appears to have a wide range of habitats. However the evidence
concerning the harmful effect on wildlife appears to be mainly anecdotal.
The site has no specific designations as regards any nature conservation
status. The retention of much of the woodland and hedgerows would give
the opportunity to maintain much of the natural habitat which currently
exists on site. As regards the generally open areas of the site, they did not
appear to me to be significantly different in habitat terms to other neighbouring land outside the development site. Again I do not consider that this
objection would justify the refusal of planning permission.[31]

Thus the extent of natural habitat diminishes year on year on land
outside designated sites, where the type, numbers and tolerance limits
of flora and fauna are unrecorded. Unless there is specific evidence,
biodiversity does not even graduate to becoming a material consideration to be weighed in the balance, let alone the key factor determining
the outcome of the appeal.

4.6 Planning conditions and obligations

In both the DoE circulars on planning conditions and planning obligations, it is stressed that the former are to be preferred because
developers may appeal against them.[32] In fact, even planning obligations are not as permanent as they may appear because they may be
discharged by agreement between the developer and the LPA,[33]
perhaps as the result of an acceptance of a new planning application.
Alternatively they may be appealed after a specified period, or five
years: for those obligations entered into after 25 October 1991, and
therefore eligible for appeal after 25 October 1996, the appeal will be
heard by the Planning Inspectorate rather than the Lands Tribunal.
Given that the former are nurtured on the presumption in favour of

[30] The Planning Inspectorate, T/APP/X2410/A/95/257472/P7, 19 September 1996.
[31] The Planning Inspectorate (Wales), APP/L6940/A/97/510700.
[32] DoE Circular 11/95, *The Use of Conditions in Planning Permissions*, para.12
and DoE Circular 1/97, *Planning Obligations*, para.B.11.
[33] S.106A, 1990 TCPA (alias s.12, P and C Act 1991).

development, unless demonstrable harm can be shown, the Inspectorate are likely to be more flexible than the Lands Tribunal.[34]

Throughout PPG 9, *Nature Conservation*, the emphasis is on making development acceptable via the use of conditions or obligations.[35] If these are the chief means of reconciling nature conservation and development, how effective are they? The RSPB has researched the issue and the findings are not reassuring. Only 12 per cent of the cases studied involved conditions to protect nature conservation interests, or avoid potential impacts. Furthermore only 0.7 per cent directly sought to provide genuine enhancement for habitats, species or features of interest. Eight per cent of the cases involved positive nature conservation measures, but these were as compensation for loss of habitat or adverse impacts caused by the development.

The majority of cases used conditions to lessen the adverse impact of the development by the use of restrictive or negatively worded conditions. However, there were instances where positive works were required, such as the creation of a buffer zone. This raised the difficulty that s.106 obligations are more efficient at delivering positive measures, but, as mentioned above, the government's preference is for conditions, and the courts have interpreted this requirement narrowly.[36] This has left planning officers in a quandary: effectiveness on the ground versus a possible legal challenge. On the other hand, government policy has recently changed, and would appear to view with favour the use of s.106 planning obligation to protect sites and species, and/or instigate measures to offset the impact of a development on wildlife.[37] During times of such financial stringency, LPAs are wont to be cautious.

4.7 Development involving licensing

In some instances, the grant of planning permission is not the final word. Applications for plants operating processes which fall within the category of Integrated Pollution Control, and also for waste-disposal sites, will require a licence granted by the Environment Agency. PPG 23 on Pollution Control repeatedly warns LPAs not to trespass into the territory of the Environment Agency or the Heath and Safety

[34] S.106B, 1990 TCPA. See also W. G. Le-Las, *Understanding the Development Jigsaw*, Appendix IX.

[35] PPG 9, paras.27, 28.

[36] C. E. Brook, *Natural Conditions: A Review of Planning Conditions and Nature Conservation* (RSPB, Sandy, 1996).

[37] DoE Circular 1/97, *Planning Obligations*, para.B11. It should be noted that whilst government policy has sought to limit the scope of s.106 to what is necessary, the courts have allowed greater discretion: see 1996 JPL 581, *Tesco Stores Ltd.* v. *Secretary of State for the Environment, West Oxfordshire DC and Tarmac Provincial Properties Ltd.*

Executive.[38] This is a legacy of the *Gateshead* judgment in 1992. However, the EC Waste Framework Directive 1991 (WFD), implemented by the Waste Management Licensing Regulations 1994,[39] has the potential to change the balance of power between the LPAs and the Environment Agency.

LPAs would appear to have a duty to establish the best environmental option for each waste stream.[40] LPAs would also appear to have a duty to recover or dispose of waste safely.[41] On neither count have the courts upheld the necessity of LPAs to be systematic in their observance of WMLR Schedule 4(4).[42] Why does this matter? The LPA is accountable to its population, and procedures under the Planning Acts are open to public scrutiny and participation. The licensing stage is a private matter between the Environment Agency and the applicant, unless it goes to appeal. Given the reluctance of the courts fully to implement the WFD, there is still a tendency for applicants at the development control stage, and at appeal, to insist that pollution matters be dealt with at the licensing stage. Unless LPAs and/or objectors are well versed in the WFD and WMLR, discussion on potential pollution, with its damaging effect on wildlife, may be limited to amenity considerations.

4.8 Enforcement

For many years forward planning was the exciting area in the field. More recently, development control has come into its own. However, as Millichap points out, there is a third party to the planning trinity: without the enforcement of the decisions made at the other two stages, their efforts are a vain show.[43] Notwithstanding, the enforcement

[38] PPG 23, *Pollution Control*, para.1.34.

[39] SI 1056, 1994, Waste Management Licensing Regulations (WMLR).

[40] Ibid., Schedule 4, 4(3), derived from Article 3 of 1991 Waste Framework Directive.

[41] WMLR, Schedule 4, (4)(1)(a):
> ...necessary measures to ensure that waste is recovered or disposed of without endangering human health and without using processes or methods which could harm the environment, and in particular without: (a) risk to water, air, soil, and plants and animals; or (b) causing a nuisance through noise or odours; or (c) adversely affecting the countryside or places of special interest.

[42] *R. v. Bolton Metropolitan Council, ex parte Kirkman*, JPL 1998 pp.787–807. Neither Carnwath J nor Schiemann LJ were sympathetic to LPAs being required in every case to test for BPO. Neither in the *Bolton* case (ibid.) nor in *R. v. Environment Agency ex parte Leam*, 8 May 1998, was the Article 4 duty of LPAs fully recognized. See P. Shiner, 'The process of environmental protection judicial review, paper to United Kingdom Environmental Law Association Seminar, 22 October 1998.

[43] Denzil Millichap, *The Effective Enforcement of Planning Controls* (Butterworths, 1991), 1–3.

branch of the planning department is usually the first to be cut in times of financial stringency: the results may not be felt for years to come. At present there are many LPAs without a full complement of enforcement officers. This must be having effects across the board, including the conservation of biodiversity.

Yet the system is loaded against the LPA: such is the British respect for private property rights that actually bringing anyone to book is an art form, for gentle persuasion is the order of the day, and taking action the last resort.[44] The RSPB research has shown that actually monitoring what is happening on the ground after a condition has been imposed is far from routine: in 38 per cent of the cases studied, it was not known whether the permission had been implemented, let alone whether the conditions or agreements had been adhered to.[45] Monitoring is regarded as a luxury when there are barely enough personnel to staff the enforcement unit.

However, a new weapon has appeared in the armoury of enforcement officers during the 1990s, namely the Breach of Condition Notice.[46] Clearly such a notice is geared to the conditions imposed. It outlines the steps to be taken and/or the activities to be attenuated or stopped. One advantage is that there is no recourse to appeal: aggrieved parties would have to go to judicial review to get the notice quashed. On the other hand the RSPB research has shown that so often the original conditions in question are not well drafted by the LPA: in many cases conditions did not meet one of the six tests prescribed in DoE Circular 11/95, or they were *ultra vires*. In particular they were expressed in vague language, such 'during the breeding season' or 'minimize disturbance to wildlife'.[47] Unfortunately the finality of a Breach of Condition Notice may also be compromised by the offending party lodging an entirely separate planning application.[48]

Although the Enforcement Notice route is fraught with difficulty, it does have the advantage of allowing Stop Notices to be used if the breach of condition is causing immediate damage, and where biodiversity is concerned the use of such a provision can be vital. None the less, there is a sting in the tail: if the Enforcement Notice is quashed on appeal, for any reason other than the fact that the planning permission should be granted, the LPA becomes liable for compensation.

---

[44] Le-Las, *Understanding the Development Jigsaw*, 101–5.

[45] C. E. Brook, *Natural Conditions*.

[46] Planning and Compensation Act, 1991, s.2 – alias s.187A of the 1990 TCPA.

[47] C. E. Brook, *Natural Conditions*.

[48] Magistrates' courts have shown a reluctance to proceed with a prosecution, preferring to wait for the result of the planning application. The higher courts have indicated that the magistrates should prosecute anyway: see *R. v. Beaconsfield Magistrates ex parte Bucks DC* [1993] COD 357.

Consequently Stop Notices are used very sparingly. In fact the compensation risk is very small: LPAs are wont to exaggerate the problem
despite advice from DoE, but it is yet another sign of local authority
penury.[49]

An even rarer animal is the injunction. The LPA now has the opportunity to ask the courts to issue a special planning injunction, and the
case law looks as though it will be given much more readily that previous remedies. An interlocutory injunction may be granted without the
LPA having to give undertakings in damages if the action is brought in
the public interest under Planning Acts.[50] Clearly this measure has
potential in terms of protecting wildlife. The traditional remedy is the
Enforcement Notice. Many are the pitfalls, however, and the RTPI has
suggested that LPAs adopt a strategic approach towards the proper
issue and service of enforcement notices, and communication with
elected members and the public. Even when things run smoothly,
proceedings are liable to go into abeyance because the accused takes
the opportunity to appeal against the notice. All this takes time: hence
the importance, for wildlife, of using Stop Notices and interlocutory
injunctions to halt damaging practices.

5 Improving the Status Quo

As has been shown, the regulation of development works within a
certain set of parameters: the boundaries of the planning system are not
necessarily where one would expect; the definition of development is
constantly evolving; and there is a bias in favour of the applicant. If
one accepts the political reality that progress is more likely to be made
by adapting an existing system rather than starting from scratch,[51] then
it is a question of addressing current deficiencies. That said, the following recommendations will appear radical, which says more about the
mores of our society than the need to conserve biodiversity.

The recommendations may be divided into two parts: changing the
culture of the institutions in any way responsible for generating or
regulating development; and making changes in planning law.

5.1 Cultural change

To be effective, change has to start with the priorities of central
government. If the Biodiversity Convention were taken seriously, it
would transform its own internal practices and its attitude towards

---

[49] Le-Las, *Understanding the Development Jigsaw*, 104.

[50] RTPI, *Enforcement Control; Practice Note 6* (February 1966), s.16.

[51] C. E. Lindblom, 'The science of muddling through', *Public Administration
Review* (1959).

statutory agencies, statutory undertakers, local government and the private sector.

Article 6(a)[52] focuses on preparing a national strategy for biodiversity. The Steering Group Reports mentioned earlier and the government's response[53] indicate progress so far. It is striking how much we have yet to learn about the natural world, and its tolerance limits towards development.[54] Assuming the government and other parties deliver in terms of the Action Plan for Key Species and Habitats,[55] then the information should become available so that everyone can make informed decisions. It will be a matter of educating not just land-use professionals in central and local government, MPs and councillors, but also landowners, developers in the public and private sectors, NGOs and the general public.[56]

Article 6(b)[57] is supposed to work in conjunction with Article 10(a): 'Each contracting Party shall . . . (a) Integrate consideration of the conservation and sustainable use of biological resources into national decision-making.'

An obvious first choice in the legislative programme is to reform nature conservation law so as to create a system of sites which are positively managed rather than just designated and left to their fate.[58]

---

[52] United Nations Convention on Biodiversity, Nairobi, 22 June 1992, Article 6, General Measures for Conservation and Sustainable Use:

Each Contracting Party shall, in accordance with its particular conditions and capabilities:

(a) Develop national strategies, plans or programmes for the conservation and sustainable use of biodiversity or adapt for this purpose existing strategies, plans or programmes which shall reflect *inter alia*, the measures set out in this Convention relevant to the contracting Party concerned; and

(b) Integrate, as far as possible and as appropriate, the conservation and sustainable use of biological diversity into relevant sectoral or cross-sectoral plans, programmes and policies.

[53] *Government Response to the UK Steering Group Report on Biodiversity* (HMSO, May 1996, Cmnd. 3260).

[54] *UK Biodiversity Steering Group Report*, Appendix G; also *A Guide to the Convention on Biodiversity: Environmental Policy and Law Paper No.10* (IUCN, 1994), Box 10.

[55] *Government Response to the UK Steering Group Report on Biodiversity*, paras.12–22.

[56] Le-Las, 'The significance of the Habitats Directive for the British planning system'.

[57] United Nations Convention on Biodiversity.

[58] A useful first step in rectifying the situation is to be found in DETR, *Sites of Special Scientific Interest: Better Protection and Management*, a consultation paper, September 1998, section C. This adopts the regulatory approach used with regard to the Habitats Directive. It is, however, unlikely that statutory change will be effected before the next election.

Only thus can the British government comply with Article 8(b) of the Biodiversity Convention.[59]

Article 14(b)[60] extends the principles of EA to all programmes and policies of government, across the board, including 'non-environmental' areas such as trade and taxation, as well of the usual suspects. It ought to result in the reform of the Common Agricultural Policy, which would do much to help biodiversity. The EC has endeavoured to introduce Strategic Environmental Assessment to do just this, but no Member State with a presidency in the next few years intends to pursue the matter.[61] If sustainable development is ever to become a reality, it is essential that the environment is no longer a 'bolt-on extra' but an integral part of decision-making on every subject, changing the framework which determines whether a project is 'viable'.

If these provisions were acted on it would affect the advice required of statutory agencies such as English Nature or the Environment Agency: they would not have to be seen to be so compliant towards proposed development. This in turn would affect the corporate culture of such organizations. It should also increase their resources so that they can undertake proper research to act as a yardstick against which to assess a given proposal, rather than having to rely on the views of the developer's consultants.

It should affect the relationship between central and local government, e.g. with regard to calling in cases likely to have an adverse effect on nature conservation. As has been shown, the policies of central government set the parameters for local government: 'policy advice' and 'policy guidance' have metamorphosed into 'soft law' long since. If government policy is more sensitive and well informed about the requirements for preserving favourable conservation status[62] for biodiversity, this will be reflected in PPGs etc. and allow LPAs more latitude, e.g. with regard to implementing Article 10 of the Habitats

[59] Article 8, In Situ Conservation: '(b) Develop, where necessary, guidelines for the selection, establishment and management of protected areas or areas where special measures need to be taken to conserve biological diversity.'

[60] Article 14, Impact Assessment and Minimising Adverse Impacts: '(b) Introduce appropriate arrangements to ensure that the environmental consequences of its programmes and policies that are likely to have significant impacts on biodiversity are duly taken into account.'

[61] This is not to say that techniques are not being developed. See DETR, *Strategic Environmental Appraisal: Report of International Seminar, Lincoln 27th–29th May 1988*. In Britain the government has been appraising the environmental effects of its own policies since 1991, and local authorities have similarly been assessing their development plans. See ibid., 14–16.

[62] This phrase originates from the EC Habitats Directive, Article 1. It is defined as meaning that the species or habitat is maintaining itself or increasing in extent, and is likely to do so for the foreseeable future.

Directive.[63] That, however, would not be sufficient. As with statutory agencies the corporate culture of LPAs has to change to a healthier balance between biodiversity and development. As in central government and the EC, LPA departments promoting economic development tend to be more politically powerful than those restraining the undesirable side effects.

It is essential that LPAs be allowed the resources to carry out their planning functions properly at every level in the planning trinity. Having the resources to do the groundwork, both substantively and procedurally, would mean that LPAs would have the confidence to refuse applications and fight appeals if necessary without fear of costs being awarded against them. The LPA would have undertaken an appraisal of the biodiversity in its area, and be able to provide accurate information to developers and to their elected members making the decision. Given that any particular proposal is the focus for discussion, biodiversity can rarely be the determining factor: it is likely to 'win' on the coat-tails of other issues, e.g. road congestion, the need for shops or houses, pollution, etc. Therefore, it is essential that the groundwork be done on the broader front, in order for biodiversity to benefit.

Such a cultural transformation of central government, the statutory agencies and LPAs, and the legislative and policy changes which would ensue, would transform the climate in which planning decisions are taken. Without them, the proposed changes to planning law, set out below, would not achieve their objective.

5.2 Technical changes

The previous section dealt with the broad swathe of law and policy changes, which would benefit biodiversity. Given that the latter tends to 'win' or 'lose' by default, during the planning process, the following section centres on changes in planning law and procedure, many of which would profit the natural world indirectly, rather than immediately.

---

[63] Now reinforced by the Biodiversity Convention, Article 8, In Situ Conservation:

(c) Regulate or manage biological resources important for the conservation of biological diversity, whether within or outside protected areas, with a view to ensuring their conservation and sustainable use;

(d) Promote the protection of ecosystems, natural habitats and the maintenance of viable populations of species in natural surroundings;

(e) Promote environmentally sound and sustainable development in areas adjacent to protected areas with a view to furthering protection of these areas;

(f) Rehabilitate and restore degraded ecosystems and promote the recovery of threatened species, *inter alia*, through the development and implementation of plans or other management strategies.

5.2.1 Permitted Development Permitted development (PD) rights have already been withdrawn for SACs and SPAs. No doubt PD does affect biodiversity in the wider world, particularly Parts 5, 6, 7, 14, 15, 16, 17, 19, 21, 22 and 32. However, further withdrawal of rights could only be justified in the light of research, such as is being done under the auspices of the Action Plans. Perhaps it would be a matter of applying Article 4 directions in specific locations rather than restructuring Schedule 2 of the General Permitted Development Order 1995.

5.2.2 Environmental Assessment (EA) Whilst UK legislation requires environmental statements to provide certain information about predicted impacts, both direct and indirect, clearer guidance (and possibly new rules) is needed on the expected outcome. This would ensure that statements explicitly set out what is expected to happen so that the actual results can be audited.[64]

Housing has never been included as a candidate for EA, yet it is one of the most common types of development. As government has decreed that there is a need for 3.8 million houses before 2021, a large number will end up on greenfield sites. This is bound to have an impact on the natural world. Housing proposals over above a certain size should qualify for EA.

Currently there is much discussion on how to determine which Annex II projects require EA. It is clear from the consultation paper that SSSIs, NNRs, SPAs, SACs and Ramsar sites will almost certainly qualify for an EA.[65] Once again the significance of prestigious designations is evident. However, there will still be the discretionary element to allow the requirement to be waived. Similarly with regard to the exclusive thresholds which have to be designed not to interfere too drastically with PD rights.[66] Thus biodiversity outside prestigious sites is still unlikely to be subject to the EA process. However, a legacy perhaps of the Dutch Dykes case is that the need, or otherwise, for an EA has to be published in every case by the LPA.[67] This means that a conscious decision has to be taken in every instance, and this should make it easier to challenge decisions with a potentially detrimental effect on biodiversity.[68]

[64] Ben Dipper, Carys Jones and Chris Wood, 'Impact predictions: do they come true?', *Planning*, 23 October 1998.

[65] DETR, Consultation Paper: 'Determining the need for environmental assessment' (EC Directive 97/11/EC), para.28. It should be noted that exclusive thresholds do not apply to development affecting SSSIs.

[66] Ibid., paras.32, 33.

[67] Ibid., paras.19, 20.

[68] *R.* v. *Secretary of State for the Environment, Transport and Regions and Parcelforce ex parte Marson* (Court of Appeal, Nourse LJ, Pill LJ, Mummery LJ, 8 May 1998) illustrates the difficulties of trying to find out why an EA is *not* required. British judges seem antipathetic to European law – see footnotes 20 and 42.

As has been shown there can be difficulties in not having an ES scrutinized by an independent body. Alone amongst the EU Members, Spain has an independent body producing ESs, which at least removes the suspicion of bias in the findings although it obviously does nothing to facilitate discussion. An alternative is to make an inquiry mandatory if the proposal is significant enough to warrant an EA: the latter is more likely to result in independent scrutiny of the problem than an agency to undertake ESs.

5.2.3 Pollution Procedures The allocation of duties under WMLR, Schedule 4(4) needs to be teased out, understood and properly implemented by all involved in the process, be they LPAs, the public, the private sector, the Environment Agency, the Planning Inspectorate or the courts.[69]

Pollution procedures need to be streamlined in such a way that the implications of a given development may be fully explored at the right stage. There are occasions when the problem begins with the development plan: if an incinerator is proposed for a site, the likelihood is that all parties know which model would be constructed but are precluded from referring to its specific pollution characteristics which could make all the difference when deciding if the site is suitable. Yet, once the site is allocated in the plan s.54A TCPA makes it difficult to stop an application if there are adverse effects, particularly on nature conservation interests which tend to be of subsidiary importance.

Given that biodiversity has suffered so much from polluting activities, some of which are regulated by these procedures, there would appear to be benefits in amalgamating the procedures, e.g. allowing all the evidence to be heard at the one inquiry.

5.2.4 Fiscal Measures A measure which could be introduced is a betterment tax: it would remove the incentive to sell green land for development. The primary beneficiary would be biodiversity outside sites graded SSSI and above. Betterment levies have had an unhappy history,[70] but equally it could be argued that they have never really been tried because measures have been overturned before they could become effective. If a workable system could be introduced the monies could help finance the clean-up of contaminated land: neither the public

[69] M. Purdue, 'The impact on planning law in UK', in J. Holder (ed.), *The Impact of EC Environmental Law in UK* (Wiley & Sons, 1997), 237–44; R. Macrory, 'Incinerator case blurs division of planning and pollution controls', *ENDS Report*, 280 (May 1998), 51, 52; Douglas Evans, 'Resurrecting the balance: planning and pollution control revisited', *Waste Management* (October 1998), 38, 39.

[70] J. Barry Cullingworth and Vincent Nadin, *Town and Country Planning*, eleventh edn (Routledge, 1988), 106–14.

nor the private sector are willing to find the necessary funds.[71] This is much needed because of the potential to cause further pollution, and to take the pressure off the demand for greenfield sites. Biodiversity would profit both ways. Another option currently under discussion is a greenfield tax.

In recent years the tenor of planning policy has shifted dramatically in the direction of sustainable development, but there is a backlog of planning permissions which are less than eco-friendly, but for which it would be too expensive to compensate the owner. In their evidence to the House of Lords Select Committee on Sustainable Development, the UK Environmental Law Association put forward two suggestions for dealing with this problem (and, indeed, environmentally unfriendly permissions which had been enacted). The first suggestion was amortization procedures to allow an undesirable development to be wound down over ten years to reduce the compensation liability. The second is for the award of compensating planning permission for a sustainable development in lieu of the current permission.[72] Given the 1 per cent turnover in the built environment, there is a great need to deal with the existing stock of damaging permissions, and those which have yet to be constructed. Here again, it is biodiversity, particularly beyond the SSSIs, which would profit from these measures.

6 Conclusions

The UK Steering Group Report on Biodiversity shows that urbanization, with its attendant problems of excessive water abstraction, water and air pollution, has accounted for the decline of a third of the most threatened species and half the most endangered habitats. This being the case, it must be contributing to a diminution in the number and range of flora and fauna which has not yet reached the danger list.

It is said that s.54A has superseded the presumption in favour of development, but the latter is still the basic principle underlying the operation of the planning system as a whole.[73] Apart from facilitating development in terms of procedures, there are two more subtle effects. There are no moratoriums on development, however precious the site,

[71] Sir Hugh Rossi, 'Paying for our past', *Journal of Environmental Law*, 7, 1 (1995), 10.

[72] *House of Lords Select Committee on Sustainable Development* (1994/5).

[73] For example, development interests dominate the formulation of development plans because they can afford the expertise required to make an effective contribution. Applications are determined in the light of the development plan, and there is no third-party right of appeal. Judicial review is not designed for rectifying substantive errors, although people attempt to use it for such, and is very expensive for third parties. See Le-Las, *Understanding the Development Jigsaw*, 208–10.

and at each stage in the procedure the onus is on objectors to prove demonstrable harm to interests of acknowledged importance. Whilst nature conservation qualifies on this score, a closer look at PPG 9 shows that the emphasis is on rare habitats and species which, by definition, have already reached a critical level. In case of dispute, it is essential that the site be designated and/or the species documented by a reputable body, in order to carry any weight. Even then it is only one of many material considerations, and compromise is the preferred course of action other than in exceptional circumstances.

Whilst there is a growing realization that special sites and species cannot flourish in isolation, and LPAs are taking steps to implement Article 10 of the Habitats Directive, nature conservation is very much a subsidiary issue when considering development proposals on the 92 per cent of the land area in England and Wales outside SSSIs. As a material consideration it is much weaker, and therefore less able to stand up to the perceived social and/or economic benefits of any proposal. Biodiversity lacks political clout because it is difficult for it to boast an economic return: traditionally economics has treated the environment as a 'free good'. Although academics have been attempting to graft environmental considerations onto cost-benefit analysis and other decision-making measures,[74] and it has been estimated that the true value of the services provided by the Earth's ecosystem must run to trillions of US\$,[75] such considerations have not filtered through to the planning committee of an LPA, or even a major public inquiry.

Thus the natural world is only likely to figure as an issue of any importance in cases where the fate of an internationally designated site is involved. Otherwise it is but an 'also-ran', usually of little significance. Hence the necessity of tackling wider issues, changing the culture in which decisions are made. Tinkering with planning law, whilst useful, cannot achieve the required result on its own. If fully implemented, the Biodiversity Convention could do much to transform the climate of decision-making in favour of the natural world.

On the other hand, the Conventions signed at Rio, and the Bruntland report[76] before them, are founded on the assumption that environment and development are not incompatible. A discussion on this key issue is beyond the scope of this chapter, but, suffice it to say that if the demands of humanity for further development prove too much for the

[74] David Pearce, Anil Markandya and Edward B. Barbier, *Blueprint for a Green Economy* (Earthscan Publications, 1989), and subsequent publications by Professor Pearce. See also Robin Attfield and Katherine Dell (eds.), *Values Conflict and the Environment*, 2nd edn (Avebury, 1996).

[75] *Independent*, 6 January 1998, 'Time to face the true cost of the Earth?'

[76] The World Commission on Environment and Development, *Our Common Future* (Oxford University Press, 1987).

ecosystem, then there will be no winners. In order to prevent this, it is likely that the enormous power of the economic machine needs to be counterbalanced by a 'presumption in favour of biodiversity'. This would require a knowledge of the tolerance limits of the natural world, and then tailoring policies and procedures accordingly. Whilst the writer has an uncomfortable feeling that this is what is really needed, she has limited herself to current political and legal realities.

5

Nature Conservation and Development in the Rural Environment

LYNDA M. WARREN

1 Introduction

Both the modern planning system and the protected-area series have their origins in the reforming legislation of the post-war Labour government acting in response to the recommendations of a series of committees on land-use policy and the countryside. The first of these, the Addison Committee, was appointed by the government in 1929 with the remit

> to consider and report if it is desirable and feasible to establish one or more national parks in Great Britain with a view to the preservation of the national characteristics, including flora and fauna, and to the improvement of recreational facilities for the people, and to advise generally, and in particular as to the areas, if any, that are most suitable for the purpose.[1]

Despite an apparently favourable response from the government to the committee's recommendation for the designation of reserves, the ideas were not taken forward until the early 1940s when the coalition government commissioned John Dower to write a report on national parks.[2] Immediately after the war the new Labour government set up a committee under the chairmanship of Sir Arthur Hobhouse,[3] to consider ways of giving practical effect to Dower's recommendations.

---

[1] *Report of the National Park Committee*, chaired by Addison, 1931, Cmnd. 3851.
[2] Dower (1945), *Report on National Parks in England and Wales*, Cmnd. 6378.
[3] *The Report of the National Parks Committee (England and Wales)* was published in 1947, Cmnd. 6628.

The Hobhouse Committee subsequently set up a separate committee to look at conservation needs.[4]

Meanwhile, a series of committees was looking at the possible reform of planning law. The first of these, under the chairmanship of Sir Montague Barlow,[5] considered the demographic effects of industrialization and measures that could be taken to direct industrial development to certain areas. It was followed by a study of rural land use and, in particular, incursions onto agricultural land by urban and industrial sprawl,[6] and a study of the difficulties of implementing policies of betterment and compensation for planning gain and loss.[7]

The outcome of all these deliberations was a number of pieces of interrelated legislation which have formed the basis of both planning and countryside law ever since, of which the most significant for the present discussion are the Town and Country Planning Act 1947 and the National Parks and Access to the Countryside Act 1949.[8]

Despite the fact that habitat protection measures and planning legislation arose out of the same policy reforms, most nature conservationists and more than a few planners would surely agree that nature conservation has been ill served by the planning system. This is somewhat ironic as both are intimately concerned with issues of land use. It might be expected that planning law, as a tool for guiding the procedural aspects of land-use policy, would play an important supportive role in promoting government policy on nature conservation. Indeed, an examination of the provisions for Sites of Special Scientific Interest (SSSIs) in the National Parks etc. Act 1949 and of the debates that helped mould them show clearly that the conservation of habitats was seen in a planning context.

It is the purpose of this chapter to look at the changing ideas about the conservation of natural habitats over the last fifty years and discuss the limitations of the planning system, which has remained relatively unchanged over the same period, as a tool for conservation objectives.

[4] The Report of the Wild Life Conservation Special Committee, chaired by Julian Huxley, *Conservation of Nature in England and Wales*, was published in 1947, Cmnd. 7122.

[5] *Royal Commission on the Distribution of the Industrial Population*, 1939, Cmnd. 6153.

[6] *Report of the Committee on Land Use in Rural Areas*, chaired by Lord Justice Scott, 1942, Cmnd. 6378.

[7] *Final Report of the Expert Committee on Compensation and Betterment*, under the chairmanship of Mr Justice Uthwatt, was published in 1942 as Cmnd. 6386.

[8] Summing up the second-reading debate on the National Parks and Access to the Countryside Bill, Evelyn King, the Parliamentary Secretary to the Minister of Town and Country Planning said, '[i]t is impossible to consider this Measure in isolation. The Town and Country Planning Act 1947 and the New Towns Act 1946, and this Bill all form part of an integrated land code ...' (HC Debs [463] 1 April 1949 col. 1655). He might also have added the Agriculture Act 1947.

2 Limitations of the Planning System

The alleged failings of the planning system to protect sites of nature conservation importance have been well rehearsed since the revised scheme of SSSIs came into being following the enactment of the Wildlife and Countryside Act 1981. The inadequacy of the planning system and law to ensure that planning authorities strike the correct balance between conservation and other interests has become something of a *bête noire* in conservation circles. The concerns listed below have been well documented in the literature but seem to arise time and time again:

(a) exclusion of most agricultural and forestry development from the planning regime;
(b) overriding of SSSI status by planning permission;
(c) the general presumption in favour of development;
(d) the ease with which the presumption against development on sites of international or European significance can be rebutted;
(e) the uneven playing field in which short-term social gains are matched against long-term conservation objectives;
(f) the difficulty of putting a financial value on nature conservation interests;
(g) the reluctance of the Secretary of State to call in applications;
(h) the delay in obtaining a decision from the court.[9]

These failings will be addressed in the next section which looks at changes in nature conservation policy over the last fifty years.

3 Changes in Nature Conservation Policy over the Last Fifty Years

3.1 The immediate post-war era

As noted in the introduction, the National Parks etc. Act 1949, which introduced the SSSI system, arose out of the review of rural land use which also led to the 1947 planning legislation. Although the motivation behind the Town and Country Planning Act 1947 was that industrial and suburban encroachment into the rural environment should be strictly controlled, the underlying philosophy was to ensure a 'proper balance between competing demands for land, so that all the land of the country is used in the best interests of the whole people'.[10]

---

[9] See, for example, Hawke, *Nature Conservation: The Legal Framework and Sustainability* (1991); Rowell, *SSSIs: A Health Check* (1991); Hatton, *The Habitats Directive: Time for Action* (1992).

[10] Second reading debate on the Town and Country Planning Bill, HC Debs [432] 29 January 1947, col. 947 *per* Lewis Silkin, Minister for Town and Country Planning.

This was to be achieved by extending the use of development plans to cover the whole country and by applying clear rules for determining planning applications. Certain types of land use were singled out for protection against development pressure. As the minister said, '[a] high level of agricultural production is vital. More land must be kept for forestry.'[11] The justification for not over-regulating these activities was the need to promote both in the immediate post-war years. Agriculture and forestry, being things to be encouraged and developed with alacrity, required legislation that facilitated their development rather than laws constraining them. Thus neither agriculture nor forestry were regarded as threats to the countryside and, therefore, were largely excluded from the planning legislation.

Apart from the need to cushion rural activities from the incursions of urban life, the government of the day wanted to ensure that a war-weary public had access to the recuperative effects of the countryside. To quote the minister again, 'it is important to safeguard the beauty of the countryside and coast-line, especially now that holidays with pay will enable more people to enjoy them'.[12] The Act made provision for the preparation of development plans and it is interesting to note that the minister spoke of these as showing 'special areas to be preserved because of their scenic beauty'[13] along with the location of principal communications and other broad land allocations such as agriculture, new towns etc. It is equally noteworthy that there was no reference in his speech to nature conservation areas of any type. In any event, detailed provisions for land-use allocation for countryside and conservation purposes were left to the National Parks etc. Act which followed in 1949.

The legislation for National Parks, included in part II of the 1949 Act, implemented the recommendations of the Hobhouse Committee. Similarly, the inclusion in the Act of measures for nature reserves and SSSIs was a direct result of the Huxley Committee's work.[14] From the very start, therefore, habitat protection was seen in the context of a broader range of provisions for rural land use. The consequences for the future of nature conservation of this close link between planning and habitat protection in this country was not appreciated at the time. During the consideration of the National Parks etc. Bill in Parliament,

[11] Ibid., col. 948.

[12] Ibid.

[13] Ibid., cols. 962–3.

[14] Note that the Huxley Committee was set up by Hobhouse. The need for particular and separate consideration of nature conservation issues of land use does not seem to have occurred to the government, and we have Hobhouse and his committee to thank for realizing that natural beauty cannot always be regarded simply in the context of public enjoyment.

there was very little debate on the SSSI provisions, which were presumably regarded as a minor, non-controversial elaboration of the main topic, public enjoyment of the countryside. In moving the Bill, the minister said that the Bill was about being able to enjoy the countryside, for its 'peace and spiritual refreshment'.[15] He considered the Bill to be necessary because of the disfigurement of the countryside by development and because of the loss of agricultural land which 'contributes very greatly through its pattern of cultivation to the unique character and the beauty of our countryside'.[16] We have here an early statement of the 'farmer as custodian of the countryside' principle, one that is easy to criticize now but which must be seen against the context of the time where the major changes in the rural scene were brought about by urbanization, not changing farming practices.

There is scant attention to nature conservation in general or SSSIs in particular in any of the contributions to the second-reading debate in the House of Commons. Indeed, the minister made no reference at all to SSSIs. In his review of the nature conservation aspects of the Bill he referred only to the newly created Nature Conservancy[17] and the need for close contact between the Conservancy and the new National Parks. The most telling comment was that made by W. S. Morrison, member for Cirencester and Tewkesbury, in reference to clause 23 on SSSIs. He commented on the notification requirements and went on to say:

That is all right, but what happens then? . . . It seems to me that, whenever the right honourable gentleman opposite comes up against a local planning authority, he seems to strike against a sort of iron curtain . . . Conservancies can notify, inform and recommend, but, if the notification, information or recommendation is disregarded, nothing happens. We are left with the pious hope that all these, together with all other relevant considerations, will be borne in mind . . . There is no surer way of asking for trouble than providing for a conflict of opinion and failing to provide some means of resolving that conflict.[18]

This far-sighted observation sums up many of the problems that have subsequently arisen with the implementation of this legislation and its replacement in the 1981 Act, as does Sir Arthur Salter's prediction that the 'Minister concerned with a particular scheme will push his scheme so far as he can; and the Minister responsible only for the more general duty of preserving beauty will almost always lose'.[19]

[15] Debate (n.8), col. 1461 per Lewis Silkin, Minister for Town and Country Planning.
[16] Ibid., cols. 1461–2.
[17] Set up under Royal Charter in 1949.
[18] Debate (n.8), col. 1493 per W. S. Morrison.
[19] Ibid., col. 1506 per Sir Arthur Salter.

3.2 From science to management – the first steps

The original SSSI regime, as provided under the 1949 Act, was nothing more than a label designed to inform the planning authorities of the scientific interest of the area in question. Presumably it was felt that such information was too technical to be apparent to the uninformed public or its elected representatives – hence the need for a special scientific body to act on the public's behalf. It is implicit in the 1949 Act, however, that the planning authorities would be able to judge the appropriate weight to be given to a nature conservation interest in comparison with conflicting interests. In other words, acquisition of the scientific knowledge and the evaluation of a site on scientific grounds were specialized activities, but assessing the significance of the stated scientific interest *vis-à-vis* other, socio-economic, interests could be dealt with by democratically elected members as part of the planning process. The fact that councillors might need help in evaluating the merits of any particular SSSI was acknowledged in the Town and Country Planning General Development Order 1950,[20] Article 9(9) of which provided that local planning authorities should consult the Nature Conservancy Council[21] over planning applications for development within notified SSSIs. These provisions were retained in subsequent development orders and extended in 1991 to cover developments outside SSSIs where these might affect the integrity of the SSSI.[22]

Until 1968, the SSSI remained as a label whose function was simply to draw attention, in planning circles, to the existing scientific interest. The link between planning and nature conservation remained intact. The Countryside Act 1968, however, introduced legal provisions for a more proactive role for the SSSI, that of management of the scientific interest. S.15 of the Act empowered the Nature Conservancy Council to enter into an agreement with the owners and occupiers of notified

[20] Town and Country Planning General Development Order and Development Charge Applications Regulations 1950, SI 1950/728.

[21] The successor body to the Nature Conservancy, established by the Nature Conservancy Council Act 1973.

[22] By the Town and Country Planning (General Development) (Amendment) (No.3) Order 1991 SI 1991/2805, Article 4 and now contained in the Town and Country Planning (General Development Procedures) Order 1995 SI 1995/419, Article 10, which provides two ways in which this may be achieved. The appropriate nature conservation agency (English Nature or the Countryside Council for Wales) may inform the local planning authority of Consultation Zones adjacent to existing SSSIs over which they wish to be consulted on any planning application. These Consultation Zones may extend for up to two kilometres from the SSSI. Alternatively, and in the absence of a Consultation Zone, the local planning authority must notify the nature-conservation agency of any application for development that it considers likely to have an effect on the nature conservation interest of the SSSI.

land which imposed restrictions, for the purposes of nature conservation, on the exercise of their rights over the land. This provision, which has since been extended to cover land adjacent to an SSSI,[23] still forms the basis of management agreements for the protection of SSSIs.

The shift in emphasis from simply flagging SSSIs for special attention under planning law to making provisions for their management received a major impetus with the enactment of the Wildlife and Countryside Act 1981. S.28, which replaced the 1949 provisions, extended the notification to owners and occupiers and introduced limited controls over the exercise of their rights over notified land. Where there are proposals to undertake activities that might damage the conservation interest, the nature conservation agency may negotiate a management agreement under which the owner or occupier is paid not to undertake the activity. Note, however, that these procedures do not apply to activities that come under planning control. Under s.28(8) planning permission is a reasonable excuse for carrying out a potentially damaging activity.

The result is that, despite the importance placed on the SSSI as the foundation of the nation's site-protection system, every notified site is vulnerable to development sanctioned by the planning authority. In many cases a proposed development has no implication for the nature conservation interest; in others, simple modifications to a proposal or the inclusion of planning conditions can safeguard the interest.[24] In a few cases, however, nature conservation and development simply are not compatible. Under these circumstances the planning authority is faced with the conflict referred to at the birth of the SSSI by Morrison.

One of the most difficult issues facing the planning authority is evaluating the particular importance of a given SSSI in the overall scale of nature conservation interest. The government's original proposals for amending the SSSI legislation in 1981[25] would have created a two-tier system in which the majority of sites remained notified under the 1949 Act with just a few being singled out for added protection that would restrict rights of ownership. The government considered that this would be sufficient to give effect to their obligations under the Berne Convention on the Conservation of European Wildlife and Natural

[23] Introduced by the Environmental Protection Act 1990 Schedule 9, para.4.

[24] Most cases can be resolved satisfactorily. Of about 1,400 planning applications referred to the Countryside Council for Wales in 1995-6, the Council lodged objections to only nineteen (Countryside Council for Wales (1996), *Annual Report 1995-96*, p.15).

[25] Only the most important SSSIs were to be notified to owners and occupiers. Notice of intent to carry out a potentially damaging operation would have triggered a twelve-month period for the Nature Conservancy Council to negotiate a management agreement, but anyone delayed for more than three months would have been entitled to compensation.

Habitats.[26] Intensive lobbying by the voluntary conservation movement, who were concerned that this would lead to the second-tier sites being neglected, resulted in the Opposition introducing amendments into the Bill to replace the 1949-type SSSI completely.[27]

S.29, however, retained the government's preferred element of discrimination, although it does not refer expressly to SSSIs. The section provides for the making, by the Secretary of State, of a Nature Conservation Order which imposes greater restrictions on the use of land subject to the order than would be available under s.28. Although s.29 does not require the land in question to be notified under s.28, in practice this is the case. Furthermore, it has transpired that not every SSSI can enjoy the protection of a Nature Conservation Order. S.29 states that such an order can be made in the case of any land of special interest for the purpose of securing the survival in Great Britain of any kind of animal or plant or of complying with an international obligation or for the purpose of conserving any of its flora, fauna, or geological or physiographical features that are of national importance.[28]

In the early days of implementation of the Act, the Nature Conservancy Council maintained that all SSSIs were of national importance. The public inquiry into the 1985 Nature Conservation Order for West Mersea Meadows held that this was not the case, however,[29] thereby opening the way for numerous challenges on the relative importance of a site.

The idea that some SSSIs might be better, or more important, than others has carried over into planning cases. If a nature conservation agency gives evidence at a public inquiry into a planning application affecting an SSSI, it is likely that that evidence will include a justification for the site notification, a comparison of its importance against other sites notified for similar reasons and an assessment of its national importance.

Where a proposed development is likely to affect a site that the nature conservation agency considers is of national or international importance, it will usually request the Secretary of State to call in the application for decision. Surprisingly, perhaps, call-in under such circumstances is not automatic. Following the case of R. v. Poole Borough Council ex parte Beebee 1991,[30] Michael Heseltine, the then

[26] UKTS 56 (1982), Cmnd. 8738; ETS 104.

[27] See the debates in the House of Lords Committee on Clause 26 of the Bill, HL Debs [417] 12 February 1981, cols. 292–340 and 351–65.

[28] Wildlife and Countryside Act 1981, s.29(1) and (2).

[29] See Withrington and Jones (1992), 'The enforcement of conservation legislation: protecting Sites of Special Scientific Interest', Howarth and Rodgers, Agriculture, Conservation and Land Use, 90–107, at p.94.

[30] Journal of Environmental Law (1991) 3(2), 293.

Secretary of State for the Environment, announced that, in future, the Secretary of State would call in applications affecting sites of national or international importance. The policy was subsequently included in PPG 9, *Nature Conservation*, para.36 of which states that, when

> weighing the case for proposed development in [National Nature Reserves] and in [Nature Conservation Review] and [Geological Conservation Review] sites against nature conservation interests, a planning authority is expected to pay particular regard to their national importance. On the advice of English Nature, the Secretary of State will normally call-in for his own decision planning applications with a significant effect on these sites. He may also call-in other applications affecting SSSIs if they raise planning issues of more than local importance.

As these words imply, one way of identifying a site as being of national or international importance will be its inclusion in the Nature Conservation Review or the Geological Conservation Review. These reviews were conducted[31] to provide a comprehensive survey and assessment of all those sites regarded as of particular importance for conservation.

PPG 9 does not apply in Wales which explains, perhaps, why the then Secretary of State for Wales, John Redwood, felt able to resist calling in the planning application for development of Mostyn Dock within the Dee Estuary SSSI. The site is of undoubted international importance. As well as being an SSSI, it is a Special Protection Area (SPA) under the Birds Directive[32] and is listed as a Ramsar Site.[33] Nevertheless, the Secretary of State was content to leave an application for such a small development to the local planning authority. It was only when the Department of the Environment (now the Department of the Environment, Transport and the Regions), which also has responsibilities for this estuary because it forms the boundary between the two national jurisdictions, exerted pressure that he agreed to the call-in.

The fact that an application has been called in does not mean that the nature conservation interest will determine the outcome of the inquiry.

---

[31] The Nature Conservation Review was conducted by the Nature Conservancy Council and published as Ratcliffe (1977), *A Nature Conservation Review*. The Geological Conservation Review was undertaken by the Nature Conservancy Council between 1977 and 1989 but publication of the outstanding volumes is now the responsibility of the Joint Nature Conservation Committee, which took on the national remit following the break-up of the Council into national bodies. Some fourteen of the proposed forty-two volumes have already been published.

[32] Council directive on the conservation of wild birds, 79/409/EEC, OJ 1979 L 103/79.

[33] Under the Convention on Wetlands of International Importance especially as Waterfowl Habitat UKTS 34 (1976); Cmnd. 6465.

The record is not encouraging, even where sites are of acknowledged international importance. In most cases, socio-economic considerations have outweighed the science. In the case of Mostyn Dock this was, perhaps, not surprising. The proposed development would affect only a tiny part of the designated area and arguments raised by the Countryside Council for Wales that the development would affect the integrity of the site overall failed to hold sway.

The courts have not assisted the conservation case, although, as we shall see below, the eventual outcome of the Lappel Bank dispute is more positive. The courts cannot, of course, insert their own view of the conservation importance of a site in place of that of the planning authorities, but there have been occasions where they might have been more critical of the procedures used by these authorities in reaching their decisions. The following cases illustrate this point.

In April 1989 Poole Borough Council granted itself planning permission for a housing development on Canford Heath. The land in question had become part of an SSSI following a boundary renotification in 1988 which had been made because the site supported a number of protected species of birds and reptiles. The Nature Conservancy Council requested the Secretary of State to call in the decision but he declined to do so. Following the planning decision, the World Wide Fund for Nature and the British Herpetological Society applied for judicial review of the decision,[34] having failed to persuade the Nature Conservancy Council to do so. Schiemann J dismissed the application. Of the first ground of challenge, that the planning authority was unaware that the site had been notified as an SSSI and mistakenly believed that it was just a proposed notification, he held that this was not material to the decision although he agreed that the complaint was well founded. Similarly, he agreed that the local authority was at fault in not considering the need for an Environmental Impact Assessment as required under European Law[35] but held that this was merely a technicality as the authority already had all the information that would have been revealed had such an assessment been undertaken. The third ground was that the planning officer had erred in advising his Council that an earlier planning permission with respect to the site remained extant when it had, in fact, expired. While this was undoubtedly true, the judge did not consider that the previous planning history had played a decisive role in the authority's decision. As Harte[36] has pointed out,

[34] R. v. Poole Borough Council ex part Beebee (n.30).
[35] As implemented in this country by the Town and Country Planning (Assessment of Environmental Effects) Regulations 1988, SI 1988/1199.
[36] See Harte's excellent analysis of this case in Journal of Environmental Law (1991) 3(2), 293, 'The extent of the legal protection enjoyed by Sites of Special Scientific Interest in England and Wales'.

Schiemann J appears to have been motivated by a reluctance to allow a challenge of a decision based on the reasoning behind that decision when there is no legal requirement to publish that reasoning.[37] It could be argued that he was taking the traditional procedural niceties a little too literally and that the failure to comply with the letter of the law giving effect to European obligations was equally worthy of his attention. Certainly the World Wide Fund for Nature thought so and were seriously considering appealing the decision when the Secretary of State stepped in and revoked the planning permission.

This case highlights the difficulties that can be entailed in bringing a successful challenge to a grant of planning permission concerning land of nature conservation interest. The real issue at Canford Heath was not whether the local authority had, or had not, followed the correct procedures or reached their decision following a full appraisal of the facts, but whether the socio-economic benefits of a housing estate outweighed the nature conservation interest. It was this case that resulted in the government's commitment to call in cases involving nature conservation sites of national or greater importance. While this is an obvious step in the right direction, it does not provide any assistance in reaching the decision. Whoever makes the decision, there is still the problem of balancing interests that are not easy to compare, i.e. the immediate benefit to the public of a proposed development and the long-term environmental interest. The former can readily be expressed in economic terms but, despite the development of environmental economics, the latter cannot be evaluated simply in monetary terms.

Similar problems arose in the public inquiries over the construction of the Newbury bypass and the M3 motorway extension through Twyford Down. Although not planning-law cases, the issue was again the balance between the desirability of protecting a site of considerable nature conservation importance and dealing with a socio-economic problem, in this case road congestion. Again, the judiciary felt unable to assist in the balancing exercise. This is well illustrated by Sedley J in *R. v. Secretary of State for the Environment ex parte Berkshire, Buckinghamshire & Oxfordshire Naturalists Trust.*[38] The Secretary of State for the Environment had received advice from the Joint Nature

---

[37] The Town and Country Planning Act requires local planning authorities to give reasons for refusing planning permission but does not require them to give reasons for granting permission. Schiemann J observed that, while Parliament had on occasion legislated to require public bodies to give reasons, it had not done so in the case of local planning authorities granting planning permission. He went on to express 'grave reservations' about challenges of decisions of this type where there was no allegation of bad faith. Ibid., p.295.

[38] [1997] Env. LR 80.

Conservation Committee that Twyford Down should be considered as a possible candidate for designation as a Special Area of Conservation (SAC) under the Habitats Directive[39] because of its populations of the pulmonate snail *Vertigo moulinsiana*. The Secretary of State had followed the usual practice of consulting the public on the proposal. Meanwhile, the Secretary of State for Transport had let a contract for the construction of the bypass across the same land. The Trust sought judicial review on the ground that the decision to let the contract placed a fetter on the exercise of the government's discretion to put the site forward to the European Commission as a candidate SAC. Sedley J was, to his regret, not prepared to interfere. He found that there was no foundation in law for the challenge nor any reasonable expectation in policy. The dispute, being simply one concerning conflicts between separate policies, was not one that could be challenged through judicial review. He concluded:

> It is one thing to say that the use of the prerogative power to put it out of a minister's power to fulfil a statutory obligation is unlawful. It is another to contend that, in a situation in which neither law nor policy affords a direct answer, it is an abuse of power to choose between two incompatible policy courses available to government after weighing the competing factors . . . once the case comes down . . . to an assault upon the bare policy choices between the road and the snail, it is only if improper motive or irrationality can be shown to have biased the choice that it can be impugned, and neither is arguably shown here.[40]

The longest-running saga has been the fight by the RSPB to prevent the extension by the Medway Ports Authority of Sheerness Docks on Lappel Bank in the Medway Estuary. This is an area of acknowledged international importance for migratory birds. Most of the area is notified under s.28 of the Wildlife and Countryside Act 1981 and, at the time of the application for planning permission, was designated or a candidate for designation as an SPA or a Ramsar site. *R. v. Swale Borough Council and Medway Ports Authority ex parte the Royal Society for the Protection of Birds*[41] was a challenge to the grant of planning permission for land reclamation of 125 acres of Lappel Bank. The proposed development would have destroyed the mudflats that were the feeding grounds for the birds. The RSPB's application was refused because Simon Brown J held that the RSPB had failed to make their application promptly enough. In reaching this decision, he was

---

[39] Council directive on the conservation of natural habitats and of wild fauna and flora 92/43/EEC OJ 1992 L 206/7.

[40] Env. LR 80 (n.38) at p.89.

[41] [1991] 1 PLR 6; [1991] JPL 39.

no doubt influenced by the financial implications for the Ports Authority should the planning permission be quashed. The judgment expresses some sympathy for the RSPB's view that they had a legitimate expectation to be consulted before the planning application was decided. Grant[42] is in no doubt that, had it not been for the delay in bringing proceedings, the RSPB might have expected the decision to be quashed in order to give them an opportunity to be consulted. He bases his conclusion on the fact that failure to consult had left the local planning authority ignorant of relevant information that the RSPB might have been able to provide. Even if the RSPB had been successful, there is, of course, no certainty that the enhanced environmental case would have swung the balance. Subsequent events strongly suggest that the socio-economic benefits would still have outweighed the environmental case in the opinion of the local planning authority. The RSPB continued their campaign on Lappel Bank by bringing a separate challenge on the ground of failure to comply with the requirements of the EC Birds Directive. Eventually, after unsuccessful challenges at first instance and in the Court of Appeal,[43] the RSPB succeeded in persuading the House of Lords[44] to refer the matter to the European Court of Justice[45] which supported the RSPB's interpretation of the directive. The decision came too late to save the conservation interest of the site, however. The 1989 planning permission had not been implemented within the five-year period allowed. Unfortunately, some time after the RSPB's unsuccessful application for judicial review in the Divisional Court, the local planning authority granted a new planning consent for the development of Lappel Bank. Their decision was no doubt influenced by the Secretary of State's decision to exclude Lappel Bank from the SPA classification, i.e. the decision that was the subject of the RSPB's then unsuccessful application for judicial review. The House of Lords' referral to the European Court of Justice was not made until work had already commenced on the site. Their lordships refused the RSPB's application for interim relief in the form of a declaration. Had this been granted, further development at Lappel Bank would have been held up pending a decision from the European Court. This would have resulted in a large commercial loss to the developers. In the main judgment, Lord

[42] Grant, 'Development and the protection of birds: the *Swale* decision', *Journal of Environmental Law* (1991) 3(1), 135.
[43] *R. v. Secretary of State for the Environment ex parte the Royal Society for the Protection of Birds*, CO/464/94 QBD 8 July 1994 (unreported) and *R. v. Secretary of State for the Environment ex parte the Royal Society for the Protection of Birds* (1995) JEL 245.
[44] [1997] Env. LR 431; (1995) JEL 262.
[45] Case C-44/95 [1996] ECR I-3805; [1997] 2 WLR 123; [1997] Env LR 442.

Jauncey made it clear that he regarded this proposal as an attempt by the RSPB to hold up the development without having to make the financial undertaking that would have been required if they had applied for an interim injunction against the Ports Authority.[46]

What conclusions can be drawn from these cases in terms of the relationship between planning law and nature conservation? First, judicial review, being essentially a device for challenging procedural aspects of the public decision-making process, is a cumbersome, inappropriate tool for dealing with disputes over the correct balance between conflicting development and conservation interests. In most situations the real issue is the actual decision; to put it in simple terms, whether sufficient weight has been given to the conservation case. Judicial review does not permit a challenge of this type, hence the reliance on procedural matters. The challenges in *Beebee* and *Swale* both hinged on the assumption that, had the planning authorities followed the correct procedures, they would have had a better understanding of the issues involved and would have reached the 'right' decision. There has been no opportunity to see if this would have been the result. In *Beebee*, it is clear that the Secretary of State disagreed with the local planning authority's decision but there is nothing in the case to suggest that the authority would, itself, have reached a different conclusion. Similarly in *Swale*, where the prospect of development leading to job creation was clearly an important material consideration for the planning authority. The judiciary, themselves, are not unaware of the problem. As Sedley J said, '. . . one can appreciate the force of the view that if the protection of the natural environment keeps coming second we shall end by destroying our own habitat . . .'.[47] Concerns of this type have led to calls for a change in the law to allow appeals against the grant as well as the refusal of planning permission as is the case in some other jurisdictions. The difficulties of getting a fair and competent hearing on the scientific merits of a case have similarly led to suggestions that we need some form of environmental tribunal.[48]

Even where successful challenges have been made, the delay in reaching a final conclusion can result in the scientific interest being lost. There appears to be a failure on the part of planning authorities and the courts

[46] (1995) JEL 262 at 266.

[47] Env. LR 80, n.40.

[48] The main proponent of this idea is Lord Woolf who first raised it in his lecture to the United Kingdom Environmental Law Association in 1991 (see Woolf (1992), 'Are the judiciary environmentally myopic?' *Journal of Environmental Law* 4(1), 1). The value of environmental courts formed the subject matter of 'Environmental Justice. New Directions in Environmental Dispute Resolution', a conference held at the University of Wales, Aberystwyth, in October 1997, the papers from which are to form a volume to be published by the University of Wales Press.

alike to appreciate that, in most cases, once a site is developed the conservation interest is lost for ever. If the decision is subsequently overturned, the damage cannot be undone. There are powerful arguments for not holding up development. It was a key principle of the Conservative government that development should not be unduly delayed by procedural requirements.[49] Both the planning and environmental assessment procedures are framed with tight deadlines for consultation and decision-making. The financial consequences of an extended delay while an issue is referred to a higher court are potentially too great to be generally acceptable. Unfortunately, such consideration of the economic circumstances of the developer makes it almost impossible to apply a precautionary approach to planning. Development proposals may only be viable if they can be carried out now. If an application is turned down after appeal then the developer will look elsewhere. A system that allowed for decisions that said 'maybe' to a request for planning permission would be commercially unacceptable.

At the heart of the problem is the fact that nature conservation interests are treated as any other material consideration whereas, in fact, it could be argued that the quality of the interest is such as to merit it being taken into account in a different way. Planning applications are about proposals to develop land, i.e. for people to undertake activities that will change the land. The decision-making process involves evaluating and balancing a variety of socio-economic interests to reach the best outcome for society as a whole. It is relevant to note that most agricultural development takes place without reference to a planning committee. So the only time the planning authority faces questions of nature conservation and the natural environment is when these are raised as material considerations inviting a refusal to grant permission. This puts the conservation interest in a negative light. It also reduces it to the equivalent of a short-term interest. There is no tradition of considering the long-term implications of habitat loss and hence no expertise in judging this in terms comparable with judgements of the value of other material interests. The system is geared towards sanctioning piecemeal loss of little bits of protected areas. Each year, approximately 5 per cent of reported cases of damage to SSSIs are the result of the implementation of planning permission. Although the overall figure is quite low, it makes up a high proportion of the sites that suffer long-term damage.[50]

[49] See, for example, PPG 9, para.18 which refers to the need for local planning authorities to 'take care to avoid unnecessary constraints on development'.
[50] According to Rowell, *SSSIs*, (n.9) at p.18, development given planning permission was the single most frequent cause of partial- or whole-site loss of SSSIs and the second most frequent cause of long-term damage, accounting for the majority of the area (59 per cent) suffering loss or long-term damage in 1989–90. Activities authorized

The United Nations Conference on Environment and Development heralded a new appreciation of the importance of the natural environment and the need for sustainable use. The next section examines the extent to which these new ideals have influenced the planning system in this country, and considers the likely effect for the future.

3.3 Nature conservation after Rio

The main results of the Earth Summit, in terms of nature conservation, were the Convention on Biological Diversity[51] and the Commission on Sustainable Development. For the first time the international community had espoused the philosophy of the Brundtland Commission[52] and its oft-repeated concept of sustainable development as 'development that meets the needs of the present without compromising the ability of future generations to meet their own needs', and the World Conservation Strategy[53] with its emphasis on the conservation of genetic resources, species and ecosystems. These international developments were being matched within Europe. The Fifth Environmental Action Programme,[54] designed to run from 1993 to 2000, was actually entitled *Towards Sustainability*. In 1992 the Council adopted a major piece of nature conservation legislation, the Habitats Directive,[55] which, along with the Biodiversity Action Strategy designed to meet the government's obligations under the Biodiversity Convention, has come to dominate the nature conservation programme in this country.

The Conservation (Natural Habitats, etc.) Regulations 1994,[56] which implement the Habitats Directive in Great Britain, go some way to shifting the balance towards the conservation interest in the planning context. Part IV is concerned with the adaptation of planning and other types of controls. Regulations 55 and 56 require local authorities to review extant planning permissions and to modify or revoke these where their implementation would have a significant detrimental effect on the nature conservation interest of a candidate Special Area of Conservation (SAC). Given the long lead in time for the identification of sites for designation under the directive, it is unlikely that there will

by planning permission caused 5 per cent and 4 per cent of loss and damage to English SSSIs in 1991–2 and 1992–3 respectively (National Audit Office (1994), *Protecting and Managing Sites of Special Scientific Interest in England*).

[51] 31 ILM (1992) 822.

[52] World Commission on Environment and Development (1987), *Our Common Future*.

[53] IUCN/UNEP/WWF (1980), *World Conservation Strategy*.

[54] OJ C 138, 17.5.1993.

[55] Council directive (see n.39).

[56] SI No. 1994/2716.

be many such outstanding planning permissions. The main exception to this is mineral planning permissions. Revocation of these could result in a considerable compensation bill for the minerals planning authority[57] which few local authorities would be willing to accept. The solution would seem to be to raise the money in other ways, as has happened with respect to Fenn's and Whixhall Bettisfield Wem and Cadney Mosses SSSI, which is already designated, in part, as a National Nature Reserve and a Ramsar site and is a candidate SAC. The site comprises the third-largest lowland raised peat bog in the United Kingdom. Planning permission to extract peat was granted in 1950 in respect of about one-quarter of the site. In 1991 the Nature Conservancy Council bought out the lease over this part of the site, and commercial peat extraction ceased in the same year. Unfortunately, the lease expired at the end of 1998. As part of the negotiations for a new arrangement, it has been necessary to consider the extent of the compensation that would be payable by the Mineral Planning Authority if the planning permission to extract peat were to be revoked. To avoid the protracted procedures that could arise if this happened, the Countryside Council for Wales has successfully applied for lottery funding to lease the site, thereby avoiding the possibility of peat extraction.

Once a site has been designated as an SAC or a candidate SAC it benefits from the guidance in PPG 9 which is designed to ensure that planning decisions do not lead to a breach of European obligations. As mentioned above, PPG 9 advises local planning authorities to give greater weight to the conservation interest of national and international recognized sites. This guidance is strengthened by Regulation 54 which requires the planning authority to consider the effects of a proposed development on a European Site.[58] Article 6(3) of the directive states that no planning permission shall be granted in respect of a proposed plan or project that is likely to have a significant effect on the nature conservation interest of the site unless an assessment has been made of the likely effects of the proposed development.[59] Planning permission should normally be refused where the assessment reveals that there will be a negative impact. The only exception for most sites is where there are imperative reasons of overriding public importance that outweigh the nature conservation interest.[60] This is a powerful weapon for the nature conservation interest. In effect it is saying that once a site has

[57] Under Reg. 59.

[58] A European Site is defined for these purposes in Regulation 10 as an SAC, SPA and candidate SAC following its adoption by the European Commission.

[59] This obligation is given effect in Great Britain by Regulation 48 of the 1994 Regulations.

[60] Under Article 6(4).

been designated as an SAC or an SPA[61] its nature conservation interest is established in a quantifiable manner. The only discretion that the planning authority has is to decide whether a proposed development is of overriding public importance such that it is imperative that it should be permitted. Following the case of *Commission* v. *Germany* (the *Leybucht Dykes* case)[62] which concerned a classified SPA, public safety and human health were the only reasons that met this requirement. Unfortunately, under Article 6(4) of the Habitats Directive, which also applies to SPAs, this condition no longer holds true. Reasons of overriding public importance can now include social or economic ones. Nevertheless, the added weight given to European sites is a powerful tool to assist their protection. The problem remains, however, that their protection may be at the expense of sites that have not been so designated – another example of the danger of a hierarchy of protected areas.[63]

4 Conclusion

The analysis above has concentrated on the limitations of the protected-area designation as a device for protecting nature conservation interests in the planning arena. The post-Rio philosophy puts greater importance on the need to apply a holistic approach to conservation and not place so much emphasis on protected areas such as SSSIs and SACs. Local Agenda 21 is designed to assist local communities to work for sustainability. Conservation of the wider environment is one aspect of this. Its importance is recognized in the Habitats Directive, Article 10 of which refers to the need to encourage the management of features of the landscape which are of major importance for wild fauna and flora, including linear features, such as hedgerows and 'stepping stones' for migratory species. However, the government has paid scant attention to implementing this part of the directive. The 1994 regulations merely repeat the words of the directive,[64] which is not very helpful for those charged with putting the words into action.

The government's Biodiversity Strategy does, however, address these broader issues. Rather than adopting a protected-area approach, it concentrates on the management needs of targeted species and habitats and then considers the most appropriate ways of addressing these. The

---

[61] Article 6(4) applies also to sites classified as Special Areas of Protection under the Birds Directive.

[62] Case C-57/89 [1991] ECR I-883; (1992) JEL 4(4) 139.

[63] Le-Las, elsewhere in this volume, similarly refers to the problems facing sites that are not given any formal protection or are SSSIs where development is not opposed by English Nature.

[64] Reg. 37.

concept has its attractions in that it highlights the actual needs in a practical way which should make it more useful as a material consideration in planning terms than a blanket designation which is often little more than a label. It should be easier, in future, to assess the effect of a proposed development on the conservation interest and to judge this against the overall strategy. The difficulty with any integrated approach of this type, of course, is its complexity. Its success will be dependent on continued monitoring of the conservation status of the targeted species and habitats.

The increasing complexity does not augur well for the prospects of decisive action from the courts to uphold the country's nature conservation obligations. If the case law described in this chapter is anything to go by, the traditional planning-law approach to dispute resolution is unlikely to provide a suitable avenue for ensuring conservation interests are properly respected. One solution, which has been proposed by various commentators over the years, is an environmental tribunal of some sort.[65] In the author's view, however, the procedural form is less important than the criteria used in reaching a decision. Until the natural environment and all its components are regarded as an important national resource, no adjudication system will solve the problem.

[65] See, for example, Woolf, 'Are the judiciary environmentally myopic?', *Journal of Environmental Law* (1992) 4(1), 1.

6

Conservation v. Access: Perpetual Litigation?

GERARD RYAN QC AND GEORGE MEYRICK

1 Introduction

Potential and actual conflict over the use of land has always been a root cause of human troubles. This chapter looks at a narrow but significant contemporary issue. It can be put simply as the demand for the provision of greater access to the countryside versus the need to conserve wildlife, habitats and places of natural beauty. Alongside this tension the longer-standing conflict between the claims of landowners and those wanting access as of right over all open country continues to reverberate.

General statutory recognition of the importance of both access for air and recreation and the preservation of places of natural beauty was generated by eighteenth-century enclosures and nineteenth-century urbanization. The enactment of the National Parks and Access to the Countryside Act put in place mechanisms designed to assist in securing public access over open country at a national level. The importance of nature conservation was first formally recognized in that Act by the establishment of mechanisms intended to protect sites of nature conservation importance. After nearly fifty years, amendments to the 1949 Act begin to make a patchwork quilt of it. Since it became law, real changes have taken place both in respect of the increased use of, and demand for access to, the countryside and the greater weight given to the need to preserve and enhance the environment,[1] a need

---

[1] The Government's White Paper on Rural England commits it to sustainable development which means 'managing the countryside in ways that meet current needs

heightened by the continued destruction of and damage to sites of nature conservation value.

Government has recognized that in this area of potential conflict it will not always be possible to reconcile competing priorities;[2] for instance, National Park Authorities are now under a statutory duty to put the interests of wildlife conservation ahead of the provision of access for recreation where the two are in conflict.[3] This results from amendments to the core provisions of the 1949 Act by part III of the Environment Act 1995: the purposes for which National Parks are now deemed to be designated place principal emphasis on conserving and enhancing their 'natural beauty, wildlife and cultural heritage' and require this to be given 'greater weight' when the possibility of conflict arises. It is not only government agencies which may put the interests of conservation ahead of recreation; the National Trust has opted to manage its properties in a sustainable manner, and it has adopted a precautionary approach whereby, if the impact of a recreational activity is suspected of causing damage, it will be modified or removed.

It is only now that some of these bodies (some with more vigour than others), in the face of pressures to provide both greater access and more protection to areas of nature conservation value, are beginning to grapple with what sustainable management means in practice. Such management is dependent upon both sufficient information, derived from relevant research, and adequate powers.

This chapter refers to the modern legislation governing access and conservation; examines some of the bodies which manage areas of importance for both access and nature conservation; illustrates some of the pressures that are experienced at 'ground level'; and indicates some of the positive steps that are now being taken to manage land affected in a way that actively seeks to reconcile competing pressures.

2 Conservation in History

Before 1949 specific protection was given only to species and habitats of interest to those hunting animals for sport. An example is given by the Game Act 1539 which made it a felony to take game whilst breeding or to steal the eggs or fledglings of hawks or falcons. The persistence today of the remnants of royal forests (such as the New Forest, Epping Forest, the Forest of Dean, and the Malvern Hills), although often now used extensively for commercial forestry, is a testament to the efficacy

without compromising the ability of future generations to meet theirs.' (DoE and MAFF, 1995 Cm. 3016).

  [2] Ibid.

  [3] Section 11A(2) of the National Parks and Access to the Countryside Act 1949 as inserted by the Environment Act 1995.

of the forest laws established as early as the eleventh century to uphold royal hunting and timber rights. Further, although the forest laws did not prevent the extermination of wild boar from their natural habitat (on account of excessive demand for meat for the royal table), the worth of forest laws can be illustrated by the consequences of the turbulent years of the mid-seventeenth century when they were in abeyance: during this time numerous deer parks were broken down, thereby causing deer to be poached and the semi-domesticated 'wild' boar to be finally exterminated whilst the veterans of the New Model Army were settled in Windsor Forest.

Many estates have long been, and continue to be, managed primarily for their sporting value, as opposed to agricultural or forestry value, which has been to the benefit of both nature and landscape conservation. Even in the nineteenth century agricultural improvement and modernization was inimical to hedgerows, trees, game and wildlife. A woodland habitat is necessary for the shooting of pheasants: much of the woodland planted in the nineteenth century was laid out with this purpose in mind. A recent study has concluded[4] both that the vast majority of 'new' plantations (within the area surveyed) were established on shooting holdings, and that the more seriously shooting has been taken on an estate, the more woodland and conservation features are to be found there.

A successful grouse moor, in terms of numbers of grouse, requires active maintenance of the heather moorland. So it may not be surprising that the nature conservation value of shooting was recently recognized by the Edwards Report;[5] although it may be noted that until recently gamekeepers were generally notorious for their antipathy to raptors (among other genera).

Animal welfare legislation, by contrast, and in particular the Animals Act 1911, has been of little conservation value.

3 Modern Legislation: Access to Open Country

A modern form of conflict arising between land ownership and use has been the attempt to secure for the general public a right of access over open country. Open country has, since 1968, included land consisting wholly or predominantly of mountain, moor, heath, down, cliff and foreshore, plus countryside woodlands, rivers and canals and, generally speaking, their banks and towpaths as well as any expanse of water through which a river, or part of one, runs.[6]

---

[4] See Cox, Watkins and Winter, 'Game management in England: implications for public access, the rural economy and the environment' (August 1996), pp.48, 51.

[5] The Edwards Report, 'Fit for the Future', p.41.

This conflict has continued between organizations such as the Country Landowners' Association on one side and the Ramblers' Association and the Open Spaces Society on the other.

The first attempt as securing public access to open country was James Bryce's Access to Mountains (Scotland) Bill 1884, the first of many unsuccessful attempts to pass access legislation. Success of a kind came with the enactment of the Access to Mountains Act 1939. This originated in a private member's bill which had the technical consequence that, not being a government proposal, no public funds could be made available to pay compensation to landowners. More significant, however, were the fourteen hostile amendments which placed numerous impedimenta in the way of securing an access order, the most notable of which was that the responsibility for and cost of securing an order (including the expense of any public inquiry) fell upon the individual or organization rather than a local authority. No access to the countryside was ever secured under the 1939 Act.

3.1 The National Parks and Access to the Countryside Act 1949

Those with the responsibility for drawing up the eventual future access legislation were determined to avoid the disappointments of the 1939 Act. The foundations of the eventual legislation were laid in the work underlying the classic reports on the creation of National Parks. The Dower report of 1945 adopted a robust approach to the provision of greater public access, characterized by the belief that the recreational needs of the few were outweighed by the recreational needs of the many;[7] and advocated the speedy passage of new legislation to confer public rights over all uncultivated land by direct and immediately operative provision.[8]

Following the publication of the Dower report, a committee was established under the chairmanship of Sir Arthur Hobhouse to consider the implications arising out of Dower's proposals for National Parks. This committee had two offshoots: one was the Special Committee on Footpaths and Access to the Countryside; the other was the Wildlife Special Conservation Committee under the chairmanship of Sir Julian Huxley. The Special Committee on Footpaths and Access to the Countryside was supportive of the provision of public access over the majority of open country and recommended that all open country should be designated access land by the relevant local planning authority. It

[6] S.59(2) of the National Parks and Access to the Countryside Act 1949 as amended by s.16 of the Countryside Act 1968. The previous definition was then enlarged to include the last four categories generally.

[7] See para.45 of the Dower report (1945), Cmd. 6628.

[8] Ibid at para.52.

proposed that after a period of consultation and, if necessary, public inquiry, the status of such land as access land would be confirmed by order of the minister. The committee also recommended that compensation should be paid if the value of land decreased as a result of being made subject to the ministerial order.[9]

The report of the Special Committee provided the basis for the eventual legislation – part V of the National Parks and Access to the Countryside Act 1949 – and the minister responsible for the passage of the legislation, Lewis Silkin, the Minister for Town and Country Planning, claimed that 90 per cent of the recommendations in the Hobhouse Report had been incorporated into the legislation. Notwithstanding this claim, the Minister, in relation to the recommended public right of access over open country, felt himself 'unable to accept the rather sweeping recommendations of the special committee'.[10] Silkin also said that this part of the Bill was the most difficult to prepare and possibly the most controversial. Thus when the Bill reached the House of Commons, it failed to provide for public access as of right over all open country. No doubt the hostility of sections of the House of Lords and the advanced stage of the parliamentary calendar ensured that a Bill advocating public access over open countryside as of right would have stood no chance of enactment, with the result that a measure of consensus had to be reached to enable the passage of some access legislation. Indeed, the disappearance of the Special Committee's recommendations for access as of right proved to be uncontroversial in the House of Commons debate and drew minimal adverse comment[11] from members of Parliament. 'In the end', as one commentator has put it,[12] 'the 1949 Act's access proposals differed from those in the never-implemented 1939 Act only to the extent that negotiating access now fell to the local authorities rather than the ramblers themselves.'

In place of public access to open country as of right, the 1949 Act established a tripartite mechanism whereby a local planning authority might provide greater access to open country: the access agreement (a commercial arrangement with a landowner); the access order, in respect of which compensation might be paid; and power compulsorily to acquire land to provide greater access.[13] In order that these powers should be used and greater access be provided thereby, the Act laid

[9] See the Special Committee Report *Footpaths and Access to the Countryside* (1947), Cmd. 7207 at paras.173ff.

[10] See Hansard, 31 March 1949, col. 1478.

[11] See the speech of H. D. Hughes MP, Hansard, 31 March 1949, cols. 1563f. for a rare example of criticism.

[12] Curry, 'A people's charter', p.59.

[13] Respectively ss.64, 65 and 76 of the 1949 Act; compensation provisions are at ss.70–3.

down a duty on local planning authorities to survey all open country within their areas and to consider what steps should be taken to secure public access for open-air recreation.[14]

3.2 After the 1949 Act

Since 1949 relatively little legislation has been passed in relation to access to open countryside. In place of the National Parks Commission, the Countryside Act 1968 established the Countryside Commission, its function being to conserve and enhance the natural beauty and amenity of the countryside and to encourage the provision of greater public access thereto.[15] The 1968 Act gave local authorities powers to provide country parks,[16] and extended the definition of 'open country' to embrace woodland, rivers and canals.[17]

Thirteen years on, the Wildlife and Countryside Act 1981 extended the ability of various authorities to enter into a management agreement[18] in relation to any area of the countryside (and not just open countryside) for the purpose of either conserving or enhancing the natural beauty or amenity of the land or for promoting its enjoyment by the public. After a similar period the Criminal Justice and Public Order Act 1994 created a new offence of aggravated trespass, committed by those unlawfully gathered on land without the permission of the owner and with the intent of obstructing a lawful activity.

The existence of other statutory powers which can provide greater access to the countryside must not be overlooked. An example is the footpath-creation order,[19] a procedure used recently to secure access to Wychwood Forest in Oxfordshire. More commonly used, however, are a number of schemes which provide a financial incentive to encourage landowners to provide a greater degree of access over their land. The Countryside Stewardship Scheme enables access to be obtained to over 220,000 acres, but has also been the subject of criticism by the access lobby; exemption from inheritance tax can be obtained for providing access to land; additional payments are available within ESA schemes to farmers for providing access to land; and, in general terms, government policy encourages both the diversification of the use of agricultural land and greater provision of land for sport and recreation.[20]

[14] S.61 of the 1949 Act.
[15] S.1(2) of the 1968 Act.
[16] S.7 of the 1968 Act.
[17] S.16 of the 1968 Act.
[18] S.39 of the 1981 Act.
[19] S.26 of the Highways Act 1980.
[20] PPGs 2, 7 and 17.

3.3 The Future

Attempts, however, to enact a general right to roam over open country continue. One example was Paddy Tipping MP's Access to the Countryside Bill which was laid before Parliament in 1997. It provided for a public right of access to all open country with the exception of National Nature Reserves and land subject to temporary prohibition orders of up to three years. No compensation would be paid to landowners as a consequence of greater access. The Bill failed.

A consultation paper on access to the open countryside in England and Wales has been published by the government. Philosophically the consultation paper is very much a continuation of the process begun by the 1949 Act; and its underlying aim appears to be the desire to extend a statutory right of access over open countryside. Whether a consensus can be reached must be open to doubt. The access lobby continued to press for new legislation conferring a right to roam over all open country; whereas the representatives of the landowning interest, the Country Landowners' Association, argue that the existing mechanisms of the 1949 Act can and should be made to work more satisfactorily. It is clear, however, that the government is committed to providing a greater degree of access over open countryside.

A more likely subject for successful legislation is the provision of a right of access over all common land. Notwithstanding both the recommendations of the Royal Commission on Common Land (1955–8) and the Common Land Forum (1986), and the then government's manifesto promise in 1987 to enact the recommendations of the latter, there is as yet no public right of access over common land outwith an area that formerly lay in a borough or urban district.

Other developments likely to provide more access to land, but of an enclosed nature, are the National Trust's intention to extend access to tenanted farmland and the growing trend towards individual commercial arrangements for limited public access to farm land.

4 Provision of Access under the 1949 Act

The way in which local authorities undertook their duty to survey open land within their jurisdiction and assess the need for access caused disappointment. For example, West Riding County Council (within whose area the Yorkshire Dales National Park is to be found) decided that no action was required to secure access agreements anywhere in the county, and it was not until 1960 that the first access agreement was entered into in relation to 2,700 acres of Barden Moor and Fell. In the early 1950s thirty councils considered no action was necessary, and another seven considered that they had no open country within their areas of administration. There has been no review since of either open country or the public's access requirements. The announcement of a new review of potential access land in 1969 was not proceeded with after the change of government in 1970.

The lack of access secured by the provisions of the 1949 Act has been well documented; and the use of compulsory purchase powers has been even more rare. By 1989 access had been secured over 34,000 hectares in England and Wales, over half of which is in the Peak District National Park. This is perhaps not entirely surprising, as much of the impetus behind the 1949 Act came from the particular access difficulties in the Peak District. However, landowners within the Peak District have become increasingly unwilling to enter into access agreements, and it is anticipated that this mechanism will be used less and less in the future.[21] This again is perhaps not entirely surprising as the access agreement is now a mechanism of some antiquity, lacking the flexibility of a management agreement. Tentative preliminary indications from Scotland have suggested that the management agreement is perceived in a more favourable light by landowners than the access agreement.[22]

Commentators[23] have suggested a number of reasons for local authorities' reluctance to use the 1949 Act's powers: these have included the noisy socialism of access campaigners; Conservative control of local authorities in the years following the 1949 Act; opposition from farmers and landowners; and the trouble and expense which the provision of public access can cause. Local authorities' reluctance to use their powers under the 1949 Act has been contrasted with their greater willingness to establish country parks and picnic sites under powers conferred by the Countryside Act 1968.

5 Rights of Way

While this chapter does not concern itself with rights-of-way legislation, one cannot help observing that, as a first step, the most practical, efficacious and legislatively undemanding way of achieving increased provision of public access to the countryside (if not *de facto* access over much open country) would be for local authorities to utilize their existing powers adequately and uniformly to secure the availability and maintenance of footpaths and bridleways. An example of what can be achieved is provided by Ynys Môn County Council's establishment of

[21] Curry, 'A people's charter', pp.136ff.

[22] Jeremy Rowan-Robinson's 'Public access to the Scottish countryside', in *Nature Conservation and Countryside Law*, ed. Rodgers (1996), p.169.

[23] See both Marion Shoard's polemic 'This land is our land', p.378, which draws on research conducted by Dr Judith Rossiter; and MacEwen's 'National parks'.

four circular walks on existing footpaths (all associated with a local saint), which are well marked, maintained and publicized.[24] An added advantage of such an approach might be a likelihood of less resistance from farmers and landowners.

6 Conservation: The Legislation

The Huxley Committee was appointed to consider the scientific problems that arose directly or indirectly from the proposal to establish National Parks. In 1947 it published its report, recognizing the need for active management of places of nature conservation interest, and it proposed the establishment of nature reserves within National Parks; a series of National Nature Reserves; a series of Conservation Areas to preserve areas of singular natural beauty and scientific interest; and Sites of Special Scientific Importance principally for the protection of a species. Further, the Huxley Committee recommended the establishment of a Biological Service whose functions would be to manage National Nature Reserves; to provide advice on nature conservation; and to conduct research.

The 1949 Act followed the recommendations of the Huxley report in most respects. The Nature Conservancy Council was created with powers to enter into agreements to manage nature reserves or alternatively to acquire them compulsorily; to make by-laws for the protection of nature reserves, including the prohibition or restriction of persons within nature reserves; and to notify local planning authorities of sites of special scientific interest.[25]

The focus of nature conservation shifted to SSSIs with the enactment of the Countryside Act 1968 which, in addition to placing all government departments and public bodies under a duty to have regard to the desirability of conserving the natural beauty and amenity of the countryside,[26] empowered the Nature Conservancy Council both to enter into agreements with landowners for the management of SSSIs, and to make payments in relation to such agreements.[27]

6.1 The Wildlife and Countryside Act 1981

This process of moving the focus of the nature conservation effort was advanced by passage of the 1981 Act, which provided a new statutory

---

[24] These walks were established with the help of a £10,000 grant from the European Regional Development Fund (all information provided by Mr Arwel Evans, a rights-of-way officer with Ynys Môn County Council).

[25] Part III of the National Parks and Access to the Countryside Act 1949.

[26] S.11 of the Countryside Act 1968.

[27] S.15 of the Countryside Act 1968.

framework for the protection of SSSIs. Where English Nature[28] are of the opinion that a site is of interest on account of its flora, fauna, or geological or physiographical features,[29] not only local planning authorities, but also the owner and occupier of a site of interest must be notified. Notification specifies both the nature of the site's interest and a list of operations likely to damage the site. Protection of the site is immediate, and if the owner or occupier of the site wishes to carry out one of the damaging operations specified, he must give notice to English Nature, which then has a period of four months to enter into a management agreement.

If, after the expiry of the four-month period, no management agreement has been entered into and the owner or occupier persists in his desire to carry out the damaging operation, the Secretary of State may make a nature conservation order[30] preventing such operation from being carried out. Such an order gives English Nature up to twelve months either to buy the site or to enter into a management agreement. If no agreement has been reached within this period or no decision has been taken to acquire the site compulsorily, the owner or occupier may lawfully carry out the damaging operation.

6.2 Other designations and schemes

There are several other designations relevant to nature conservation on an international, European and local level.

In June 1992 the United Kingdom signed the Biodiversity Convention at the Earth Summit in Rio de Janeiro. Following from this, 'Biodiversity: the UK Action Plan' was launched in January 1994 at which it was announced that a Biodiversity Steering Group would be established which would be chaired by the then Department of the Environment. The steering group would oversee a number of tasks, one of which was developing costed targets for key species and habitats. One such key habitat is lowland heathland (which comprises 20 per cent of the international resource). Key targets of the Heathland Habitat Action Plan (HAP) are to maintain and improve by management all existing lowland heathland (58,000 hectares); and encourage the re-establishment of a further 6,000 hectares of heathland by 2005, with the emphasis on key lowland heathland counties. The Heathland HAP indicates a number of action points for lead agencies and their partners, which include asking the Department of Transport, the

[28] The successor to the Nature Conservancy Council: see part V of the Environmental Protection Act 1990. Its full title is the Nature Conservancy Council for England.
[29] S.28 of the Wildlife and Countryside Act 1981.
[30] Wildlife and Countryside Act 1981, s.29.

Environment and the Regions (DETR) and the Welsh Office to simplify
the process for submission of applications to the Secretary of State to
fence lowland heathland comprising common land to enable grazing to
maintain its wildlife interest; and a requirement that relevant local
authorities should incorporate heathland wildlife site-protection policies
in development plans by 2000.

At the European level, European directives have been incorporated
into English law: the Birds Directive established Special Protection
Areas, and the Habitats Directive establishes Special Areas of Conservation. A further international designation under the Ramsar
Convention attaches to wetlands of international importance. And there
are informal local designations identified in the planning system.

One scheme of particular importance to nature conservation is that
which operates within Environmentally Sensitive Areas. In areas designated as ESAs farmers can enter into ESA management agreements
whereby they are paid to farm in a less intensive and more environ-
mentally-friendly manner. The scheme has three tiers. Tier 1 is
obligatory and aims to retain valuable wildlife and landscape features
such as ponds, heathland, and bogs; Tier 2 is voluntary and offers
higher rates of payment for the enhancement of certain types of land by
specific management practices; and Tier 3 pays farmers for providing
access. But by way of example, take-up of the third Tier in the three
ESAs in north Wales (Anglesey, the Llŷn Peninsula and the Clwydian
Range) has so far been non-existent, which would suggest that if
farmers' antipathy to greater access is to be overcome, Tier 3 payments
need to be increased. Another important scheme is the Wildlife
Enhancement Scheme, described as English Nature's flagship project,
which covers 12,057 hectares, whereby landowners are paid for remed-
ial works to SSSIs.

7 Conservation: 'The Toothless Regime'

By September 1997 there were 4,000 SSSIs in England which covered
an area of 955,000 hectares, or 7 per cent of the land area of England.
Damage to and destruction of SSSIs has only been documented in part:
for example, in Wiltshire by 1977 35 per cent of SSSIs had been
partially destroyed; and 5 per cent had been wholly destroyed. A
Nature Conservancy Council survey in 1980 estimated that 15 per cent
of SSSIs nationally were being damaged on an annual basis. The most
recent estimate by English Nature (its successor) is that 45 per cent of
SSSIs are deteriorating.[31]

The protection given to sites of conservation value by the 1981 Act

[31] See 'A muzzled watchdog?', a WWF-UK Report (November 1997), 5 and 15.

has been subject to much criticism, and was famously characterized as 'toothless' by Lord Mustill.[32] The most common criticism is that the protective regime is founded on the principle of voluntarism, and contains no coercive powers (aside from the power of compulsory purchase) which can in the long run prevent damaging operations. Accordingly the 1981 Act has failed to prevent the continuing destruction of SSSIs. Indeed, until the Wildlife and Countryside (Amendment) Act 1985 gave immediate protection to SSSIs upon notification, SSSIs were vulnerable to deliberate destruction by landowners determined to thwart confirmation of a site's status. The only protection that the 1981 Act provides is that of delay, to enable English Nature to have the opportunity of exerting moral pressure on the landowner to enter into an agreement and abandon the destructive operation in question. Compulsory-purchase powers have, to date, never been used although the threat of their use has, on occasion, been enough to persuade a reluctant owner to enter into an agreement.

An ancillary criticism has been the great expense of agreed acquisitions and the compensation paid in respect of management agreements. The purchase of 6,000 acres of the Ribble Marshes apparently cost the Nature Conservancy Council £1.75 million; and entry into a management agreement in the case of the Halvergate Marshes was prevented by English Nature's unwillingness to pay the amount demanded by the particular landowner. That particular impasse was resolved by the Secretary of State suspending the relevant exemption from planning control in respect of that particular piece of land. In 1995–6 English Nature paid £5.5 million to landowners.

Weaknesses in the current SSSI regime have been recognized by the present government which has published a consultation paper on better protection and management of SSSIs. The consultation paper includes proposals which would bring to an end the entitlement of landowners to compensation for not carrying out operations which would damage an SSSI; rather payments will only be made to secure appropriate management of the site, to ensure that its nature conservation value is preserved. Further, the consultation paper proposes to increase penalties for deliberate damage and to provide legal means to require restoration where this is practicable, and invites consideration of how to secure positive management of SSSIs where the landowner neglects the site. Suggestions have included the use of orders, and options for public purchase and management; compulsory purchase orders, however, continue to be seen as a last resort. These proposals are both welcome and overdue, as neglect of sites of nature conservation importance is both prevalent and difficult to resolve and to enforce.

[32] *Southern Water Authority* v. *Nature Conservancy Council* [1992] 3 All ER 481; 65 P & C R 55.

A more profound criticism of the protection afforded to SSSIs is that the statutory conservation regime was based upon the assumption that farming benefited the environment and that farmers were natural conservationists. This led to perhaps the greatest weakness of nature conservation legislation which continues today, and which originated in the Scott Report of 1942 into land utilization in rural areas: namely that reliance should be placed on planning control to protect areas of nature conservation importance, and the failure to appreciate the destructive potential of modern farming and forestry,[33] which have caused the most damage to SSSIs, and which are well exemplified by the ploughing up of moorland in Exmoor in the 1970s.

Since the establishment of milk quotas in 1984 and the passage of the Agriculture Act 1986, the farming industry has moved away from its previous productionist bent. With the likely future accession of the countries of central Europe to the European Union, it would seem likely that pressure to produce ever more food within the UK is unlikely to return in the immediately foreseeable future. Notwithstanding the more benign nature of farming, it appeared for a time that the Department of Transport would inherit MAFF's mantle as the government department most destructive of areas of nature conservation importance; there has, however, been a notable shift in policy in relation to the provision of roads.

In addition, and no doubt both because of the weakness of the 1981 Act, with its emphasis on reaching agreement, and its lack of provision of human and financial resources, English Nature has come in for severe criticism in relation to its protection of sites of importance to nature conservation.[34]

This is something which the consultation paper on better protection and management of SSSIs sets out to deal with, and it is notable that as part of the Comprehensive Spending Review, English Nature will receive an additional £6.1 million in 1999 to support its work.

8 Reconciling Access and Conservation Pressures

8.1 Bodies

A number of bodies have the combined responsibility of managing land in the interests of both public access for recreation and for nature conservation; they include the National Park Authorities; the National Trust, which owns 235,000 hectares (or 1 per cent of the United Kingdom); English Nature (which manages a number of National

---

[33] See paras.214 and 236ff. of the Huxley report (1947), Cmd. 7122.
[34] WWF-UK, 'A muzzled watchdog?'

Nature Reserves); the Epping Forest Conservators; the Malvern Hills Conservators; and the various bodies exercising management functions over the New Forest, including the Forestry Commission (over Crown land) and the Verderers. The New Forest Committee, a non-statutory body, performs co-ordinating functions.

8.2 Purposes and powers

Whilst there is a degree of variance, these bodies are in general under a dual duty both to provide for as great a degree of public access as is reasonably possible and to conserve the natural aspect and interest of the areas under their control. Some bodies are more explicit as to the priority of these purposes and the way in which these duties are to be fulfilled; but most make nature conservation a priority over recreation. The statutory duties of National Park Authorities were noted in the Introduction; achieving a balance with nature conservation became a statutory duty of the Forestry Commission with the passage of the Wildlife and Countryside Act 1985; and the National Trust's current policy on access and conservation can be summarized as follows:

(a) The duty and primary purpose of the Trust in the countryside is to promote permanent preservation for the benefit of the nation. It will regard access as a fundamental way of providing this benefit and as a principal purpose.

(b) The Trust's Acts establish the responsibilities for conservation. If serious conflict arises, conservation will take precedence over access.[35]

By contrast, nature conservation occupies the less exalted position of consideration, rather than priority, in the Malvern Hills Conservators' Management Plan.

8.3 Conditions on the ground

Conditions on the ground vary. For example, the North Yorkshire Moors National Park has a thriving farming community and contains large stretches of land over which the public have no right of access, whereas the public have an unrestricted right of access to all the land within Epping Forest and the Malvern Hills, and in the case of the former the agricultural economy is in a moribund state. What is common to all bodies managing open countryside in the interests of

[35] The National Trust, 'Open countryside', report of the Access Review Working Party (April 1995).

both nature conservation and recreation is a political condition in which there is pressure for greater public access, heightened recognition of the importance of nature conservation and the need to preserve the value, interest and amenity of the areas within their control. Pressures on National Trust land are typical: there are currently demands for more rights of way, more access to lowland farmland, and more provision for walking, field studies, horse riding, cycling and canoeing.

Since the passage of the 1949 legislation, much has happened to make the countryside ever more accessible to the population. People have moved out of inner cities into the suburbs, bringing them closer to rural areas for their recreation. Car ownership, the extension and improvement of motorways and trunk roads, and the popularity of rural recreation have combined to bring increasing numbers of people into the countryside. Many of them have little understanding of its dynamics.

8.4 Management

A number of these bodies have over a long period had the management of their areas reviewed in the light of this increasing pressure. Both the National Parks and the New Forest were beneficiaries of general management reviews in the 1970s (respectively the Sandford and Baker reports), and were again reviewed in the 1980s and 1990s (the Edwards report in relation to the National Parks and the current strategy being prepared for the New Forest). The National Trust has established an access-review working party. Effective management is dependent on knowledge of the state of the land managed, the demands placed upon that land, and the damage that it suffers. A prerequisite to successful management is research of the particular areas in question over a prolonged period. Research is being carried out into recreational pressures, or demand, on the open countryside;[36] a good understanding of the effect of various types of recreational activity on nature conservation is, however, in its infancy. In fact, much of the research currently being carried out itself bemoans the lack of adequate previous research.

8.5 Powers

An obvious prerequisite to proper management is the existence of a management organization equipped with adequate and sufficient powers. Some areas, and in particular much common land, have no management structure or plan in place at all. Legislation which would

[36] See, for example, the University of Portsmouth's study of sport and recreation in the New Forest (1994–6), *The New Forest Sport and Recreation Study* (1996).

have provided the required management has fallen victim to a dispute over public access as of right over all common land. The Dartmoor Commoners' Council, established by the Dartmoor Commons Act 1985, which provides the requisite management over common land in and adjacent to Dartmoor, is an example of the managerial organization required; the 1985 Act provided a right of public access to the common land subject to the Commoners' Council. An attempt to create a similar body to manage common land on Bodmin Moor is currently languishing in limbo, a victim of an unresolved dispute over a public right of access to this land.

Other already established bodies, such as the Malvern Hills Conservators, have tried to secure additional powers to equip them for the demands of modern management. These attempts have not always met with complete success: a House of Lords Committee was not persuaded of the Conservators' need to restrict or prohibit public access to protect depastured animals. Yet another body, the Epping Forest Conservators, finds itself facing changes of a social, economic and cultural nature that cannot all be remedied by legislative change.

Competing pressures have been discussed in general terms. It may be useful to look at examples of particular pressures experienced by some of the bodies previously referred to: these pressures are the disturbance caused to birds and the establishment and maintenance of grazing regimes. Both are directly affected by the most popular form of rural recreation – walking, and in particular the walking of dogs – which has been recognized as one of the foremost problems to conservation and recreation managers.

9 Birds

The choughs of the Pembrokeshire Coast National Park are particularly vulnerable to disturbance from human recreation. Choughs nest and feed in a narrow zone of the cliff-face and cliff-top pastures, through which runs a coastal path along which some of the National Park's annual three million day-visitors walk. It is clear that choughs are disturbed by human presence both on the nest and while feeding; unfortunately, however, the effect of such human impact is not fully understood as no relevant research has been conducted.[37] One of the few studies which has been carried out, in relation to ground-nesting birds on upland moors, concluded that some species, for example the golden plover, were more adversely affected by human presence than others, such as the red grouse. Other research tends to suggest (perhaps

[37] Jane E. Hodges, 'A chough conservation strategy for Pembrokeshire' (November 1994), p.16.

unsurprisingly) that birds which live on water are particularly sensitive to disturbance from water-based recreation.[38] The general lack of research into the effect of human disturbance on bird populations is disturbing and really needs to be rectified urgently so that appropriate management regimes can be established in areas of nature conservation importance.

Some restriction on access forms an inevitable part of the proper management of habitats of importance to birds, especially in the breeding season. If the habitat is well managed and well resourced, restrictions on access can be adequately explained, mitigated and enforced, and should not cause undue problems to either visitors or birds.

RSPB reserves are the best examples of the successful coexistence of nature conservation and 'passive' recreation, in the form of bird-watching. In 1990 the RSPB managed 118 reserves covering an area of 74,400 hectares, which in 1989 received 1,008,000 visits.[39] Indeed the RSPB has a policy of maximizing public access to those reserves that can accommodate a large number of visitors; in other reserves access is restricted. Accordingly sites are designed to optimize viewing conditions and to minimize disturbance. Some even have installed closed-circuit television systems to allow viewing of species which are either awkward to observe, for example, the cliff-nesting birds at South Stack in Anglesey, or of particular prominence, such as the ospreys at Loch Garten (which have been viewed by one-and-a-half million people).

Another example of successful coexistence occurs in the New Forest where round-the-clock protection of a nesting Montagu's harrier by wardens has not unduly inconvenienced walkers, who were asked to avoid the area in question.[40] Other good examples of co-operation between the interests of conservation and recreation come from the Pembrokeshire Coast National Park. The park's cliffs are a favoured area for climbers, and a voluntary ban on climbing during the breeding season is observed, which is of benefit to the chough population. In addition climbers help avian ecologists by ringing nestlings otherwise inaccessible to researchers. Again for the benefit of the resident chough population there has been a voluntary footpath diversion over a hundred-metre stretch of National Trust land which has on the whole been observed by walkers.

[38] See, for example, Tanner, 'Water resources and recreation' (1973), and L. A. Batten, 'Sailing on reservoirs and its effects on water birds', in *Biological Conservation* (1977), II, 49–58.

[39] Anthony Chapman and Jon Haw's 'Showing birds to people', in RSPB, *Conservation Review*, 4 (1990).

[40] Personal communication, Martin Noble, chief keeper employed by Forest Enterprise, Lyndhurst.

RSPB reserves well illustrate what can be achieved by good management of an area of importance. They are, however, somewhat unusual in that in the reserves the interests of birds come first, and people visit the reserves with this in mind. By contrast, problems arise in relation to sensitive species within areas that have become accessible for public recreation, and where the access regime is not sufficiently restrictive. Terns are such species, and the shingle beaches, on which they nest, are often popular recreation areas. The decline of the Little tern is well known and has been attributed to recreation.[41]

The decline in tern numbers has occurred even in a National Nature Reserve, primarily, it is thought, as a result of recreational pressure from walkers and beach-goers. Niwbwrch[42] National Nature Reserve was established in 1955 and covers an extensive mobile sand dune system, an estuary and an island promontory, Ynys Llanddwyn. Access to a number of beaches has been restricted on a voluntary basis, and the local authority has passed a by-law banning the presence of dogs on the beaches in the summer months. Nevertheless, since 1955 the three species of terns (Sandwich, Common and Little) have abandoned the reserve, the last Sandwich terns leaving their nesting site at Abermenai in 1979; and the population of ringed plovers and oystercatchers has declined to six pairs of each.[43]

At present the management strategy for the reserve seeks only to maintain the status quo for birds, and there are no plans to enhance, or rather restore, the habitat which the terns require. Any restoration project would necessitate a more restrictive access regime for the beaches. Visitor pressure is intense, with approximately 10,000 people per month visiting Ynys Llanddwyn in July and August. Any attempt to close off more of the beaches would be likely to founder on inevitable local opposition and lack of resources to police a more restrictive regime. It is not yet clear whether, in Wales, the fusion of the functions of the Countryside Commission and English Nature into one agency, the Countryside Council for Wales, impedes a more dynamic management of National Nature Reserves in the interests of nature conservation.

Notwithstanding the deleterious effect of greater public access in the instance of Niwbwrch NNR, it is clear that loss of habitat caused by agricultural change has had a far more serious impact on avian ecology than human disturbance. This has certainly been the case for choughs.[44] One agricultural change of particular importance to nature conservation has been the transformation of grazing patterns in Britain.

[41] Nature Conservancy Council review of declining bird species since 1950 (1984).
[42] The English version is 'Newborough'.
[43] Personal communication, Will Sanderson, warden of the Niwbwrch NNR.
[44] Jane Hodges, 'Chough conservation strategy', 15.

10 Grazing

Grazing is an essential habitat management tool for both the creation and preservation of the natural beauty of the landscape, for nature conservation, and, less obviously, for the requirements of public access (for access and recreation cannot be enjoyed over land that is covered in scrub or gorse). Many of the most important landscapes and richest habitats have been created by centuries of grazing. A notable product of traditional grazing is the New Forest with its variety of lawns, open heath and other features typical of wood pasture. Another example is the mobile sand dune system at Niwbwrch National Nature Reserve mentioned above, which before the decimation wrought by myxomatosis, was traditionally grazed by rabbits (and is now under active grazing management with the aim of both encouraging the return of a rabbit population and re-creating the bare patches of sand required by species of nature conservation importance).

Excessive grazing, however, can damage vulnerable soils by poaching or by stripping the land of essential vegetative cover,[45] especially in winter, and excessive grazing will also prevent the natural regeneration of woodland. This has caused some concern in upland areas of National Parks.

Insufficient grazing can lead to the invasion of bracken, gorse and other scrub which can degrade a site of its nature conservation interest. This was recognized by the Royal Commission on Common Land 1955–8 which heard evidence that there was no method of destruction of brush and scrub as efficient as grazing; and then went on to conclude that:

> Even where preservation of wildlife is an important consideration, grazing may be necessary to maintain a properly balanced use and although it may be otherwise unprofitable [grazing] has got to be looked upon as the most suitable mowing machine for such areas as are essentially public open spaces.[46]

This extract illustrates the falsity of a prevalent belief[47] that a landscape that is grazed is either of less conservation value or somehow less natural than an ungrazed area which is colonized by scrub and which might, decades later, become reforested. Such a belief is often a product of confusion as to what constitutes the natural state of the land, and, according to one commentator, led the Epping Forest Conservators to adopt a management policy that destroyed much of the richness, diversity and character of that particular forest.[48]

[45] Edwards report, 19.
[46] Royal Commission on Common Land 1955–8, Cmnd. 462 at para.109.
[47] See, for example, Shoard, 'This Land', 448.
[48] See Oliver Rackham's *History of the Countryside*, 150.

To emphasize the point, grazing is not only consistent with the preservation of wildlife, but often essential. An illustration of what happens when grazing goes into decline is provided by the Pembrokeshire Coast National Park, where fencing between the coast path and the adjacent pasture has excluded cattle from the cliff-tops and so allowed bracken, gorse and scrub to spread, to the detriment of the chough population.

Traditional lowland grazing regimes have been under considerable pressure in Britain and throughout Europe. Particular pressure has been experienced by lowland commons, which are important areas both for the recreation requirements of urban and suburban populations and for nature conservation. The New Forest provides the most graphic example of the pressures experienced. It is adjacent to the urban areas of Bournemouth and Southampton and is accordingly an important area for the provision of open-air recreation. Following highway improvements to the M3 and the A34, the New Forest is now within the day-trip range of fifteen million people. It had been thought that the New Forest received seven million day-trips annually;[49] more recent research, however, includes calculations that the New Forest receives eighteen million day-trips from local residents alone.[50] The New Forest is also extremely important in nature conservation terms on both a national and international basis. It contains some of the largest concentrations of heathland, wood pasture and valley mire in western Europe. This richness has been recognized by both national and international designation: a Special Area of Conservation (under the EU's Habitats Directive) has been proposed for both the New Forest itself and the adjacent maritime environment of the Solent and the Isle of Wight. The majority of the land within the New Forest perambulation has also been designated as a Wetland of International Importance (under the Ramsar Convention) and as a Special Protection Area for Birds (under the EU's Birds Directive). Part of the coastline is designated as the North Solent National Nature Reserve. Approximately half of the total area within the New Forest is classified as SSSI. Furthermore, the traditional process that has shaped the landscape, grazing and the exercise of other rights of common, has given some cause for concern as the younger generation of commoners finds it difficult to compete for land and housing with more affluent settlers. Other areas with similar pressures are the Malvern Hills (albeit not lowland) which are close to the urban centres of the West Midlands, and Epping Forest which is on the boundary of north-east London.

The problems affecting grazing on common land were recognized by

---

[49] Ecotec survey (1992).
[50] *The New Forest Sport and Recreation Study* (University of Portsmouth, 1996), 44–5.

the Royal Commission on Common Land 1955–8. Among the problems experienced are the transformation of agriculture and the rural economy (and hence rural society), the increase of traffic on the numerous roads that bisect commons, and the predation of dogs, which the NFU calculates kill 10,000 head of stock annually. All these have contributed to a sharp decline in grazing on common land,[51] and the situation has not improved since the publication of the Royal Commission's recommendations.

Conditions on the ground vary. Some areas such as the New Forest are in a relatively healthy state, with an active community of commoners and a sufficient number of beasts (for the most part, ponies and cattle) to maintain its natural landscape, although the numbers of active commoners and of animals depastured do ebb and flow. The New Forest is managed by both the Forestry Commission and the Court of Verderers (who have responsibility for managing the commoners' affairs). Despite the moribund state of the market for New Forest ponies, the fall in the price of beef consequent upon BSE, and the problems young commoners experience in being able to find property in which to live, the New Forest and its grazing community is on the whole in a healthy state. In addition a number of steps have been taken to protect grazing animals, including the fencing of major roads and the introduction of a 40 m.p.h. speed limit on all minor roads within the Forest.

By contrast, 1997 was the final year in which commoners grazed in Epping Forest. The Epping Forest Conservators recognize the importance of grazing as a habitat management tool, and wish to reintroduce grazing on an extensive basis. Indeed, SSSIs which cover Epping Forest are likely to include the standard requirement that the grazing regime should not be changed. To counteract the deficiency in commoners' grazing, proposals under consideration include the establishment of experimental grazing sites, the licensing of local graziers, and even, although presently rejected, the acquisition by the Corporation of London of its own herd of cattle. The Conservators' management plan is due to be published at the beginning of 1998.

11 Fencing

The New Forest and Epping Forest exemplify areas which have traditionally been commonly grazed. In lowland Britain there are many areas like Epping Forest where grazing has declined to the level of extinction. The reintroduction of grazing often requires fencing, although it should be noted that this is not always the case (on cliff-top

---

[51] Cmnd. 462, para.108.

land belonging to the National Trust in the Pembrokeshire Coast National Park the fence between pastureland on the one side, and the coastal path and cliffs on the other has been taken down to allow grazing animals to keep down the scrub growing up on the seaward side of the fence, but contrast the position where it has not, mentioned above). Accordingly the utility of erecting fencing for managed grazing has been generally recognized: for example, by the Huxley report,[52] by the National Trust,[53] in Paddy Tipping's Access to the Countryside Bill,[54] by the Royal Commission on Common Land,[55] and by the Secretary of State, when considering, as he is bound to do, the 'benefit of neighbourhood' and giving his consent (when required for the fencing of most common land) under s.194 of the Law of Property Act 1925. Furthermore if the recommendations of the Royal Commission and the Common Land Forum had been enacted, bodies managing common land would have been given the power to fence. As it is, the Dartmoor Commons Act 1985 has provided such a management body with the power to fence.

Fencing does, however, have its opponents, at both a local and at the national level, as it can interfere with public access, whether *de facto* or as of right, and the aesthetic of open spaces. For example, one farmer grazing on a water meadow on the outskirts of Christchurch, part of which has been designated an SSSI, has had his fences cut on a number of occasions, and on one occasion has even had his cattle attacked and mutilated.[56] Accordingly, part of the site in question is no longer grazed, with the result that over the longer term it is likely to become degraded in nature conservation terms. Furthermore, in the same locality some landowners are reluctant even to consider instituting necessary grazing regimes on common land on the urban fringe, which has been overrun by scrub, because of fears that any fencing will inevitably be destroyed.[57]

At the national level the Open Spaces Society, which is consulted by government departments in relation to all applications under s.194, is hostile to the fencing of common land.[58] Indeed it has launched a campaign to change the law in relation to s.194: it proposes that the current consideration of benefit to the neighbourhood be replaced by a

---

[52] Cmd. 7122, para.191.

[53] National Trust, 'Open countryside', 24–5.

[54] Clause 5(5)(a).

[55] Cmnd. 462, paras.315 and 329.

[56] Personal communication from farmer affected, Jack Bailey, Staple Cross Farm, Christchurch.

[57] Personal communication from director of MEM Ltd.

[58] *Open Space*, 25, 8 (Spring 1997), 2.

requirement that the Secretary of State's consent should be given only if there is an overriding need and no alternative to fencing.

All bodies that manage common land ought to have the power to fence. Some bodies are under a duty to keep land within their control permanently open to the public, and at the same time to preserve the natural aspect of beauty of the land. Such bodies include the National Trust,[59] and the Conservators of both the Malvern Hills and Epping Forest. It might at first sight appear that management requirements of fencing might clash with either or both of these statutory duties. However, closer examination shows that the fencing for grazing is not only consistent with, but is essential to the fulfilment of both these duties. If fencing comes equipped with stiles and gates, it ought not to cause an insurmountable impediment. If land is both to be kept open, and free from encroaching scrub, for public recreation it can usually only be so kept by grazing. Many of the bodies which are under a statutory duty to preserve the natural state or beauty of the areas they control were established at a time when the landscape of the areas for which they were established resulted from a long-standing grazing regime, illustrating how grazing has been essential in preserving the natural aspect of the land.[60] The compatibility between the provision of fencing for managed grazing and the performance of these statutory duties, was, in the case of the National Trust's duties in relation to commons in its control, recognized by the High Court in a recent judgement.[61]

12 A Wider Context

The disturbance of birds and the difficulties associated with grazing illustrate but by no means exhaust the problems experienced at the interface of access and recreation with conservation. Another notable problem caused by the weight of numbers of people is erosion and physical degradation of the land. This problem is widespread, whether on popular footpaths in the upland National Parks or in the New Forest (at nine of the ten base sites examined and monitored by the University of Portsmouth). Indeed in 1987 it was calculated that 9.7 hectares were being lost annually in the New Forest to erosion, the leading culprit being identified as horse-riding. Another serious and widespread problem is that caused by dogs which are out of control.

In neither case, however, has a firm and necessary management policy, which would have entailed unpopularity, been adopted. In

---

[59] National Trust Act 1907, s.29.
[60] Report of the Royal Commission on Common Land, Cmnd. 462, para.109.
[61] *National Trust* v. *Ashbrook* [1997] 8CL 264.

relation to equestrian erosion in the New Forest a code of practice has been drawn up, but in relation to dogs the report prepared for the New Forest Committee interestingly did not propose that all dogs be kept on a lead in the Forest. By contrast, management has been more creative where there is less likelihood of resultant unpopularity or opposition, for example, in relation to the promotion of the remote-areas policy or restoration of heathland in the New Forest.

It remains to be seen whether roads will be closed or charges introduced by the various managerial authorities, let alone attempts to solve some of the more intractable problems such as the gradual undermining of the social and economic basis of commoning or controlling the 95 per cent of visitors who come to the New Forest in their cars.

13 Conclusion

This chapter has sought to discern and to welcome the gradual emergence of a priority from an area of actual and potential conflicts, the priority that is now being given to the conservation of biodiversity.[62] The conflict between the need for conservation and the ever-extending nature of human recreational activities has grown sharper with the increasing sophistication of internal combustion engines. Within England and Wales clearer indications of legislative, administrative and practical recognition of this priority for conservation can now be seen. These indications are significant, albeit modest, steps towards an ultimate objective of restraining humankind from totally overrunning the remainder of the natural world, and from destroying most of it in the process.

---

[62] Biodiversity is taken for this purpose as meaning the range of indigenous plant and animal species and their associated communities together with the ranges of variations within species.

7

Protection of Hedgerows:
Biodiversity or Rupert Bear?

CHARLES MYNORS

1 Introduction

'There is an unnecessary prejudice against trees and hedges, and if those who dislike them were better informed, they would be more alive to their advantages and less fearful of their disadvantages.'[1] That was the view of a government committee reporting over forty years ago, as life returned more or less back to normal after the end of the last war, and changing farming methods began to make an impact on the rural landscape. However, whilst it may have been the view current amongst civil servants in Whitehall, it was not widely shared by those who mattered – the farmers. They knew perfectly well that hedgerows took up space; they required time-consuming and expensive maintenance; they harboured pests; and they impeded the creation of larger, more sensibly shaped fields suitable for being worked with modern agricultural machinery.

So, in the following two decades, little changed, and hedgerows continued to disappear. The influential Countryside Commission study, *New Agricultural Landscapes*, reported in 1974 that

> since 1945 there have been fundamental changes in the structure and methods of farming which have brought about changes in the landscape almost as extensive as those which have occurred during the 'enclosure movement'. Many mourn the loss of traditional landscapes, and believe that the emerging landscapes will be of poorer quality.[2]

[1] *Report on the Committee on Hedgerow and Farm Timber* (HMSO, 1955).
[2] *New Agricultural Landscapes*, study by Westmacott and Worthington for the Countryside Commission (1974), para.1.1.

And indeed it has been alleged that half of the hedgerows that were present in 1946 had been destroyed by the mid-1970s – some through removal, but the majority through neglect. Some were replaced, but replacement hedges were in many ways no substitute for those that were lost.

But was this a true loss? The chairman of the Commission, in his foreword to the 1974 study, noted that 'many of the lowland landscapes inherited from earlier generations have been, or soon will be, replaced by new landscapes of greatly reduced scenic and wildlife interest'. And government advice four years later was that 'losses of trees and hedgerows since the war years represent an erosion not only of land-scape quality, but also of important wildlife habitats'.[3] Both comments reflect a theme which constantly recurs: hedgerows are of value because they are of scenic and wildlife interest. But these are concerns of non-farmers, who therefore have to find apparently practical arguments in their favour.[4] Hedges can be barriers against soil erosion; but in Britain this is scarcely a problem. They provide shelter to animals; but not as effectively as even the humblest shed. They control the movement of animals; but to remain stock-proof they need attention, and they are not as efficient as barbed wire and electric fences – which of course are readily movable.

And barbed wire and electric fences are not attractive – at least not to the eyes of urban dwellers, who are used to a landscape of small fields bordered by old hedges, rich in wildlife, and laid by hand so as to allow the emergence of trees at intervals. Further, as public aware-ness of history has grown, hedges are valued also as archaeological evidence of past land-use patterns.

Concern has thus been widely and continuously expressed over the loss of hedgerows in the last fifty years. It might be thought that, in the light of that, the destruction would have slowed down or stopped. But no. Not only did it continue, it did so at an accelerating rate. The average net loss of hedgerow each year (destruction less replacement), which was 4,000 km in the period 1947–69, rose to an average of 4,600 km in 1969–80, 6,200 km in 1980–5, and 7,600 km in 1985–90. The reasons for the loss are very simple, and were summarized thus by Lord de Ramsey of the Country Landowners' Association, who farms 7,000 acres in East Anglia:

Essentially you have a traditional landscape feature trying to survive in a twentieth-century environment. There used to be hundreds of cows around

---

[3] Department of the Environment Circular 36/78 (Welsh Office 64/78), *Trees and Forestry*, Memorandum, para.30.

[4] See, for example, Nan Fairbrother, *New Lives, New Landscapes* (Penguin, 1972).

here when I was a boy, but now there are just seven dairy herds in the whole of Cambridgeshire. Once you no longer have animals, you don't need field boundaries. Potatoes, after all, don't wander across the road. In practical terms, hedgerows are an anachronism and an attractive luxury. In 1946 we had thirty-five miles of hedgerows on the farm. Now we have fourteen, but it still costs us £4,000 a year to maintain them.

Throughout this post-war period, as the widespread debate continued about landscape change in the countryside, the statistics on which many assertions were loosely based appeared increasingly inadequate. More recently, therefore, the Department of the Environment commissioned two survey reports from the Institute of Terrestrial Ecology (ITE). The first revealed that between 1984 and 1990, the total hedgerow length fell by over 20 per cent in England, and 25 per cent in Wales: in both, 9 per cent of hedgerows were removed or destroyed, and 19 per cent ceased to be classified as hedgerows as a result of neglect or conversion into another form of boundary (23 per cent in Wales). The only good news was that the position improved significantly in the following period, 1990–4: the average annual loss dropped from 9,500 km to 3,600 km.[5]

Against this loss should be set replacement planting of an average of 1,900 km per annum in 1984–90, rising to 4,400 km in 1990–3.[6] The official government line is that this means that 'the rate of gains from new planting [were] more than outweighing the losses from removal in numerical terms';[7] but David Gear from the Countryside Commission has pointed out that 'it is a continuing source of surprise how some commentators have attempted to equate a newly planted hedge with one which has just been lost and may have taken centuries to develop'.[8]

This chapter will review the attempts that have been made to give some measure of protection to the vanishing hedgerows. Until 1997 these measures took two forms, the classic 'carrot and stick' approach: the former in the shape of grants being available for hedgerow retention, and the latter by means of various forms of legislation, largely ineffectual. The one possible exception to that criticism is the Enclosure Acts themselves, which brought into being many of today's hedgerows, and which have recently enjoyed a renaissance, since it has

[5] *Changes in Hedgerows in Britain between 1894 and 1990* and *Hedgerow Survey 1993*, contract reports for the Department of the Environment by the Institute of Terrestrial Ecology.

[6] Ibid.

[7] DoE Guide (see below), para.2.5.

[8] In a talk at a seminar on 'The Implementation of Hedgerow Protection' organized on 19 May 1997 by Reigate and Banstead Borough Council in association with the Arboricultural Association.

been argued that they can still be enforced so as to provide a means of protecting those hedgerows from removal.

The remainder of the chapter then considers the new Hedgerows Regulations, the final creation of the last Conservative government, which came into force in mid-1997. They are designed to provide specific protection only for 'important' hedgerows; the question of which hedgerows are sufficiently important to merit such protection is therefore considered in some detail, followed by an outline of the statutory machinery by which the protection is achieved.

Before proceeding further, however, it may be helpful to put the matter in a broader historical context, and to try briefly to dispel some of the mythology that abounds on this subject.

2 The Development of Hedgerows

It should no longer be necessary to refute in detail the theory that all, or nearly all, hedges are modern, the product of the Enclosure Act movement of the eighteenth and nineteenth centuries . . . The fact is that innumerable maps and pictures, as far back as the sixteenth century . . . plainly depict hedges and hedgerow trees as the normal furniture of the countryside. To trace them back further calls for a little specialised knowledge; but it is no great feat of scholarship to show that they were already part of England as far back as the written record goes.

Thus starts the chapter on hedges in a recent work by one of the greatest experts on the subject, Dr Oliver Rackham.[9]

The Romans probably found Britain already a hedged land; and there are many references in Anglo-Saxon charters to hedges. However, the pattern of the countryside varied. In the central, more crowded area of lowland England, stretching from York and King's Lynn to Weymouth, there were by the time of the Norman Conquest few heaths, few hedges, less woodland, downland, thorn, elders and apples. This area, referred to by Rackham as the Planned Countryside, was still broadly open when, centuries later, following the Enclosure Acts, it was carved up into hedged fields and straight roads, laid out hurriedly in a drawing office. Not all the hedges even in this area, however, are recent; and there are within it still some Anglo-Saxon hedges, medieval woods and ancient trees that the enclosure commissioners failed to destroy.

In the Ancient Countryside, on the other hand – the western part of England from the Fylde down to Exeter, and the south-eastern section up to the New Forest, the Chilterns and Thetford Chase – there is a hedged and walled landscape dating from any of forty centuries

---

[9] *Trees and Woodland in the British Landscape*, revised edn (1990). It will be obvious to anyone familiar with his work that this section of this chapter owes much to Rackham's authoritative work in this field.

between the Bronze Age and the Stuarts; a landscape of hedgerow oaks, limes, wild pears and birches. The highland zones of England, from the Peak District to the Scottish border, together with West Devon and Cornwall, are different again. And it should also be borne in mind that not all hedges were consciously planted; a few are relics of woods, since grubbed out, leaving their edges as field boundaries, and others are hedges that have developed naturally at the edges of fields.

Hedges increased during the Middle Ages. In some areas of Ancient Countryside, they were at that period as numerous as they have ever been; and in the Planned Countryside, although less numerous, hedges were present round most villages, and often on parish boundaries. In Tudor and Stuart times, hedges were increasingly valued for the timber in them – penalties for 'hedge-stealing' increased to include whipping and the stocks. In the ancient countryside, losses of hedgerows were roughly balanced by additions; but in the Planned Countryside, hedges increased as individual fields, and here and there a whole parish, were enclosed.

But of course it is true that the Great Enclosures were a time of more new hedging (and walling) than ever before or since. More than 300,000 km of hedges were planted between 1750 and 1850 – approximately equal to (but, note, not more than) all those planted in the previous five hundred years. The hedges themselves, at first quite elaborate, became more commercialized and perfunctory as the enclosure movement advanced. And although many were planted, others were destroyed; in the Ancient Countryside, particularly, existing fields were enlarged. In addition, from 1750 the number of hedgerow trees gradually declined, so that by 1870, after a century of agricultural prosperity, there was a maximum number of hedgerows and a minimum number of hedgerow trees. The mechanisms by which this enclosure was achieved are considered below.

In the eighty years after 1870, which were in general times of agricultural adversity, very few hedges were destroyed except those immediately required for urban development or wartime airfields, and the numbers of hedgerow trees increased to a new peak around 1950. Thereafter, the numbers of hedges and hedgerow trees declined dramatically, as has already been described.

The result of this historical evolution is that in the Ancient Countryside the majority of hedges are older, much older, than 1700; and even in the Planned Countryside, pre-enclosure hedges are not uncommon. Dr Max Hooper has shown that there is a surprisingly close correlation between the number of tree and shrub species in a hedge and its age in centuries – at least in some areas of England. Enclosure Act hedges thus typically have two, for example, hawthorn (often used) and ash; whereas a hedge with ten or more tree species in a thirty-yard stretch is likely to be pre-Conquest. This rule, although handy, should be treated with some caution, as other research suggests that woody plant diversity is only weakly related to age.

3 Grants

Given the various practical benefits accruing from the removal of hedgerows, already noted, it is not surprising that, until 1976, financial assistance was available from central government to assist farmers to 'improve' their farms in this way. Thus one farmer in the early 1970s had on his farm of 242 hectares more than three km of hedges, which cost £150 a year for maintenance. He accordingly grubbed up all the hedges and trees, and piped the drains to fill in the ditches, at a cost of £200 per hectare for the area involved, partly paid for by grants. That land was then worth £1,200, and increased the total farm yield by 900–1,000 kg per hectare. All this was in addition to the more efficient and therefore less costly working of the land, which was his original motive.[10]

That has all changed now. The Hedgerow Incentive Scheme, introduced by the government in 1992, was designed to combat the problem of losses through neglect. It is now part of the Countryside Stewardship Scheme, administered in England by the Ministry of Agriculture, Fisheries and Food (MAFF), which offers grants for the planting and restoration of hedges – although, as noted, new planting may not of itself be of any great benefit for a while. In Wales, Cyngor Cefn Gwlad Cymru (the Countryside Council for Wales) (CCW) operates Tir Cymen and the Hedgerow Renovation Scheme.

The House of Commons Environment Sub-Committee recently considered in detail the whole issue of the funding of incentive schemes, the balance between funding maintenance and restoration, and the design of a fair and effective cross-compliance scheme which places upon farmers a basic duty to care for the field boundaries (both hedgerows and walls) on their holdings; and the Sub-Committee's report[11] makes a valuable source of further information.

4 Existing Relevant General Legislation

There was already some legislation giving a small measure of protection to hedgerows, prior to the introduction of the Hedgerows Regulations 1997 – and it should be noted that any requirements arising

[10] Fairbrother, *New Lives*, 67–8.
[11] Thirteenth Report of House of Commons Environment, Transport and Regional Affairs Committee, Environment Sub-Committee, Session 1997–8, HC 969-I; see particularly paras.163–210.

under the earlier legislation have not been superseded by the new provisions.

There is thus at least some control over works to individual trees in the hedgerows. Firstly, a felling licence would be required from the Forestry Commission (for which an application should be made to the Forestry Authority) under s.9 of the Forestry Act 1967, as amended in 1979, for the removal of any tree with a diameter of 8 cm or more at a height of 1.3 m. A licence is not required, however, where the volume of clearly identifiable 'trees', as opposed to woody shrubs, felled by one owner in any quarter is less than 5 m³, and the amount sold is less than 2 m³ – which in practice equates to two or three large trees.

It would also be possible for a local authority to make a tree preservation order to protect a specific tree or group of trees within a hedge, under powers in Part VIII of the Town and Country Planning Act 1990. This procedure is not frequently adopted, at least in rural areas, although it is by no means unheard of. Where an order has been made, consent for the carrying out of almost any works to the tree or trees (not just felling) would be required from the authority that made the order – which would probably be difficult to obtain. If a hedgerow is in a conservation area (again, unusual but not unknown), notice of the carrying out of works to any tree will need to be given to the authority.[12]

Hedges may also be important habitats for wildlife. The Conservation (Habitats etc.) Regulations 1994 implement in the United Kingdom the requirements of the EU Habitats Directive, so that it is now an offence to kill, injure, take or disturb the listed animal species, or to destroy their resting places or breeding sites; or to pick, collect, cut or uproot the listed plant species. For details, see Annex G to Planning Policy Guidance note PPG 9; that PPG gives useful guidance (for England) as does Technical Advice Note TAN 5 for Wales. In addition, there are specific controls relating to badger setts; any interference with a sett requires a licence from English Nature or the CCW – see the Protection of Badgers Act 1992 and Home Office Circular 100/91.

Some 8 per cent of the land area of Britain is within areas that have been designated as sites of special scientific interest (SSSIs) – which include national nature reserves, special protection areas under the Birds Directive, and special areas of conservation under the Habitats Directive.[13] Where a hedgerow is in an SSSI, the landowner and occupier will have been provided by English Nature or the CCW with a list

---

[12] Town and Country Planning Act 1990, ss.211–14.

[13] Wildlife and Countryside Act 1981, s.28; Conservation (Natural Habitats etc.) Regulations 1994. See also PPG 9, Annex A.

of operations likely to damage the special interest of the site – which might well include the destruction or pruning of a hedge. Owners and occupiers must then give four months' notice if they intend to carry out any of the operations specified. Further, where an owner undertakes not to carry out the work, he or she may negotiate a management agreement and be paid compensation based on profits foregone, including an element for the costs of the maintenance of the hedge.[14] Some farms are protected by voluntary schemes within environmentally sensitive areas.[15]

Finally, where a hedgerow is on the site of an archaeological monument that is of sufficient national importance to have been scheduled by the Secretary of State, any works affecting that monument (which would probably include the grubbing-up of a hedge) would require scheduled monument consent to be obtained from the Department of Culture, Media and Sport (formerly the Department of National Heritage). For further details, see the Ancient Monuments and Archaeological Areas Act 1979, PPG 16 (in England), and Welsh Office Circular 60/96.

5 The Enclosure Acts

It has already been noted that a significant proportion of the hedgerows that now exist in lowland England (at least in the Planned Countryside) are the result of the Enclosure Acts. In general, in the early stages of the enclosure movement, land was enclosed by agreement; but this gradually gave way to what is sometimes referred to as parliamentary enclosure; that is, enclosure by award, associated with an Act of Parliament. The first Enclosure Act is probably 4 Jas 1, c. 11, which authorized the enclosure of nearly one-third of Herefordshire. Thereafter, it has been estimated, there were in the region of 4,500 or more Acts, almost all of which are still in existence – that is, they have not been repealed. The process by which this all took place has been reviewed by a number of historians, many of whom were motivated by indignation at the perceived injustice of it all.[16]

It had been supposed until 1996 that the Enclosure Acts were of no continuing significance. However, in June of that year an action was brought in the Hull County Court[17] to enforce the terms of an Act of

---

[14] 1981 Act, s.15.

[15] Under Agriculture Act 1986, s.18.

[16] For a helpful overview, from a legal perspective, see two articles in the *Journal of Legal History*: 'An Introduction to the Enclosure Acts', Sharman (1989), 10(1), at pp.45–70; and 'Enclosure: Agreements and Acts', Brown and Sharman (1994), 15(3), at pp.269–86.

[17] *Seymour* v. *Flamborough Parish Council* (1996) unreported.

1765, relating to a hedge at Flamborough, in Yorkshire. It had been planted under the terms of the Act; and under the relevant award, the owner of the land on which the hedge was planted was required to 'make and forever maintain a ditch and fence to divide the allotment from the Bempton Road'. Further, the award provided that the boundary was to be a live hedge, not a fence (in the modern sense of that term). The land was now in the ownership of the Parish Council, which wished to remove the hedge, and replace it with a close-boarded fence, to create a better bowling green. The action was brought by Mr Seymour, who (as well as being something of an expert in this area of the law) happened to own land elsewhere in the village that had also been the subject of the same award, and by the Yorkshire Wildlife Trust.

The Court (HH Judge Cracknell) first concluded that the 1765 Act was still in force. It then noted that it had been commonly accepted that it was possible for two adjoining landowners to agree by mutual consent that a fencing obligation in an enclosure award should not be enforced, as happened in, for example, *Garnett* v. *Pratt*[18] (although that decision does not explicitly authorize the practice); but that even in that situation it was possible for the award to be later enforced. However, where the boundary in question adjoins a highway, the Court considered that any aggrieved local resident was entitled to seek the enforcement of the award, and accordingly granted the declaration sought, so that the Council was required to maintain the hedge 'forever'.

The decision in the Flamborough case was unsatisfactory for a number of reasons. In the first instance, the plaintiff was representing himself, and the defendant Council was not represented at all, so the law was not fully argued. Secondly, it is arguable that the action was essentially a public-law dispute, and should therefore have been by way of an application for judicial review; indeed, the judge made it clear that he considered that the matter should go to the High Court. However, it was widely reported (in the popular press, not the law reports), in terms that suggest it had established that all Enclosure Acts were fully enforceable. As a result, sometimes the mere threat of litigation is sufficient to lead to the desired result – the industrious Mr Seymour, it appears, had taken up two cases prior to his battle in Flamborough, but the councils concerned (Garforth and Methley, both near Leeds) both decided to replant the hedges in question rather than pursue the matter to court.[19]

On the other hand, the decision in *Seymour* certainly was not

---

[18] [1926] 1 Ch. 897.
[19] HC 969-I (above), para.115.

followed in the one other known case under the Enclosure Acts, *Marlton* v. *Turner*.[20] That case, decided by HH Judge Langan in the Norwich County Court, related to an enclosure award under an Act of 1808, which required the owners of certain land at Field Dalling in Norfolk to 'forever keep in good repair and condition' a hedge between it and the adjacent highway. The obligation was laid upon the then owner of the land 'and his heirs'. The action was brought to stop the owner of the land who now wanted to block up an existing opening in the hedge and replace it with another one nearby.

The first question was whether the burden of the obligation still applied to the present landowner. The Judge followed *The Earl of Cadogan* v. *Armitage*[21] in holding that the phrase 'heirs' was equivalent to what are now more usually known as 'successors in title'. However, he went on to find that an award under an Enclosure Act was similar in character to a normal conveyance, so that the positive obligations imposed within such an award may be enforced only as much as similar obligations imposed in contractual agreements between neighbouring landowners. And of course, under normal common law principles, such obligations may only be enforced where they are negative in character.[22] It followed that the obligations were no longer enforceable on the present owner.

Secondly, even if such an obligation were enforceable (for example, where the owner of the land at the time of the award still owned the land), it would not prevent the replacement of one opening in a long hedge with another; by far the greater part of the hedge would remain. Finally, the court held that a private landowner A, albeit a local resident, had no right to challenge the duty of landowner B to maintain a boundary between his (B's) land and the public highway. This was so even if, as was the case in this instance, A and B were neighbours – it was after all not the boundary between them that was in dispute.

The court accordingly dismissed the claim. This decision, which was not picked up by the press, nevertheless seems much more satisfactory than *Seymour*. And even if a whole hedge is being removed, so that the second of the arguments used in *Marlton* v. *Turner* would not apply, a court might well find that the conscious consent of the highway authority (on behalf of the inhabitants at large) to the removal of the hedge, to enable the carrying out of development for which planning permission had been granted, would be sufficient to bring any potential dispute into the same category as that in *Garnett* v. *Pratt*.

More recently, the effect of old Enclosure Acts has been considered

[20] Noted briefly at [1997] CLY 4233.

[21] (1823) 2 B&C 197 at pp.213, 214.

[22] *Austerberry* v. *Oldham Corpn* (1885) 29 Ch D 750; *Jones* v. *Price* [1965] 2 QB 618 per Willmer LJ at p.633.

by the High Court in *R* v. *Solihull BC, ex parte Berkswell PC*[23] (1998) 77 P&CR 312, which concerned an application for judicial review of a decision to grant planning permission for development that inevitably led to the loss of hedges that were said to be subject to an Enclosure Act of 1802. Sullivan J carefully avoided the question of what was the effect of the 1802 Act in isolation, and whether its terms were enforceable by a parish council, or simply by the private landowners concerned, or by their successors in title – although he did point out that any application for a declaration on such an issue should be brought promptly.[24] Instead, he dismissed the application on the grounds that, even if the provisions of the Act were enforceable in relation to the hedge concerned, that would only constitute a private law restriction on implementing the permission – in the same way as the existence of a restrictive covenant or a ransom strip might frustrate a development proposal for which permission had been granted.[25] The environmental consequences of implementing the present proposal, including the loss of the hedge, had been carefully considered by the planning authority, and there was thus no basis on which to impugn the grant of permission.

In the light of *Marlton* v. *Turner*, which was incidentally not cited to the Court in *ex parte Berkswell PC*, it now seems less likely that the argument that was successful at Hull will succeed again. But if it does, and particularly if it is in a higher court, so that enclosure awards are considered to be generally enforceable, at least in some circumstances, it is likely that Parliament will act to change the law. It cannot be in the public interest that the intention of planning authorities can be thwarted by legislation passed many years ago for quite different purposes. It is noteworthy that the hedge in the *Seymour* case itself was 'undistinguished . . . barely maintained, unkempt and straggly' – it would for a number of reasons not be within the scope of the 1997 Regulations at all, let alone 'important' enough to merit protection. Whilst the industry of Mr Seymour at Flamborough, and of others who have used the same tactics elsewhere to halt unwanted development proposals, has to be admired, the use of eighteenth- and nineteenth-century Enclosure Acts cannot be a sensible way to provide for the protection of hedges now.

The conclusion of the House of Commons Environment Sub-Committee was that 'the Government should as a matter of priority investigate the nature and typical incidence of the legal responsibilities

---

[23] (1998) 77 P&CR 312.
[24] P.318.
[25] See also *Vasiliou* v. *Secretary of State for Transport* [1991] 2 All ER 77, CA, and British *Railways Board* v. *Secretary of State for the Environment* [1993] 3 PLR 125, HL.

for the protection and maintenance of field boundaries in the Enclosure Acts with a view to issuing guidance on the matter'.[26]

6 Specific Legislation Relating to Hedgerows

Whilst the alterations to the grants regime in recent years have been welcomed by the conservation lobby, they are not enough to secure the retention of the most important hedgerows in the face of commercial pressures, ignorance and simple neglect. Nor are the existing powers under other legislation (including the Enclosure Acts) described above. There have therefore been a succession of attempts to protect hedgerows by means of more specific legislation. There were thus during the 1980s three unsuccessful private members' bills, including one promoted in 1987 by Peter Hardy which survived four committees before falling, and which provoked a commitment to action by the government of the day – a pledge that was to take ten years to come to fruition.

There was then a proposal by Mr James Batho, in his report to the Secretary of State on tree-preservation policies and legislation, that local authorities should be allowed to make hedgerow management orders, subject to the payment to owners of compensation similar to that payable in respect of management agreements under the Wildlife and Countryside Act 1981. That suggestion was taken up in a consultation document on the Batho proposals issued by the Government in December 1990. In reliance on that, the Government resisted calls in the House of Lords for the extension of tree preservation legislation to be extended to cover hedgerows, in the debate on what became the Planning and Compensation Act 1991.[27]

Two more private members' bills followed in the early 1990s, promoted by Peter Ainsworth and supported by the Countryside Commission. They too were unsuccessful, but they led directly to Mr Gummer, the then Secretary of State for the Environment, confirming in 1994 that the Environment Bill would include 'an enabling power for the preservation of hedgerows of particular value'. That in turn led to the enactment of what is now s.97 of the Environment Act 1995, which enables the appropriate ministers[28] to make regulations for the protection of important hedgerows. Such regulations are not to be made without consultation with all the appropriate bodies (including representatives of those likely to be affected, local authorities, and

[26] HC 969-I (above), para.119.

[27] Hansard, 29 January 1991, cols. 652–6.

[28] In England, the Secretary of State for the Environment and the Minister for Agriculture, Fisheries and Food, in Wales the Secretary of State for Wales: 1997 Act, s.97(8).

environmental conservation groups), and require to be approved by a resolution of each House of Parliament.

Draft regulations were duly published in the autumn of 1996. Considerable concern was expressed regarding the mechanics of the new control regime and, in particular, over the criteria for evaluating 'important' hedgerows. Revised regulations were placed before Parliament in March 1997, which still raised many of the same concerns – in particular, that there should be allowances to mitigate the economic impact of the new controls, that local authorities should not be allowed to interfere in the countryside, and (on the other side) that there should be a reference to the contribution of hedgerows to the landscape.

Recognizing that there was an election just around the corner, a move was made to defer the whole matter, to be considered afresh by the next government. However, it was also recognized that a new government might have other priorities, and that such a tactic would postpone the whole issue for months if not years. Overall, it was generally accepted that, whilst the regulations were far from perfect, they were only a first attempt, and better than nothing. Accordingly, in the last debate of the last day of the previous Parliament, the Hedgerows Regulations were finally approved, to come into force on 1 June 1997.[29]

From that date, important hedgerows have received statutory protection for the first time, so that to remove such a hedge is a criminal offence, punishable in some circumstances by an unlimited fine. The government has also issued a useful publication, *The Hedgerows Regulations: A Guide to the Law and Good Practice*[30] ('the DoE Guide'), which explains the working of the new system and provides useful practical advice.

7 The Structure of the Hedgerows Regulations

This is not the place to consider in detail the precise mechanisms by which hedgerows are protected.[31] It may be helpful, however, to outline the broad structure of the new control regime.

The purpose of the new regulations is to protect 'important' hedgerows from unnecessary removal. There are two ways in which

---

[29] Hedgerows Regulations 1997, SI No.1160; 16 pp., £3.20.

[30] Published 1997, by the Department of the Environment, Ministry of Agriculture, Fisheries and Food, and the Welsh Office (available, price £5.50, from Department of the Environment, Transport and the Regions, Publications Sales Centre, Unit 21, Goldthorpe Industrial Estate, Goldthorpe, Rotherham, S63 9BL). A Welsh-language translation is also available from the same address.

[31] See DoE Guide, chapters 4–6, 8–14; also the forthcoming book by Mynors, *The Law of Trees, Forests and Hedgerows*.

this could have been achieved. First, it would have been possible to require that 'lists' or 'schedules' should be drawn up of all important hedgerows, and then to provide that consent should be obtained to remove a hedgerow thus identified. That is the method that has been used in Britain to protect buildings,[32] ancient monuments[33] and trees.[34] It has, however, the disadvantage that it is a very slow process for all the items of value to be identified; and that in the mean while many are lost.

The alternative approach, which has been adopted in the 1997 Regulations, is to require that almost all works to almost any hedgerow are notified to an appropriate authority, which then has a specified time in which to decide whether the hedgerow is important enough to merit protection and, if it is, whether the works proposed are sufficiently important to justify removing the hedgerow. The first of those decisions could be made by an authority, or an officer, as an ad hoc professional judgement (as is done with selecting buildings for listing and trees for 'preserving'), but it is in fact to be done on the basis of theoretically objective criteria.

The next matter to be considered, therefore, is which hedgerows fall outside the scope of the regulations altogether, and which are important enough to be protected.

8 Hedgerows subject to the Regulations

The word 'hedgerow' itself is not defined in the Regulations. The DoE Guide suggests[35] that the definition in the *Oxford English Dictionary* may be used as a guide: 'a row of bushes forming a hedge, with the trees etc growing in it'. During the parliamentary debate on the Environment Bill, the Government confirmed that a wall or bank on its own would not qualify for protection – even though in some parts of the country stone walls are every bit as important in historical and land-scape terms as living hedges. Subject to that basic uncertainty, however, all hedgerows are within the scope of the Regulations, unless they are excluded either because of the type of land they border, or because of their length.

The Regulations thus apply, by virtue of reg. 3(1), only to hedge-rows growing on, or adjacent to, any of the following: common land; protected land; land used for agriculture or forestry; or land used for the keeping or breeding of horses, ponies or donkeys.

[32] Under what is now the Planning (Listed Buildings and Conservation Areas) Act 1990.
[33] Under the Ancient Monuments and Archaeological Areas Act 1979.
[34] Under Part VIII of the Town and Country Planning Act 1990.
[35] See paras.3.3–3.5.

The first two of these are defined in the regulations.[36] 'Common land' means common land or a town or village green within the meaning of the Commons Registration Act 1965. 'Common land' is itself defined in that Act as land subject to rights of common and waste land of a manor;[37] and 'town or village green' as (in summary) land used by the inhabitants of a locality for exercise and recreation.[38] 'Protected land' means land protected as a local nature reserve[39] or as an SSSI (see above).

'Agriculture' is also defined in the Regulations, and has the same meaning as in the Town and Country Planning Act 1990. It thus includes land used for allotments[40] and fox farming.[41] It does not itself include the breeding and keeping of horses, but use for those purposes is included in its own right.

The Regulations do not apply, however, to any hedgerow within or bounding the curtilage of a dwelling-house.[42] A 'dwelling-house' is not defined in these Regulations; it is elsewhere defined as not including a building containing one or more flats or a flat within such a building.[43] A 'curtilage' is a small area about a building; and there need not be a physical enclosure of the land within the curtilage, but the land in question at least needs to be regarded in law as part of one enclosure with the house.[44] The result is that garden hedges are not protected, even if they are important, and even if they form the boundary between the garden of a dwelling-house and one of the relevant types of land (common, etc.). The reason for that exclusion is far from clear.

The other preliminary matter is that a hedgerow is only subject to the Regulations if it has a continuous length of at least twenty metres; or if it meets (by intersection or junction) another hedgerow at both ends; or if it is part of such a hedgerow.[45] For the purposes of calculating the

[36] Reg. 2(1).
[37] Commons Registration Act 1965, s.22; 'rights of common' are there further defined.
[38] 1965 Act, s.22(1); see for example *New Windsor Corporation* v. *Mellor* [1975] 1 Ch. 380; *R.* v. *Oxfordshire CC, ex parte Sunningwell BC* (1999), unreported, HL.
[39] Under National Parks and Access to the Countryside Act 1949, s.21; see PPG 9, para.A22.
[40] *Crowborough Parish Council* v. *Secretary of State* [1981] JPL 281.
[41] *North Warwickshire BC* v. *Secretary of State* [1984] JPL 434.
[42] Reg. 3(1).
[43] Town and Country Planning General Permitted Development Order 1995, Article 1(2); although Greater London Council (General Powers) Act 1984, s.5 provides that 'dwellinghouse includes a flat'.
[44] *McAlpine* v. *Secretary of State* [1995] 1 PLR 16; see also *Dyer* v. *Dorset CC* [1988] 3 WLR 213.
[45] Reg. 3(1).

length of a hedgerow, a gap in it (whether or not it is filled) of less than 20 m is to be considered as part of the hedgerow.[46] The above is a summary of the provisions of reg. 3; but working out whether a hedge is subject to the Regulations can in practice be less than straightforward; and the DoE Guide contains a helpful Annex (B) explaining how the definition works out in practice, with illustrative diagrams.

The result of these provisions is that, as a broad generality, the Regulations apply to all hedgerows in rural areas that are of a reasonable length, and a few in urban and suburban areas. The main threat to the latter is urban development, and they will thus largely be protected by the normal planning process.

9 Important Hedgerows

The terms of the enabling power in the Environment Act make it clear that the purpose of any regulations made under the Act is not to protect all hedgerows, but only 'important' ones, for which replacement planting is no substitute. The Act also provides that the question whether a hedgerow is or is not 'important' for the purposes of this section shall be determined not on the basis of an ad hoc on-site judgement by an appropriately qualified professional, but in accordance with prescribed criteria.[47] And the 1997 Regulations do indeed prescribe a number of criteria, which are designed to be objective, and thus render unprofitable any argument as to whether a particular hedge merits protection.

The first criterion, in reg. 4(a), is that a hedgerow should be at least thirty years old – presumably as at the date on which notice is given of the intention to remove it. The DOE Guide[48] implies that anyone seeking to remove a hedgerow relying on a claim that it is less than thirty years old will have to provide suitable evidence to prove it – and makes some suggestions as to the type of evidence that may be relevant. It is at least arguable that it is actually up to the authority, if it wishes to prevent the removal of such a hedge, to prove that it is more than thirty years old, and not up to the applicant to prove that it is less.

The other criteria are set out in Schedule 1 to the Regulations. Part II contains the eight criteria themselves – 1 to 5 relating to archaeology and history, and 6 to 8 relating to wildlife and landscape. Relevant definitions are in Part I of Schedule 1.

Many of the criteria relate to documents and information at 'the relevant date' – that is, 24 March 1997, when the Regulations were made.

---

[46] Reg. 3(4).
[47] 1995 Act, s.97(2).
[48] DoE Guide, para.5.11.

That is unfortunate, as it means that the position will become gradually more and more detached from the latest state of knowledge as to, for example, whether an archaeological feature is or should be included in a Sites and Monuments Record (SMR), or which birds and insects are of special significance. It is to be hoped that in any revision of the Regulations this time limit will be removed, as suggested in comments on the draft regulations made by a number of bodies, including the Association of Local Government Archaeological Officers (ALGAO) and the Planning and Environment Bar Association (PEBA).

The commentary which follows is only a summary of the detailed provisions of Schedule 1; the Regulations themselves should be consulted, along with chapter 7 of the DoE Guide, to check the detailed provisions relevant to any particular case.

10 History and Archaeology

Criterion 1 is that a hedgerow marks the boundary of a parish or township existing before 1850; the best evidence in relation to this will be the historical maps mentioned below. The year 1850 was selected so as to pre-date the rationalization of parish boundaries which created current civil parishes. The effectiveness of this criterion will be limited in heavily populated areas by the exclusion from protection of hedgerows bounding residential curtilages.

Criterion 2 is that a hedgerow incorporates an archaeological feature that is a scheduled monument at the date of the proposal[49] or that was recorded in an SMR at the relevant date. Criterion 3 is that a hedgerow is wholly or partly on land that is within a site that is a scheduled monument at the date of the proposal or that was recorded in an SMR at the relevant date, and is associated with any monument or feature on that site. 'Archaeological feature' and 'incorporates' are not defined.

SMRs are usually maintained by the English county councils outside the metropolitan areas; by groups of metropolitan district councils; and by the six archaeological trusts in Wales. They often include scheduled monuments as well as other items of archaeological interest, and are regularly consulted in the course of the normal development-control process; they are, however, not always up to date, and the 'relevant date' approach means that information subsequently recorded in an SMR cannot be taken into account, which is absurd. The boundary of a scheduled monument is the red line on the schedule entry,[50] but the boundaries of sites in SMRs are not defined.

The results of the field test carried out by ADAS for the Department

---

[49] Under s.1 of the Ancient Monuments and Archaeological Areas Act 1979.
[50] R. v. Bovis Construction Ltd. [1994] Crim. LR 938, CA (Crim. Div.).

of the Environment suggest that in practice criteria 2, 3 and perhaps 4 will have very little effect.[51]

Criterion 4 is that a hedgerow marks the boundary of a pre-1600 estate or manor recorded at the relevant date in an SMR or in a document held in a record office, or is visibly related to a building or other feature of such an estate or manor. The record office means the Public Record Office, the British Library (Manuscript Collection) and the National Library of Wales (Department of Manuscripts and Records) and other national and local record offices and libraries. The most fruitful source of information is likely to be the Public Record Office at Kew and the relevant County Record Office.

Relevant documents are likely to be estate maps (from 1580 onwards), tithe maps and awards (usually from the 1840s, and usually where there had been no previous Enclosure Acts), enclosure maps and early Ordnance Survey maps (together with their field books, now in the British Museum). Earlier charters and manorial records will need to be translated into modern English, but this has been done in some cases; and they sometimes provide useful information by their description of estate boundaries in the form of 'perambulations', which may mention hedges and other features.

Criterion 5 is that a hedgerow is recorded in a document held in a record office as an integral part of a field system pre-dating the Enclosure Acts, or that it is part of such a system which is substantially complete, or which is identified by the local planning authority in a relevant development control document as a key landscape characteristic. It is not clear what is meant by 'integral' or 'substantially complete'; it will be interesting to see whether in practice this criterion proves to be of any significance. Nor is it clear what will be the scope of documentation prepared by the planning authority for the purposes of development control. Yet again, it is unfortunate that research subsequent to the relevant date cannot be taken into account.

11 Wildlife and Landscape

Criterion 6 relates to the presence in the hedgerow of one or more rare species of plant or animal. It thus requires that a hedgerow should now contain species listed in para.6(3), or be recorded as having done so at some date in the period leading up to the relevant date; the period is five years in the case of animals and birds (presumably including insects and other invertebrates), and ten years for plants. The species in para.6(3) are:

[51] *The Hedgerow Evaluation System: A System for Identifying Important Hedgerows*, a contract report by ADAS for the Department of the Environment (1996), para.4.2.2.

(a) birds listed in part I of Schedule 1 to the Wildlife and Countryside Act 1981;
(b) animals listed in Schedule 5 to the 1981 Act;
(c) plants listed in Schedule 8 to the Act;
(d) birds classified as 'declining breeders' in the Red Data Book *Birds in Britain*;
(e) species classified as 'endangered', 'extinct', 'rare' or 'vulnerable' in the books known as the British Red Data Books entitled *Plants*, *Insects* and *Invertebrates other than Insects* and in the Red Data Book of Britain and Ireland on *Stoneworts*.

The Red Data Books were published for the Nature Conservancy Council (the predecessor to English Nature) and the Joint Nature Conservation Committee. The Department of the Environment[52] can supply a single list of all the relevant species. Once again, it is unfortunate that the picture is effectively frozen at the relevant date; no new information can be taken into account.

Criterion 7 relates to the number of woody species present, which is an indication both as to the richness and interest of the hedge in terms of its biodiversity and as to its age. To be classified as 'important' on this count, a hedgerow must be in one of the following groups:

(a) it has at least seven of the woody species listed in Schedule 3 to the Regulations;
(b) it has six woody species, together with three of the features specified in para.7(4);
(c) it has six woody species, including a black poplar, a large-leaved lime, a small-leaved lime or a wild service; or
(d) it has five woody species, together with four of the features specified in para.7(4).

The number of species required is reduced by one for hedgerows in the north of England (north of a line roughly from the Ribble to the Humber). As might be imagined, there are complex rules as to how to ascertain the number of species in a hedgerow; but, roughly, the technique is to count those in the central 30 m stretch (or the central 30 m stretch of each half where the hedgerow is between 100 m and 200 m long, or the central stretch of each third where the hedgerow is more than 200 m long).

It will be noted that the choice of 30 m correlates with Hooper's rule, noted above, relating to the age of a hedgerow. Indeed the ADAS

[52] Alasdair Robertson at Eland House, Bressenden Place, London SW1E 5DU (tel. 0171-890-5616).

study[53] suggests that criteria 7 and 8, and particularly 7, will probably protect more historic hedges than the 'archaeology and history' criteria. The features specified in para.7(4) are:

(a) a bank or wall supporting the hedge for half its length;
(b) gaps which in aggregate do not exceed 10 per cent of the length of the hedgerow;
(c)–(e) an average of at least one standard tree per 50 m of hedgerow;
(f) at least three of the woodland species listed in Schedule 2, within 1 m of the outermost edges of the hedgerow;
(g) a ditch along half the length of the hedgerow;
(h) links with neighbouring hedgerows, ponds or woodlands; and
(i) a parallel hedge within 15 m of the hedgerow.

Criterion 8 is similar; it relates to hedges along a bridleway, byway or footpath, and requires that a hedgerow must have within it at least four woody species (even in the north of England!) and at least two of the features listed in para.7(4)(a)–(g).

As will be readily appreciated, these criteria, whilst (relatively) straightforward in theory, will require considerable investigation to work in practice. Further, in spite of the title given to these three criteria, they actually hardly relate to 'landscape' at all.

12 Proposals for Removal of Hedgerows

If a hedgerow is one to which the Regulations apply (as to which, see s.8 above), almost any proposal to remove it or any part of it must be notified to the local planning authority.[54] 'Remove' means 'uproot or otherwise destroy',[55] which might include any act resulting in the destruction of a hedgerow – whether on the hedgerow itself, or other land nearby. It has been held that a tree is 'destroyed' when an act, such as the severing of its root system, is carried out as a result of which it ceases to have any further use as an amenity, that is, it is no longer worth preserving;[56] and the same would presumably apply to the woody plants comprising a hedge.

The exceptions to this requirement are set out in reg. 6(1), and are as follows:

---

[53] See n.48 above; para.4.2.2.
[54] 1997 regulations, reg. 5.
[55] 1995 Act, s.97(8).
[56] *Barnet LBC* v. *Eastern Electricity Board* [1973] 1 WLR 430.

(a) the making of a new opening in substitute for an existing one (which must be filled up promptly with a new hedge);[57]
(b) the obtaining of temporary access to land (including cables etc.) in an emergency;
(c) the obtaining of access to land where other access is unavailable or is disproportionately expensive;
(d) works for national defence;
(e) the carrying out of development for which planning permission has been granted in response to an application or under parts 11 or 30 of Schedule 2 to the GPDO;[58]
(f) the carrying out by drainage boards, local authorities and the Environment Agency of works for flood defence or land drainage;
(g) the eradication of, or the prevention of the spread of, a plant or tree pest;[59]
(h) works carried out by the Highways Agency in relation to trunk roads and motorways;
(i) works to prevent obstruction of or interference with electric lines or plant;[60] or
(j) the proper management of the hedgerow.

The last of these is likely to be controversial in practice; but a number of organizations have published booklets and other guidance on proper techniques of hedgerow management.

Where proposed works do not fall within any of the above categories, the notification of the works (known as a 'hedgerow removal notice') must be served by 'an owner' of the hedgerow. This is distinct from the provisions relating to the various permissions required under the planning Acts, for which an application may be made by anyone (such as a contractor or a prospective purchaser); it is not entirely satisfactory, as what matters is that the notice is served, not that anyone in particular serves it. 'Owner' is defined as the freeholder or agricultural tenant of the land on which the hedgerow is growing.[61] Where the hedgerow was planted on A's land but has encroached on B's, A is the owner, but where it actually forms the boundary between two areas of land in different ownership, the two owners will be entitled to the

---

[57] Reg. 6(2); failure to fill the gap within eight months is an offence punishable by a fine of up to level 3 (£1,000) (reg.7(5)).

[58] Respectively development under local or private Acts, and toll road facilities.

[59] See Plant Health (Great Britain) Order 1993, Articles 22, 23; and Plant Health (Forestry) (Great Britain) Order 1993, Articles 21, 22.

[60] In consequence of an order under para.9 of Schedule 4 to the Electricity Act 1989.

[61] Reg. 2(1).

hedge as tenants in common.[62] It follows that the requirement for the notice to be served by 'an' owner rather than by 'the' owner means that, in such a boundary case, it can be served by either of the two owners.

The planning authority for this purpose will be the district or borough council, where there are two tiers of councils, and the national park authority and the Broads Authority in their areas.

13 Responses to Notification

Once the authority has received a hedgerow removal notice, together with relevant supporting documents, photographs or other evidence, it has six weeks in which to decide what to do – either to issue a 'hedgerow retention notice' or to state that it has no objection to the work going ahead.

A notice that the hedgerow may be removed could be issued either because the authority has concluded that the hedgerow is not important or because the applicant has made out a sufficient case to justify its removal. In that case, the proposed removal must take place within two years of the service of the removal notice – observe that the latter provision[63] could cause problems where the matter takes a long time to be resolved (with the possibility of an appeal, and a High Court challenge).

A retention notice may only be issued in relation to an important hedgerow (within the meaning of the Act and the Regulations); but if the hedgerow is important, a notice must be given unless there is a good reason to suggest otherwise.[64] The DoE Guide suggests some examples of what might be sufficient reasons to justify removal; personal financial loss and change of land ownership are specifically rejected.

The authority must consult with the parish or community council where there is one, but does not have to take any other specific action. In practice, however, it will no doubt carry out a site visit to ascertain the status of the hedgerow, its length, the number of species in it, and so forth, to decide whether it is an important hedge within the meaning of the Act and the Regulations.[65] There is power for the authority to enter any land for this purpose.[66] The six-week period for response

[62] *Waterman* v. *Soper* (1697) 1 Ld Raym 737; *Holder* v. *Coates* (1827) Moo and M 112; *Lemmon* v. *Webb* [1894] 3 Ch. 1, affirmed in HL, [1895] AC 1.

[63] In reg. 5(1)(d).

[64] Reg. 5(5); DoE Guide, paras.8.15–20.

[65] See DoE Guide, paras.6.10–15, for a useful checklist of information to be collected on a site visit.

[66] Regs. 12–14; and see DoE Guide, paras.6.16–24.

may be extended by agreement; but it is unclear why an owner would ever want to agree to an extension. If the authority has not obtained sufficient evidence within six weeks, that is its problem; it cannot simply issue a retention notice to gain more time.

The removal of a hedgerow without a removal notice having been given to the authority, or in spite of it having issued a retention notice, is an either-way offence punishable by a fine (of up to £5,000 in the magistrates' court or unlimited in the Crown Court).[67] If an authority considers that such an offence is about to be committed, it may apply to either the High Court or the county court for an injunction.[68]

Where a hedgerow has been removed in contravention of the Regulations by a landowner or utility operator, the authority may require the owner or operator to plant a replacement, of specified species and position.[69] Once the replacement has been planted, it is for the next thirty years to be regarded as an 'important' tree – so that, in effect, it cannot be removed again. It should be noted that a replacement notice could in theory be issued where a hedgerow that was not important was removed without notice having been given, but it would presumably not be appropriate to take action in those circumstances.

Finally, if an owner receives a retention notice, or if an owner or utility operator is required to plant a replacement hedge, an appeal may be made to the Secretary of State against the notice or the requirement, within twenty-eight days of the notice being given.[70] No grounds of appeal are given; but otherwise the provisions are much as are found in relation to the various appeal mechanisms in other legislation.

14 The Way Forward

The Regulations are but a first step in attempting to protect hedgerows of value. They constitute a complex system of control; and it remains to be seen whether it will be effective in achieving its stated purpose. It may be that there will be a significant number of hedgerow removal notices served; or it may be that the system will be seen to be so convoluted that it will simply be ignored.

Partly because of the timing of the arrival of the Regulations, immediately before the general election, they were in a number of respects (some more important than others) technically far from perfect. To resolve these defects, many possible drafting improvements were drawn to the attention of the Government at the time the draft regula-

---

[67] Reg. 7; DoE Guide, ch.10
[68] Reg. 11; DoE Guide, ch.13.
[69] Reg. 8; DoE Guide, ch.11.
[70] Reg. 9; DoE Guide, chs.9 and 12.

tions were circulated for comment in November 1996; it is unfortunate that almost all were ignored, or at any rate not incorporated. Some of those defects have been pointed out above.

The incoming Government recognized the problems, however, and announced on 29 May 1997, the day before the Regulations came into force, the setting up of a review group to see how more effective protection might be given to hedgerows in general and important hedgerows in particular. Its brief focused on: whether the time limits within which authorities have to respond to removal notices should be extended; and whether the criteria for defining important hedgerows could be improved and simplified.

The group issued its conclusions in June 1998.[71] As to the first issue, it unsurprisingly recommended extending the time limit from six to eight weeks. As to the second, it put forward a number of suggestions for revising the criteria, and recommended that they should be field-tested. It also urged the introduction of a prohibition on action to convert an important hedgerow into a non-important one – for example, by removing a single woody species – as that was a clear loophole that should be blocked. But the ambit of the group's review was severely restricted, in that it was directed to consider only the Regulations, rather than the 1995 Act itself. It nevertheless did point to the need to consider the amendment of primary legislation – to enable local author-ities, as well as ministers, to define important hedgerows; to introduce criteria relating to landscape character; and to expand the definition of hedgerow to include other types of field boundary. The Government generally welcomed the group's recommendations, and instigated research into the effect of the proposed new criteria – the results of which are expected in the summer of 1999.

More recently, the House of Commons Environment Sub-Committee has also concluded that the present system (including the primary legislation) be reformed.[72] The Government response to that Sub-Committee is awaited. Once that has emerged, and the conclusions of the research on new criteria have been taken on board, it is hoped that there will be a general consultation on proposals to alter the Regulations. New secondary legislation will then follow in due course; although new amendments to primary legislation (said by almost all to be needed) will obviously take longer.

It would surely be desirable to try to achieve a set of criteria which reflected more closely the values of hedgerows as seen by lay people,

---

[71] *Review of the Hedgerows Regulations 1997*, available (price £16) from the DETR Publications Sales Centre (see note 27 above); executive summary available free of charge from DETR Free Literature, PO Box 236, Wetherby, West Yorkshire L23 7NB.

[72] HC 969-I (above), paras. 75–102.

as well as the perspectives of experts. In particular, it would be good to recognize that some hedgerows are simply attractive features in the landscape – regardless of the number of woody species that they may or may not possess. Indeed, it may be that one day it would be possible for there to be enough recognized experience and judgement available to enable a system to be adopted which does not rely solely on quanti-fiable criteria, but simply evaluates the historic interest and amenity value of a hedgerow on a subjective basis – that, after all, is the basis of the tree preservation order system which has for many years worked well enough in concept, if not always in detail.

15 Conclusion

On the face of it, the implementation of the new Hedgerows Regulations reflects the targets set by the previous government in the UK Biodiversity Action Plan,[73] which were partly to implement Article 10 of the EC Habitats and Species Directive. That in turn required Member States to encourage the management of linear features, such as hedges, in land-use planning and development policies. Under the terms of the Action Plan, the Government is thus pledged:

(a) to halt the loss of species-rich hedgerows by neglect or removal by the year 2000, and all loss of hedgerows which are both ancient and species-rich by 2005;

(b) to achieve the favourable management of 25 per cent (that is, around 47,500 km) of species-rich and ancient hedges by the year 2000, and 50 per cent (95,000 km) by 2005; and

(c) to maintain overall numbers of hedgerow trees within each county or district at least at current levels, through ensuring a balanced age structure.

However, if these targets are to be met, far more needs to be done, both through boosting incentive schemes and through raising interest and awareness among land managers.

But, alongside these noble sentiments, it is hard to resist entirely the suspicion that the implementation of the new Hedgerows Regulations reflects the enthusiasm of a largely urban and suburban public to protect the countryside as a picturesque backdrop, as an arcadian land-scape – part of the cosy and changeless world that is country churchyards and Ann Hathaway's Cottage, cricket on the village green and cream teas in dappled sunshine; that countryside, and those hedgerows, that we all recall from *Cider with Rosie*, not to mention the

---

[73] *Biodiversity: The UK Steering Group Report* (HMSO, 1995); see also PPG 9.

illustrations in *Rupert Bear* Annuals. Ultimately, do we perhaps value hedgerows simply because they provide incident, and make the countryside more interesting? They are part of what makes the landscape of, say, Herefordshire preferable to that of the Isle of Ely.

In any event, those living and working in rural areas need to be aware of the new rules, and to watch out for changes, as they may fundamentally affect – for good or ill – the way in which their land is managed.

8

Off-Line Planning Blight: An Instance of Uncompensated Loss

CHARLES GEORGE QC

My purpose here is to identify and explore the perceived injustice presently suffered by a category of persons affected by the development process. Following a brief consideration of the adequacy of compensation for those whose land is compulsorily taken for development, I shall review the position of those whose property is *not* taken for development, but who suffer an adverse effect. My review will start with the Land Compensation Act 1973; then turn to the Planning and Compensation Act 1991; and finally consider the Interdepartmental Working Group on Blight (IDWGB)'s Final Report of December 1997.[1]

At first sight, this chapter may appear to have more to do with the urban than with the rural environment. But although off-line blight is also experienced in urban situations, it is at its most acute when public works conflict with the seclusion that has been sought (and found, often at high price) in the countryside. Two properties to which this chapter will repeatedly return (because their owners have had the misfortune to be the subjects of recent case law on off-line blight)[2] are Ashgrove at Baunton situated on a minor Roman road, The Whiteway, some two miles from Cirencester in Gloucestershire, adjoined by

---

[1] Interdepartmental Working Group on Blight: Final Report, December 1997 (DETR).

[2] For Ashgrove, see *R.* v. *Secretary of State for Transport ex parte Owen and another* [1995] 2 EGLR 213; for Swans Harbour, see *R.* v. *Parliamentary Commissioner for Administration ex parte Morris and Audrey Balchin* [1997] JPL 917. See also below n.11.

farmland and purchased by Col. Owen in 1990; and Swans Harbour, a converted outbuilding with a river frontage to the east of Wroxham in Norfolk, purchased by Mr Balchin in 1984. The recent focus for off-line blight (and the genesis of the IDWGB report) has been rural Kent, in villages such as Boxley, immediately north of Maidstone, of which it has been claimed that 'in relation to the question of wide application of any compensation for generalised blight there cannot be many, if any, other areas related to the CTRL (Channel Tunnel Rail Link) studies which suffer such an appalling history'.[3]

Those who specialize in the law relating to compulsory purchase and compensation have sometimes been accused of complicating what ought to be simple, and in particular of mystifying by their use of language. The meaning of 'compensation', 'disturbance', 'injurious affection', or 'blight', requires, in almost every instance, careful exegesis and is understandably incomprehensible to the person claiming redress. Just over a century ago, the then Lord Chancellor commented that 'a whole nomenclature' had been 'invented by gentlemen who devote themselves to the consideration of such questions'.[4] He went on to say: 'we, however, must be guided by what the language of the legislature is', a reminder that the ambiguities and anomalies of this area of the law derive from statute, leaving for the common law (and sometimes even common sense) only a limited role. Unfortunately, as was said by a recent Chief Justice of Ireland: 'These statutes are drafted for an elite cognoscenti – those who in either central or local government are accustomed to the exercise of the powers prescribed and the language used. For others the ascertainment of what is laid down involves an arduous journey into the obscure.'[5] This chapter represents an attempt at elucidating an area of law and practice in which David seldom outwits Goliath.

1 Direct Land-Take

Ownership or enjoyment of land can be affected by public works in many ways. A distinction can be drawn between two cases: (a) where

[3] Letter from Mr R.W. Howard to the chairman of the committee, Appendix 8 to the Sixth Report of the Select Committee on the parliamentary commissioner for administration, Session 1994–5, 'The Channel Tunnel Rail Link and exceptional hardship', HC270.

[4] Per Lord Halsbury LC in *Inland Revenue Commissioners* v. *Glasgow and South-Western Railway Co.* (1887) 12 App.Cas. 315 at 321. See also the finding of the Scott Committee, set up in 1917, that the existing, largely judge-made system of compensation had given rise to 'fanciful valuations and conventional allowances': Cd. 9229, para.7.

[5] Per Higgins CJ in *Portland Estates (Limerick) Ltd* v. *Limerick Cpn* [1980] ILRM 77.

there is dispossession from land, as where an owner is compelled to sell; and (b) where enjoyment of land is materially affected, but without dispossession. The rules governing the first case are not only firmly settled, but also until recently generally recognized as reasonably fair.

> [A] claimant is entitled to be compensated fairly and fully for his loss. Conversely, and built into the concept of fair compensation, is the corollary that a claimant is not entitled to receive more than fair compensation . . . It is ultimately by this touchstone, with its two facets, that all claims for compensation succeed or fail.[6]

Thus, uncontroversially, the underlying principle has been recently summarized by the Privy Council. It has also been said that 'It is a very simple principle, when certain largely verbal complications have been cleared out of the way.'[7]

Over the last quarter-century or so, legislative change in this area has been minimal, but a series of judgments have eliminated aberrations and unfairnesses, in relation, for example, to the relevant date for rule 2 and rule 5 compensation; treatment of ransom strips; and loss of profits in the 'shadow period'.[8]

2 Off-Line Blight

(a) Introduction to the problem

The position in relation to the second case, where the enjoyment of land is materially affected but where there is no dispossession, is very different. Here to its credit Parliament has been relatively active in the last quarter-century. Previously (where no land was taken) off-line blight was compensated only under s.10 of the Compulsory Purchase Act 1965

---

[6] Per Lord Nicholls of Birkenhead in *Director of Buildings and Lords* v. *Shun Fung Ironworks Ltd* [1995] 2AC 111 at 125. A recent development is that DETR has published the Interim Report, Fundamental Review of the Laws and Procedures Relating to Compulsory Purchase and Compensation, January 1999, which refers to 'a widespread perception that the process of compulsory purchase and compensation in the UK is slow in operation, inefficient and not always fair to those whose property is acquired', para. 3.1. A revised and consolidated framework for compulsory purchase and compensation seems likely in due course.

[7] Per Pearson LJ in *Hull and Humber Investment Co. Ltd* v. *Hull Corporation* [1965] 2 QB 145 at 161.

[8] Relevant date, see *Birmingham Corporation* v. *West Midland Baptist (Trust) Association (Inc.)* [1970] AC 874; ransom strips, see *Batchelor* v. *Kent CC* (1990) 59 P & C R 357; 'shadow period', see *Director of Buildings and Lands* v. *Shun Fung Ironworks Ltd*, above.

(subject to the restrictive *McCarthy* rules).[9] A s.10 claim can solely be entertained in respect of the execution, rather than the use, of works, although some Private Acts promoted by London Underground Ltd and its predecessors have included special provision in relation to use.

Eventually there was enacted the Land Compensation Act 1973 (hereafter LCA), including the power to acquire land conferred by s.26 of the LCA, as supplemented by s.62 of the Planning and Compensation Act 1991 (hereafter PCA).

As the history of the CTRL shows,[10] there remains a widespread perception that, whatever else it may be, the law in relation to off-line blight is not fair. Such doughty champions of recent case law as the Owens and the Balchins, despite initial successes before the courts, suffered severe financial disadvantage from public works without redress from the schemes' promoters.[11] This suggests that neither Parliament nor central government can be confident that the problem has been resolved. Indeed the establishment of the IDWGB demonstrates that all is not well in this area.

(b) Public works and public infrastructure projects

I shall not differentiate between 'public works' and 'public infrastructure works'. Public works are defined in the LCA thus:[12] '(a) any highway; (b) any aerodrome; and (c) any works or land (not being a highway or aerodrome) provided or used in the exercise of statutory powers'. Since private, as well as public bodies, can operate aerodromes, as well as works or land, and since the process of privatization has in any event muddied previous distinctions between the public and private sectors, it is the nature of the works themselves, rather than the nature of the person responsible for them, that determines whether they are public works within the LCA.

More recently, attention has focused on major infrastructure projects. Annex C to the IDWGB's Discussion Paper,[13] after conceding that there is no formal definition of 'major infrastructure project', states:

[9] *Metropolitan Board of Works* v. *McCarthy* (1874) LR 7 HL 243. The rules are conveniently analysed at para.2–1572 of vol. 1 of the *Encyclopedia of Compulsory Purchase and Compensation*.

[10] The Channel Tunnel Rail Act 1996 was the result of a process which began in 1988, and which is discussed later in this chapter.

[11] *R.* v. *Secretary of State for Transport ex parte Owen and another (no. 2)* [1996] 1 EGLR 52; report of the PCA to Mr Michael Lord MP of the results of a redetermination of an investigation into a complaint made by Mr and Mrs Balchin, 14 July 1997, C.57/94. See also above n.2.

[12] Land Compensation Act 1973 s.1(3).

[13] Interdepartmental Working Group on Blight Discussion Paper, June 1996 (Department of the Environment).

Whether a project is major or minor is relative; as to whether it constitutes infrastructure, a typical economic textbook definition is 'a public capital asset' (although the public/private divide is arguably less clear – or even relevant – now than it was a decade or so ago). Under any reasonable interpretation, the Channel Tunnel Rail Link (CTRL) is a major infrastructure project, as is a new motorway (including, if it were to happen, a motorway or other major toll road constructed and operated by the private sector). A single house, on the other hand, is neither. But in between those extremes it could be argued that, for instance, an oil refinery constitutes a – or even *the* – major part of the infrastructure of a local economic community ... Conventional planning usage, and the context within which the present review is established, both suggest a focus on major transport and utility infrastructure projects. Undoubtedly, those claiming to suffer from generalised blight are concerned more with the severity of the effects rather than the nature of the causes or the semantic classification of the project. As for major/minor, what separates the two in the eyes of the individual complainant is probably the scale of the adverse effects on property caused by the project, rather than cost or size.

This definition properly ignores the distinction drawn elsewhere[14] between 'infrastructure projects' and 'other projects', in which (curiously) a 'yacht marina' constitutes the former, whilst a 'waste-water treatment plant' is an 'other project'. Both waste-water treatment plants and sites for depositing sludge are properly categorized as infrastructure, and capable of being both public and major.[15]

The IDWGB focused on major transport infrastructure projects, roads, railways, airports etc. But as its Final Report states: 'given that much of the ensuing discussion concerns matters of general principle, the relative precision of the review's focus does not necessarily preclude wider extrapolation of the Group's findings.'[16]

(c) Part 1 of the Land Compensation Act 1973

The general purpose of this Act is to introduce improved arrangements for dealing with the impact of new or altered public works on their surroundings and to secure that where private rights or interests are still nevertheless affected reasonable compensation will be provided.[17]

This statement would, on any literal reading, convey the impression

[14] Schedule 2 of the Town and Country Planning (Assessment of Environmental Effects) Regulations 1988.
[15] But both appear in Schedule 2, para. 12 as 'Other projects'.
[16] Para.3.19.
[17] Para.1 of Annex to DoE Circular No. 73/73 (Welsh Office Circular No. 132/73) Land Compensation Act 1973.

that even those who were not dispossessed by public works were now to be 'compensated fairly and fully'.[18] That is, however, far from being the effect of Part I. For Part I claims are hedged about with restrictions. To mention but six:

(1) The interests which qualify for compensation are restricted, so that, in the case of all non-residential (and most residential) property, compensation is only payable to a qualifying owner-occupier. A non-occupying landlord of commercial property can make no claim, notwithstanding that his property has been massively devalued by public works.[19]

(2) Even where there is occupation, claims cannot be made in respect of non-residential property above a particular valuation threshold, unless it forms part of an agricultural unit.[20] This cut-off certainly affords protection to the most vulnerable, as well as saving the public purse, but injustice to the bigger fry remains. The IDWGB received responses claiming that 'there are fundamental, arbitrary and inequitable flaws in the current system in that it treats business and investment owners affected by a confirmed development less favourably than residential owner-occupiers', whilst itself pointing out that no discussion of the cost implications of such a change had been received.[21]

(3) The physical factors which can depreciate land are wider than those in respect of which compensation is claimable under Part I. Thus a visual obstruction (for example, an embankment outside one's sitting room), or visual intrusion (a view of a municipal waste site from the same room), or a change in the character of an area, will inevitably reduce the value of property, as will an increase in danger or an increased apprehension of danger: but for none of these is compensation payable.[22] The standard answer to this is that given by the IDWGB, that

[18] Lord Nicholls's phrase, see above n. 6. The view of the parliamentary commissioner for administration is that 'an owner of property which cannot be sold except at a substantially lower price than would otherwise be realised because it lies in the path of, or close to, the proposed route of road or railway development works or is devalued because of physical factors during the construction of the works or their use expects to receive equitable compensation.' (Fifth Report of the PCA, Session 1994–5, 'The Channel Tunnel Rail Link and blight', HC 193, para.22)

[19] S.2(2) and (3).

[20] S.2(3).

[21] Progress Report, 20 November 1996 (Department of Environment), para.7.24. In its Final Report, para.3.6, the IDWGB recognized that 'the current compensation code does provide to residential owner-occupiers redress which is not available to all businesses' but rejected criticism that this was inappropriate.

[22] S.1(2); see *Hickmott* v. *Dorset CC* (1975) 30 P & C R 237, affirmed (1977) 35 P & C R 195.

compensation for compulsory acquisition or injurious affection under the existing compensation code is available only where, but for the statutory authority lying behind the development, the recipient would be entitled to damages for nuisance;[23]

[I]f the developer's action would not, in other circumstances, be actionable in law for nuisance there are, by extension, no grounds for the compensation regime to provide a proxy remedy.[24]

Whilst understanding the logic, I have always found it less than compelling.

(4) No claim can be made in respect of devaluation from construction activities as opposed to the use of public works, something only imperfectly mitigated by the McCarthy rules.[25]

(5) No claim can be made until one year after the date when the public works were first used after completion.[26] From start of planning to opening of a major trunk road scheme, the average is about fourteen years, and twenty or more years in the case of the more controversial ones.[27] Thus there can be a prolonged period pending completion (and often even start) of the public works during which there is depreciation because of apprehended impacts of the user of the works, but no entitlement to claim. This is exacerbated when the public works concerned are eventually abandoned, whereupon property values do not always bounce back immediately, or completely, or sometimes at all. Fear of a scheme's resuscitation may provide a form of ongoing uncompensatable blight.[28]

(6) Save in the case of highways, compensation is not payable unless immunity from actions for nuisance in respect of the use is conferred expressly or impliedly by the enabling statute.[29] For example, a claim for compensation in respect of depreciation caused by a new school cannot be maintained, because the Education Act 1944 does not confer such immunity, notwithstanding that the problems in bringing an action for private nuisance in respect of noise from a children's playground would deter most prudent litigants.[30]

---

[23] Progress Report, para.7.23.

[24] Final Report, para.2.4.

[25] S.1(1); see above n.9.

[26] Ss.1(9) and 3(2).

[27] Fifth Report of the PCA, Session 1994–5, 'The Channel Tunnel Rail Link and blight', HC 193, Appendix 4, para.14.

[28] As the Balchins have experienced since abandonment of the scheme in 1996.

[29] S.1(6).

[30] *Marsh* v. *Powys CC* [1997] 33 EG 100. But see the limited success of the plaintiff in playground-related nuisance proceedings in *Dunton* v. *Dover DC* (1977) 76 LGR 87.

This list is not intended to suggest that the benefits of Part I of the LCA are illusory. Furthermore, the LCA is not always niggardly: for example, through an anomaly in the drafting, compensation is payable to an owner, notwithstanding that he acquired his interest at a price which already took account of the proposed works.[31] As the IDWGB comment, 'In such cases justice suggests that the Part I [compensation] should have been paid to the original vendor who is the one bearing the loss.'[32]

Nevertheless, the list serves as a reminder of Sachs LJ's dictum that 'a particular statute may blandly apply the word compensation to some payment which no man in his senses would regard as a reasonable compensation'.[33] Strictly, in the case of the LCA, the criticism is not so much of the quantum of compensation where it is payable, but rather of the areas of loss which it leaves uncompensated, temporarily or permanently.

(d) Part II of the LCA

Part II is not concerned with compensation properly so-called, but rather with mitigation of the injurious effect of public works. It is hard now to conceive of a highways scheme or related public inquiry without sound insulation being provided under the Noise Insulation Regulations: yet these derive from s.20. For more than twenty years after 1973, promoters of railway schemes, both surface and underground, had to improvise in respect of railway noise, until, as concomitant of the CTRL scheme, the Noise Insulation (Railways etc.) Regulations 1996 were eventually brought into operation. Since these apply also to light rail (tram) schemes, the full range of transport works is now covered.[34] The first public inquiry to consider the approved railway noise regulations was that into the Greater Manchester (Light Rapid Transit) System (Airport Extension) Order, held in the summer of 1995 and approved in February 1997; amongst the first schemes constructed in accordance with these regulations was the extension of the Greater Manchester (Light Rapid Transit) System to Eccles via Salford Quays, on which work commenced in 1997. Urban though both schemes are, the former crosses extensive areas of countryside. Other

[31] *Fallows* v. *Gateshead MBC* [1993] JPL 1157.

[32] Final Report, para.7.18.3 b.

[33] *West Midland Baptist (Trust) Association (Inc.)* v. *Birmingham Corporation* [1968] 2 QB 188 at 220E.

[34] At the public inquiry into the proposed London Underground (East London Line Extension) Order in 1994, LUL undertook to comply with whatever railway noise regulations were eventually made: para.2.38 of the Secretary of State's interim decision letter, 27 September 1995.

important mitigating matters within Part II include the power to pay expenses of persons moving temporarily during construction works, where the works affect the enjoyment of an adjacent dwelling to such an extent that continued occupation is not reasonably practicable.[35] In reality, this provision has probably had less effect than was contemplated. First, because it is a purely discretionary power, not a duty.[36] Second, because with careful programming of construction works, prolonged periods of disruption should be avoidable, and the criteria set by promoting authorities will thus seldom be triggered. Third, because the onus to find suitable alternative accommodation lies upon the occupier, not the promoting authority;[37] besides, to move himself and members of his household elsewhere, whether for all or part of the construction period, is likely to involve unwelcome upheaval, compared with the occasional disruption of sleep or amenity by noisy construction works. In the case of the London Underground (East London Line Extension) Order, eventually made in 1997, following a public inquiry in 1994, the promoters agreed to pay for the tenants of Weaver House, a block of flats adjacent to the proposed line, to be temporarily rehoused during the works.[38] However, the Secretary of State declined to compel the promoters temporarily to relocate a photographic studio which might be rendered temporarily unusable through the effects of construction dust and vibration. Such relocation was outwith s.28 of the LCA and 'As a general principle, the Secretary of State does not consider that it would be right to use secondary legislation, such as an order under the 1992 Act [the Transport and Works Act 1992], to sanction departures from the statutory compensation code.'[39]

Part II also conferred the power to carry out works for mitigating the adverse effect which the construction, alteration, existence or use of any public works will have on the surroundings of the works.[40] The works which can be carried out under this provision include planting of trees and shrubs, as well as earth-mounding (which, whilst perhaps artificial in appearance, will often achieve significant visual and aural mitigation).[41] This power was complemented and given teeth by at the same time conferring on promoting authorities the power to acquire

[35] S.28(1).

[36] S.28(2).

[37] S.28(2).

[38] Para.2.6 of the Secretary of State's interim decision letter, 27 September 1995.

[39] Para.3.4 of the Secretary of State's second interim decision letter, 13 June 1996.

[40] S.27(1).

[41] S.27(2) does not expressly refer to earth-mounding, but in para.16 of Annex to DoE Circular No. 73/73 (Welsh Office Circular No. 132/73) reference was made to 'the erection of physical barriers – walls, screens, mounds of earth etc'; see also para.18.

land by agreement for the purpose of mitigating any adverse effect which the existence or use of any public works has or will have on the surroundings of the works.[42]

But, for present purposes, the most important provision in Part II as originally enacted was s.26 (2):

> Subject to the provisions of this section, a responsible authority may acquire by agreement: (a) land the enjoyment of which is seriously affected by the carrying out of works by the authority for the construction or alteration of any public works; (b) land the enjoyment of which is seriously affected by the use of any public works . . .[43]

At last Parliament had recognized, in a single provision, the dual problems of construction and use faced by those whose land was not itself subject to compulsory acquisition for the public works.

Four deficiencies, however, were:

(a) that the phrase 'in *their* opinion' (emphasis added) explicitly leaves to the promoting authority the task of defining and appraising degrees of severity of effect, with no appeal mechanism save in cases of *Wednesbury* unreasonableness;

(b) that only owner-occupiers whose enjoyment of land is seriously affected are given the benefit of the provision, with a ceiling on the value of non-residential premises;[44]

(c) that (once again) this is a power not a duty, making extremely hard the task of any landowner who wished to compel acquisition against a recalcitrant promoting authority. Imposition of a duty need not have threatened the proprietary rights of an unwilling occupier; for the duty could have been couched in terms which made it exercisable only upon receipt of a notice from the occupier requesting exercise of the power;

(d) the use of the present tense ('*is* seriously affected') in relation to both construction and use which effectively delays the first time when any agreement to acquire could be entered.[45] In the case

---

[42] S.26(1).

[43] In Part II of the LCA as originally enacted, powers similar to those in ss.26 and 27 were conferred on highway authorities under s.22. These are now contained in s.246(1) and (2) of the Highways Act 1980.

[44] The relevant qualifying interest is now defined by reference to s.149(2) and (3) of the Town and Country Planning Act 1990: see LCA s.26(2) and (2B), as amended by PCA s.62(1).

[45] 'The only power to make agreements . . . under the previous section 146 (2) [of the Highways Act 1980 was] where the property was already being seriously affected': *R.* v. *Secretary of State for Transport, ex parte Owen and another* [1995] 2 EGLR 213 at 215A per Neill LJ.

of s.26(2) (b) (use of works) this is less important, though it means that advance acquisition during the period of blight is not possible. In the case of s.26(2) (a) (construction) the time-scale involved in negotiating, agreeing serious effect, and exchanging contracts is likely to make the provision otiose save in the case of exceptionally lengthy works of construction.

The Planning and Compensation Act 1991

S.62 of the PCA inserted into the LCA and the Highways Act 1980 a new protection in respect of off-line blight. S.26 of the LCA as amended includes:

> (2A) Where the responsible authority (a) propose to carry out works on blighted land for the construction or alteration of any public works, and (b) are, in relation to the land, the appropriate authority, they may, subject to the provisions of this section, acquire by agreement land the enjoyment of which will in their opinion be seriously affected by the carrying out of the works or the use of the public works if the interest of the vendor is a qualifying interest.

S.246 of the Highways Act as amended includes:

> (2A) Where the highway authority propose to carry out works on blighted land for the construction or improvement of a highway, they may acquire by agreement land the enjoyment of which will in their opinion be seriously affected by the carrying out of works or the use of the highway if the interest is a qualifying interest.

As expressed by Neill LJ,

> It will be apparent from reading section 246(2A) that the question as to whether or not an agreement should be entered into by the highway authority requires to be considered in two stages. First, it is necessary to consider whether, in the opinion of the highway authority, the enjoyment of the land will be seriously affected by the carrying out of the work for the use of the highway. At the second stage the question is whether, once that criterion is met, the department should exercise their discretion to acquire the land by agreement.[46]

The significance of s.62 of the PCA was that it recognized the defect identified above in relation to the use of the present tense in s.26(2) of the LCA (and s.246(2) of the Highways Act 1980). The test becomes whether the enjoyment of land 'will' be seriously affected, thereby

---

[46] Ibid. at 215L–M.

enabling purchase in advance of the serious effects. The wording glosses over a real issue, namely that frequently enjoyment itself will be seriously affected *before* construction commences: as for instance where the prospect of public works on adjoining land immediately reduces the value of the adjoining land (making it difficult to sell or mortgage). In such cases the reason for acquisition is not that enjoyment of the land *will* be seriously affected, but that it already *is* affected.

However, it seems to have been intended from the outset that s.62 should embrace also the position where the serious effect on enjoyment already existed. As recorded by Henry LJ,

> When section 246(2A) was introduced by the minister to parliament, in answer to a Parliamentary question, he paraphrased the new statutory test thereby introduced (namely as to whether the enjoyment of land *is* seriously affected) as being whether the land *is* suffering from serious blight by proximity. That was an accurate paraphrase. (emphases added)[47]

Similarly, in the same case, Neill LJ referred to the first question to be considered as being 'whether or not the enjoyment of the land *is* seriously affected'.[48]

It is possible to conceive of circumstances where a property's value is seriously depreciated as a result of an imminent road scheme because would-be purchasers are apprehensive about future noise (whether during construction or from the use of the road), whereas expert evidence shows that in fact noise would at all times be barely perceptible at that property. Or there may be an expectation of excessive dust levels, which will in fact be abated by dust-suppression techniques.[49] On those facts, it is submitted that the criterion of s.246(2A) is not met, in that enjoyment of the land will *not* be seriously affected. This runs contrary, however, to a dictum of Simon Brown LJ in the *Owen* case that

> any significant depreciation of property consequent upon a road scheme indicates of itself that, looking at the matter prospectively, the scheme has a serious effect on the enjoyment of land. Why else would the property be unsaleable or at any rate unsaleable save at a very substantially depreciated price?[50]

---

[47] Ibid. at 218G–H.

[48] Ibid. at 215M. A few lines previously, Neill LJ correctly used the future tense of the subsection.

[49] In the *Owen* case, at 216L, there was evidence of 'Mrs Owen's reasonable fear of being exposed to the dust and debris of roadworks close to her home ...'

[50] Ibid. at 217L.

The answer to the question posed is surely this: that potential purchasers may well misunderstand and exaggerate the future impact of the road. This was also the view of the inspector in the case of the Greater Manchester (Light Rapid Transit System) (Airport Extension) Order, whose conclusions record:

> 8.69 Other properties which might be 'seriously affected' by physical factors such as noise or smell from the MAE are protected by GMPTE's 'off-line blight' policy. This 'off-line blight' policy has been used to assess the effects of the MAE on properties close to but not required for the scheme – no properties were found to be so seriously affected by the MAE that they needed to be acquired by agreement under s.62 of the Planning and Compensation Act 1991. The arguments of Ms Morris of 12 Millers Close showed that she would suffer limited nuisance and hardship during construction of the MAE, but that there was insufficient justification to acquire her property. *The problems she seems to be facing in not being able to sell her house are not covered by current Government regulations or legislation.* If prospective purchasers of her property are genuinely put off simply by the pending construction of the MAE, there appears to be no redress for Ms Morris. *On the face of it this does not seem to be entirely fair as she would have to wait some 7 years before a claim for any loss of value could be made* ... (emphases added).[51]

Deficiencies in the new statutory code

In discussing s.26(2) of the LCA, four deficiencies have been identified. Three of these are equally applicable to the new power under s.26(2A).

First, in the words of the IDWGB,

> In contrast to those whose property will be acquired for a development, the position of those whose property will not be acquired but which will be affected is much less predictable. This is not least because the degree to which a property can be said to be 'affected' to its detriment – ignoring statutory definitions – is a matter for subjective judgment.[52]

Under s.62 of the PCA, it remains for the promoting authority to form the relevant 'opinion' as to serious effect.

As is the position under s.26(2) of the LCA and s.146(2) of the Highways Act 1980, the new provisions are silent as to how the opinion is to be formed. Inevitably objectors to public works will frequently disagree with the promoting authority's opinion (not usually

---

[51] The inspector's report was dated February 1996.
[52] Progress Report, 20 November 1996, para.7.22; Final Report, para.7.18.3 a.

disputing the figures, but rather the promoting authority's judgement as to serious effect which is derived therefrom). This will particularly be the case where visual impact is concerned.

Various guidelines have been issued, first by the Department of Transport as to how the Highways Agency would assess the matter; then by the same department in relation to the CTRL project. These in turn have been adopted or incorporated, whether expressly or implicitly by other promoting authorities.[53] The initial Highways Agency guidelines were the subject of judicial criticism in the *Owen* case, where they were castigated as 'at best . . . ineptly drawn'.[54] The Court of Appeal stressed that 'the first question to be considered is whether or not the enjoyment of their property would "be seriously affected by the carrying out of the works or the use of the highway"';[55] and that 'the crucial question is . . . not whether some particular guidelines, however sensible, have been complied with'.[56] However, the Manchester inspector, whose report has already been referred to, attached considerable importance to adhering to 'the criteria in the latest Government guidance';[57] and a fundamental part of one member of Parliament's objection to the approach of the CTRL promoters was not to the existence of guidelines, but rather that 'in the case of the Channel Tunnel Rail Link "hardship" is being interpreted very much more restrictively than in the Department of Transport's current section 62 guidelines for road schemes . . . The two should clearly be brought into line'.[58]

A promoter of public works cannot readily operate without guidelines, particularly in relation to noise. Col. Owen complained about the physical effects of the proposed roadworks in terms of noise, smell and vibration. But, as Neill LJ said,

> although I have great sympathy with his comments, it does not seem to me, *having regard to the guidelines which the department was using for the purpose of judging serious effects through noise or other similar causes*, that there is any basis on which the decision reached by the department could be impeached. The highest figure which the expert instructed on behalf of Col. Owen could put for construction noise was something in the order of

---

[53] The IDWGB's Progress Report contains at paras.7.28–30 and paras.7.32–3 a summary of the terms of the Highways Agency Discretionary Purchase Scheme and the CTRL Discretionary Purchase Scheme. In Greater Manchester three Transport and Works Orders have been promoted expressly on such a basis in the period 1995–7.

[54] [1995] 2 EGLR 213 at 217K–L per Simon Brown LJ.

[55] Ibid. at 217J per Simon Brown LJ; at 215L–M per Neill LJ.

[56] Ibid. at 217F per Neill LJ.

[57] See above n.51, para.8.69.

[58] Supplementary Memorandum submitted by the Rt. Hon. Sir John Stanley MP in Appendix 15 to the Sixth Report of the Select Committee on the PCA, Session 1994–5, 'The Channel Tunnel Rail Link and exceptional hardship', HC 270.

74 dB(A), whereas, it will be remembered, the department's figure was 78 dB(A) and it was to the figure of 78 that guideline 1 referred. (emphasis added)[59]

There should always, however, be a preparedness to sanction a departure where strict application of the guidelines would not involve excessive expense or cause injustice. No point seems to have been taken against Col. Owen that (contrary to the guidelines) his property had not been marketed prior to the decision, because, in the circumstances, his agents had advised against such marketing as being 'a foolish thing to do'.[60]

Second, there are limitations on who can seek to have blighted property acquired under s.62 of the PCA. 'Qualifying interest' is given the meaning in s.149 of the Town and Country Planning Act 1990, the position being consistent with that under s.26(2) of the LCA and s.246(2) of the Highways Act 1980, though slightly different from that for claimants under Part I of the LCA.[61]

Third, authorities have taken advantage of the discretionary nature of the power. They have prayed in aid arguments such as constraints on local authority funding and risk of setting a precedent. They have contended that the compensation provisions under s.10 of the Compulsory Purchase Act 1965 and under Part I of the LCA make it unnecessary to exercise the new power.[62] Whilst none of these matters is wholly irrelevant to the exercise of their discretion, together they tend to negate the rationale of the new power. A bolder view has been expressed (obiter) by Sedley J, who said (of a decision of Norfolk CC, possibly taken under s.246(2) of the Highways Act 1980, that to acquire property would set a precedent which would have enormous revenue consequences for the council): '[it] was based upon a reason which, if it were admissible, would justify all public bodies in refusing ever to exercise a discretion to make a payment for fear that others would want to be similarly treated – a textbook example of a fettered discretion.'[63]

The IDWGB comment upon the working of s.62 of the PCA in its Final Report:

---

[59] [1995] 2 EGLR 213 at 216M–217B.

[60] Ibid. at 217C–D.

[61] Though partly superseded by later legislation and case law, the commentary in *Nutley and Beaumont* Land Compensation Act 1973 (1974) remains of value, and draws attention to the fact that the interests qualifying for compensation under the LCA 'are *not* exactly the same ...'

[62] The Secretary of State for Transport appears to concur: see para.57 of his decision letter of 24 February 1997 on the Greater Manchester (Light Rapid Transit System) (Airport Extension) Order.

[63] *R. v. Parliamentary Commissioner for Administration ex parte Morris and Audrey Balchin* [1997] JPL 917 at 928.

as the powers are discretionary there are inevitably some unsuccessful applicants ... The Group believes that the result is divisive and potentially
unjust to the extent that some are compensated and others are not, even
though the unsuccessful applicants may suffer as much (or greater) loss as
the successful.[64]

Whilst I consider this criticism to be warranted, the way to reduce division and injustice lies in taking steps to ensure that the power is more
readily, and equitably, used.

This reluctance to compensate under s.62 runs contrary to the indications given by the government as to how it envisaged the new power
being used. In a written answer to a parliamentary question from Sir
John Stanley MP (a long-standing campaigner on behalf of those whose
homes in Kent were blighted by the CTRL project), the then roads and
traffic minister said: 'My Rt. Hon. Friend *will* use the new power of
earlier and wider acquisition to alleviate hardship by buying off-line
property which in his opinion is suffering from serious "blight by proximity"' (emphasis added).[65] Ministerial guidance to local authorities in
relation to the new power was that 'Authorities will wish to consider
exercising their discretionary powers to acquire property seriously
affected – or likely to become seriously affected – *wherever* this is
warranted to alleviate associated hardship' (emphasis added).[66]

It remains to be seen whether, as confirming authority, the Secretary
of State will be prepared to make confirmation of local authority
highway schemes or Transport and Works Orders conditional upon
exercise by the authority of the new power, or at any rate draw the
authority's attention in clear terms to its new power and to departmental advice about its exercise. Government lawyers are hesitant as to the
extent of ministers' powers in such circumstances.[67] There is an even
greater risk of unfairness if orders are confirmed in reliance upon the
existence of powers, but without examination of whether the powers
are likely to be exercised, the very situation in which Mr and Mrs
Balchin became, in Sedley J's words, 'innocent victims of the road
scheme', something which 'Nobody disputes'.[68]

[64] Para.7.18.3 a.

[65] Department of Transport Press Notice No. 16, 17 January 1992.

[66] Para.3 of Annex to DoE Circular No. 15/91 (Welsh Office Circular No. 50/91)
Planning and Compensation Act 1991 Land Compensation and Compulsory Purchase.

[67] *R.* v. *Parliamentary Commissioner for Administration ex parte Morris and
Audrey Balchin* [1997] JPL 917 at 928. Whilst the concern is understandable in relation to express conditions purportedly attached to an order, it is less clear why
assurances should not be a precondition of making or confirming an order. In relation
to undertakings, see *Augier* v. *Secretary of State for the Environment* (1979) 38 P & C
R 219.

[68] [68] JPL 917 at 924.

Where an offer is made at a public inquiry by a promoting authority to exercise discretionary powers, the Secretary of State has on occasion invited the authority to confirm this offer in writing as soon as practicable, and has done so *before* confirming the scheme in question.[69]

In the decision letter of 24 February 1997 in which he agreed to make the Greater Manchester (Light Rapid Transit System) (Airport Extension) Order 1997, the then Secretary of State for Transport stated, in respect of the objection to which reference has already been made, that 'He agreed with the Inspector that there is insufficient justification to require the GMPTE to acquire Ms Morris's property.'[70] Since s.62 was the power under consideration, the inference from the Secretary of State's language appears to be this: that, had the impacts been more severe, he would (or at any rate might) have been prepared to impose on the promoting Passenger Transport Executive a requirement of acquisition, as sought by the objector. But since the Secretary of State was deciding *not* to require acquisition, it was perhaps unnecessary for him to scrutinize zealously the scope of his powers.

The challenge brought by Col. and Mrs Owen ultimately failed. It was held, in later proceedings, that, when they purchased (over a year before the draft statutory orders were issued), they had sufficient information for the Secretary of State to be able to conclude

> that they knew or ought to have known that there would be a substantial road scheme passing very close to the property which they proposed to purchase. The detrimental effects of a road scheme close to property are well known; they may have disagreeable consequences for the owners of property either in relation to noise, health, or diminution in value.[71]

Such foreknowledge was held to be a matter the Secretary of State could take into account in declining to agree to a s.246(2A) acquisition, notwithstanding that it was an admitted fact that there was no diminution in value of the property at the time of purchase by reason of the proposed bypass, so that the purchase had been made without a discount.[72]

This was a harsh and unfair result. The Owens have suffered an uncompensated loss. Presumably the department's view is that they ought either to have declined to buy, or ought to have insisted on a marked reduction in price. But the latter is unrealistic. The proposals

---

[69] Interim decision letter on the proposed London Underground (East London Line Extension) Order, 27 September 1995, para.2.12.

[70] At para.57. The reference to s.62 of the PCA is at para.53.

[71] *R. v. Secretary of State for Transport ex parte Owen and another (No. 2)* [1996] 1 EGLR 32 at 56F–G.

[72] Ibid. at 55K–L and 56A–B.

were still inchoate and they had no means of negotiating a discount equivalent to that which ultimately resulted from the scheme.

It would be wrong, however, to leave s.62 of the PCA without recognition of the advance towards fairness which it, warts and all, represents. It provides a mechanism for smoothing some of the blunter edges of new schemes.

The background to CTRL

The 1990s have been a period when many major infrastructure schemes have been threatened and then abandoned. The East London River Crossing; CrossRail; the huge M25 widening; and countless other road schemes. These have raised public consciousness of blight, as has the sympathetic publicity engendered by the predicaments of the Owens and the Balchins.

But the principal generator of reform (or at least review) has been the 'problem of snowballing blight' created in rural Kent by the CTRL project.[73] It was to be expected that the construction of the first major stretch of surface railway for very many years would present problems. The undulating, high-quality landscape of Kent between Folkestone and the suburbs of London posed particular challenges, as did the government's doctrinaire starting-points that the scheme should be private-sector-driven and virtually self-financing (only the former of which survived as a principle). The inexperience of those planning the enterprise was exacerbated by delay, indecision, and tergiversation on the part of their political masters.[74]

Although a preferred route was announced in March 1989 (destination, London's King's Cross Station), the Secretary of State for Transport announced in July 1990 that the route was to be further considered, leaving open the possibility that it would change. The Department of Transport's policy was castigated as maladministration by the Parliamentary Commissioner for Administration because 'The effect . . . was to put the project in limbo, keeping it alive when it could not be funded.'[75]

The scheme development included widespread blighting in Kent from 1988. The blighting was exacerbated by the U-turn at party-conference time in 1991 by which Mr Heseltine's pet project, to (so it was claimed) regenerate East London and Thames-side Kent, caused the

[73] Fifth Report of the PCA, Session 1994–5, 'The Channel Tunnel Rail Link and blight', HC 193, Appendix 4, para.23.

[74] When the papers become available, there is a Ph.D. thesis to be written by a political scientist in relation to the promotion and then abandonment of the southern route and the associated King's Cross terminal.

[75] See n.73, para.46.

abandonment of the former southern route and the adoption of an alternative, different in almost every respect and piercing the North Downs in the Boxley region (destination, London's St Pancras Station).[76]

The Parliamentary Commissioner also concluded that

> Persons not covered by the compensation schemes may have suffered as a result of the delay in settling the route. DOT [Department of Transport] had a responsibility to consider the position of such persons suffering exceptional or extreme hardship and to provide for redress where appropriate. They undertook no such consideration. That merits my criticism.[77]

This critique was shared by the House of Commons Select Committee which investigated the matter and recommended 'that the Department of Transport ... accept his conclusion that maladministration has occurred and consider arrangements to determine whether there are householders who merit compensation on the grounds of exceptional hardship'.[78]

The government responded by undertaking to the Select Committee to consider afresh whether a scheme might be formulated to achieve redress for those affected to an extreme and exceptional degree by generalized blight from the CTRL in the period 1990–4, and a scheme was introduced in 1997.[79]

The problem of generalized blight

The CTRL problem identified by the Parliamentary Commissioner, and endorsed by the Select Committee, was different from the 'proximity blight' with which this paper is principally concerned:

> Compensation schemes from BR and Union Railways were in place but they extended only to the proximity of proposed routes. The 'generalised blight', that is, the widespread blight caused by the uncertainties of the planning and

[76] In Mr Howard's letter (see above n.3), he says: 'We believe that the history of blight in the Boxley valley is exceptional in lasting for over eight years and in being raised in two separate tranches so that it has become increasingly deeprooted.'

[77] See n.73, para.46.

[78] Sixth Report of the House of Commons Select Committee on the PCA, Session 1994–5, 'The Channel Tunnel Rail Link and exceptional hardship', HC 270, para.26.

[79] IDWGB's Final Report, para.1.4. Proposals were put to the Parliamentary Commissioner and to the Select Committee on the Parliamentary Commissioner for Administration in early 1997 and were published in the Second Report of the House of Commons Select Committee on the PCA, Session 1996–7, 'The Channel Tunnel Rail Link and exceptional hardship – government proposals for redress', HC 453. After the general election of May 1997, the proposals were considered by the new Select Committee, which accepted the new government's proposals to increase the level of payments for redress: Press Notice: 187/Transport (12 August 1997).

consultation process, remained. It was Government policy not to compensate those affected by such generalised blight.[80]

Both the Parliamentary Commissioner and the Select Committee disclaimed any intention to question the policy not to compensate for generalized blight save in the exceptional circumstances of CTRL.[81] Nevertheless, the expression 'generalized blight', once coined, took currency. The House of Commons Select Committee on the Channel Tunnel Rail Link Bill expressed concern about those whose properties decline in value because of the perception of potential purchasers rather than because of any physical effects:

... the problems of those whose homes are needed for construction of the railway, and those whose properties will experience direct negative impacts ... are not so severe. The difficult cases are those on the margins: those ... whose properties have declined in value because of the perception of house buyers, who will not buy because the railway is nearby.[82]

This is almost the same as the problem identified above and raised by the objector, Ms Morris, in connection with the Manchester LRT scheme. It lies outwith s.62 of the PCA.

The setting up of the Interdepartmental Working Group on Blight

The IDWGB, to whose work I have already made several references, was established

To review the scope, cause and effects of blight arising during the various stages of major infrastructure projects and to consider whether any practical changes can be made to the existing arrangements for property purchase and compensation, bearing in mind the concerns of the House of Commons Select Committee on the Channel Tunnel Rail (CTRL) Bill about those whose properties decline in value because of the perception of potential purchasers rather than because of any physical effects.[83]

The establishment of the IDWGB implied that 'generalized blight', if it

---

[80] See n.78, para.8.

[81] Ibid., para.20.

[82] Special Report from the Select Committee on the Channel Tunnel Rail Link Bill, Session 1995-6, HC 204, para.75. At para.77 the present law was described as 'totally inadequate'. In the House of Lords Special Report from the Select Committee on the Channel Tunnel Rail Link Bill, Session 1995-6, HL Paper 118, para.34, particular attention was drawn to certain individuals who had 'undoubtedly suffered severe financial hardship ... It is not right that major public infrastructure projects should result in such individual distress.'

[83] IDWGB's Final Report, Annex A. The terms of reference were extensive.

were properly identifiable and compensatable, could not be ring-fenced to the CTRL project. This ring-fencing had been the intention of the parliamentary commissioner when he made his suggestion of discretionary compensation 'for an isolated number of cases of exceptional suffering'.[84] His view had been that 'The position [in relation to the CTRL] was not the same as that pertaining when a road scheme is introduced – the project raised exceptional difficulties and exceptional measures were called for.'[85]

This contrasted with the view of civil servants and the government in 1995 that 'the generalised blight effects of CTRL were not materially different from those of many other projects . . .'[86] It also contrasted with the view of the Royal Institution of Chartered Surveyors that

'Blight' frequently results from informal proposals or from studies carried out by or for public authorities – particularly in relation to road schemes . . . Immense uncertainty is caused to owners and occupiers of affected properties when such specific proposed or alternative schemes are 'floated', particularly when the plans enable individual properties affected to be identified.[87]

One of the matters for the IDWGB was to define generalized blight:

The term 'generalised' or 'perceived' blight has been coined, mainly in the context of major infrastructure projects, to describe the blighting effects – which are usually said to extend over a geographical area wider than that covered by the statutory blight provisions – consequent upon uncertainty about either the siting of that project or its effects.

The group initially suggested the following definition of generalized blight in a discussion paper: 'any actual or assumed depreciation in value of property which may be attributed to a proposed infrastructure scheme'.[88]

Consultees made the point that the phenomenon of generalized blight was not restricted to the capital value of properties, and that lost profits were part and parcel of the overall effect.[89] Loss of profits are not compensatable directly under either s.10 of the Compulsory Purchase Act 1965 or Part I of the LCA.[90]

---

[84] See n.78, para.17.
[85] Ibid., para.6.
[86] See n.73, Appendix 4, paras.17 and 21.
[87] 'Compulsory acquisition and compensation', RICS 1995.
[88] IDWGB Progress Report, para.1.4 (see also Final Report, para.3.4).
[89] Progress Report, para.7.25.
[90] See *Argyle Motors (Birkenhead) Ltd* v. *Birkenhead Cpn* [1975] AC 99 at 132D–E (though not itself a case on s.10), and s.1(1) of the LCA.

In its three reports the IDWGB has demonstrated the complexity of the subject of generalized blight. There are problems in reconciling public participation and environmental appraisal of alternatives with speedy decision-making and consequent blight-reduction, as well as philosophical problems in reconciling any new form of compensation with the traditional basis on which compensation has been paid. For, as IDWGB point out, 'The policy of successive governments has been that statutory compensation should only be payable for public works which act to a person's disadvantage and, but for the statutory nature of the authorisation, would otherwise be actionable in law (e.g. for nuisance).'[91] (True though this is of Part I of the LCA, it is less clear that it is the jurisprudential basis behind s.62 of the PCA.)

The Final Report of the IDWGB

The Final Report, published in December 1997, is a slim and elegantly drafted document, the tone of which is to dampen expectations of radical reform.

The group adopts the following definition of generalized blight, into which I have introduced square brackets for the purposes of exposition:

a phenomenon characterised by
  – [1] a significant depression in the capital values of properties; [2] in any instance, the circumstances giving rise to the loss being of a nature distinct from those surrounding non-infrastructure developments,
  – [3] in a circumscribed geographical area and one in which the loss being
  – [4] realised, and
  – [5] wholly and demonstrably consequent upon a proposal for a major infrastructure development,
  [6] is not offset by quantifiable benefits associated with the proposal, nor [7] is it of a duration so short as to constitute, in any rational assessment, a normal and reasonable risk associated with the ownership of property.[92]

Criterion [1] is unsurprising, though it leaves open for debate where the threshold for 'significant depression' should be set. In the case of Part I of the LCA, there is a £50 threshold, which the IDWGB considered to be 'too low'. In respect of Part I claims, the IDWGB recommended a review and a debate on methodology (in particular

---

[91] IDWGB Discussion Paper, para.16.iv. There are indications that a change to the basic theory of compensation is under review, see paras.8.8.4 to 8.8.24 of the Interim Report, Fundamental Review of the Laws and Procedures Relating to Compulsory Purchase and Compensation (see n.6 above).

[92] Para.3.18.

between a threshold of, say, £2,500 or a figure which is a percentage of the unaffected open-market value of the property).[93]

Criterion [2] represents the group's attempt to confine claims to the consequences of infrastructure developments. The group noted that the lawful use of property often affected the value of neighbouring property: 'The possibility that one's neighbour may wish to develop the land in a way which one considers disadvantageous is one of the risks of property ownership.'[94] The group realistically stated that

> It would clearly be impossible for a nation to carry out business on the principle that any person or body may claim or *should repay* the difference in any case where the lawful use of another's property affects the value of neighbouring property, for better of worse.[95]

On the other hand the group recognized that major infrastructure projects had the potential to affect property prices and were sufficiently *sui generis* for a specific form of redress to be contemplated.

Criterion [3] seems to have flowed from twin sources: a desire to confine the phenomenon within narrow compass, so as to prevent onward and outward escalation, and a desire to limit financial exposure. As the group states, 'When one house is deemed to be sufficiently devalued to warrant intervention by a buying agency, its neighbour will be tainted by proximity.'[96] To the present writer it is not clear how the geographical area is to be circumscribed, nor why criterion [3] is essential to the definition.

Criterion [4] is presumably included to preclude claims arising from unrealized losses, that is losses which might have been realized had a sale taken place at a particular historical moment, but which were in fact avoided because no such disposal took place at that time. A householder is expected to endure with fortitude a temporary 'significant depression' in the capital value of his property, upon the basis that in the longer term there will in fact be no loss *at all*. One can see the good sense of this, though it underestimates the problems faced by those who wish to sell their property at a particular time, but for whom the project has temporarily destroyed *any* market. To this, no doubt the IDWGB would retort that there will always remain a market, albeit one which may be exceedingly depressed.[97]

Criterion [5] sensibly recognizes the need for a test of 'proven causation' rather than 'the rather imprecise concept of "attribution"'.

[93] Para.7.9.

[94] Para.2.4.

[95] Para.3.13.

[96] Para.17.19.1 (also see para.2.8).

[97] The IDWGB's proposal for a 'fully tradeable guarantee of compensation' is also relevant here: para.7.18.4.

Criterion [6] attempts to deal with the difficult problem of set-off/betterment.[98] However, the word 'quantifiable benefits' raises as many questions as it answers. If my home-to-work journey will be reduced by ten minutes as a result of the infrastructure project, is this a 'quantifiable benefit' and how is it to be offset against the 'significant depression' in value which my house may have endured by reason of the blighting effect of the project?

Criterion [7] re-emphasizes a matter already part and parcel of criterion [2], though rational people could differ upon what is 'so short as to constitute, in any rational assessment, a normal and reasonable risk' (in which case, on normal *Wednesbury* principles presumably the would-be compensator's view would prevail over that of the would-be compensatee).

A framework for this definition is set by the group's treatment of the position of business losses more generally. The group is at pains to point out the variety of circumstances in which development decisions lead to business loss or 'non-realization of speculative profits' (for instance where improved transport infrastructure in one area reduces the attractiveness of available properties in another, or where a small shopkeeper's business is affected by the development of a supermarket in its vicinity).[99] It also points to the occasions when development brings gratuitous or windfall benefits. 'One speculator loses, another gains.'[100] The group dismisses claims from the business community that the current compensation code unfairly neglects business by comparison with residential owner-occupiers: 'in the Group's view, it is entirely appropriate that, to the extent that compensation funded out of the public purse exceeds the value of the property being acquired, decisions have to be made as to where that relief should be targeted.'[101]

This passage may reveal what I consider to be the underlying – but elsewhere unstated – philosophy of the group towards off-line blight, namely that (a) compensation where land is *not* being acquired should be exceptional; (b) its scope has to be limited by financial consider-ations; and (c) perceived anomalies and injustices are likely whatever modest changes are made to the existing system.

The group believed that the phenomenon of generalized blight was capable of description and definition 'in isolation from any consider-ation of redress'.[102] And when it comes to redress, the Final Report is

---

[98] For betterment under Part I of the LCA, see s.6(1).
[99] Para.3.10.
[100] Paras.3.11–12.
[101] Para.3.6.
[102] Para.3.17.

opaque. Fifteen pages are devoted to 'Suggestions for change'.[103] The reality is less radical, for the Final Report is primarily reviewing the representations of others that particular changes should be made.

The Final Report makes four, rather banal recommendations in relation to off-line blight that (a) a code of practice on the dissemination of information on major infrastructure developers be drawn up (which ministers have accepted); (b) safeguarding directions should be defined as narrowly as possible (which the group believes to be current practice); (c) the £50 threshold under Part I of the LCA should be reviewed; (d) consideration should be given to codifying all non-statutory schemes and procedures and consolidating the statutory provisions.

More significantly, the group advances the concept of 'a fully tradeable guarantee of eventual compensation under Part I'.[104] This idea is developed more fully in the draft Property Purchase Guarantee and Compensation Scheme, published by the group in a separate document, which suggests:

> Owners of properties which may be affected by the proposed development but not actually threatened with compulsory acquisition would be able to demand from the promoter a fully transferable guarantee that any future loss of value caused by physical effects arising from the use of the development would be compensated in full one year after the development is completed. In such circumstances, the compensation would be not less than an amount stated in the guarantee (which would be the promoter's best estimate of the likely devaluation caused by the physical effects arising from the proposed development).[105]

Modestly, but surely realistically, the group accepts that whilst such a guarantee might alleviate inequalities, they would 'probably not [be] removed entirely'.[106]

3 Off-Line Blight in Other Jurisdictions

In the Republic of Ireland, whose compensation law is largely derived and modelled on the UK example, s.68 of the Lands Clauses Consolidation Act 1845, together with the *McCarthy* rules, alone

---

[103] Para.7. The Interim Report, Fundamental Review of the Laws and Procedures Relating to Compulsory Purchase and Compensation (see n.6 above) accepts that 'a total solution to the problem of blight – if a solution is achievable – would necessitate a wholesale recasting of the law', para.3.2.

[104] Para.7.18.4.

[105] Interdepartmental Working Group on Blight: Draft Property Purchase Guarantee and Compensation Scheme, December 1997 (DETR), para.27.

[106] Final Report, para.7.18.4.

apply.[107] The absence of any equivalent of Part I of the LCA or s.62 of the PCA is a striking lacuna and potential source of objection to the promotion of public works, such as a new tramway for Dublin.[108] Consultation recently carried out by the IDWGB concludes that (a) In France 'no compensation was payable where land was not required for development';[109] (b) In The Netherlands 'no compensation was payable to those whose property values were affected by development without their property actually being acquired'.[110]

It is worth quoting in full the conclusion in the IDWGB's Final Report:

> 5.5 Detailed enquiries into the German, Dutch, Belgian, Japanese and US systems, and briefings received from other countries all reveal systems under which compensation for compulsory acquisition is based on the open market value of the interest in property being acquired. We found no evidence of any country paying compensation for generalised blight.
>
> 5.6 The Group concludes that adoption of the French system of compulsory acquisition and compensation . . . or the system of any other country in respect of which we have evidence, would bring no net increase in benefits.

Thus if I have emphasized the negative aspects of the British code in relation to off-line blight, some Kiplingesque complacency may also be excusable relating to 'lesser breeds without the law'.

4 Some Conclusions

My purpose has been descriptive, neither predictive nor prescriptive. There are no easy answers to the deficiencies posed by Part I of the LCA and by s.62 of the PCA; nor to the generalized-blight problems considered by the IDWGB.

I believe there is a need for: (a) a much greater preparedness by promoting authorities to utilize s.62 of the PCA. There are too many cases where promoting authorities set the hurdle of 'serious effect' too high or fail to exercise their discretion at all; together with (b) an additional power on promoting authorities along the lines of (but wider than) s.62 of the PCA, but limited to cases of exceptional hardship. This power would mirror the discretionary power which the Secretary of State now exercises on an *ex gratia* basis in respect of certain

---

[107] See *McDermott and Woulfe Compulsory Purchase and Compensation in Ireland: Law and Practice* (1992), p. 271. The quotation at n.5 above is derived from this excellent book.

[108] The public inquiry into the first section of the route reported in 1998.

[109] Progress Report, para.5.4.

[110] Ibid., para.5.5.

aspects of CTRL generalized blight.[111] Civil servants and ministers initially opposed such a discretionary power, asserting: 'Providing compensation which is based purely on subjective judgments about the personal suffering of individuals raises serious administrative and financial problems.'[112] They have also claimed that it is invidious and impossible to distinguish exceptional suffering caused by blight from suffering which lacks that additional element of 'extreme personal distress'.[113] I believe the difficulties have been exaggerated; (c) a willingness to accept that such expenditure, whether on purchase or compensation, properly forms part of the project costs and should be budgeted for and provided. Yet it is funding (or its absence) which time after time has exacerbated blight (statutory, off-line and generalized). For it is a truism that 'The progress of major projects is often determined by expectations and aspirations for the availability of funding for construction . . . So projects which have been announced or approved sometimes remain unimplemented.'[114]

The road scheme which blighted the Balchins' property was abandoned in 1996;[115] and, as this essay goes to print, though the newly privatized Railtrack Group plc has come forward as 'white knight' to salvage the CTRL for London and Continental Railways (following fierce debate in Westminster, Whitehall and the City as to whether, when and how the CTRL would be built), blight still clouds the Kentish sky.

---

[111] See above n.73.
[112] Letter from Rt. Hon. Sir George Young MP, Secretary of State for Transport to the chairman of the committee, 10 July 1995, in ibid., App.14.
[113] Ibid., para.24.
[114] IDWGB Discussion Paper, June 1996, para.17.v–vi.
[115] [1997] JPL 917 at 924.

9

Planning Appeals, Section 54A and the Rural Battleground

STEPHEN CROW

1 Statutory Rights Relating to Appeals and Similar Proceedings

The right of appeal to central government for applicants for planning permission who are disappointed in the decision of the local authority is of long standing. It originated in the 'interim development control' in pre-war planning legislation, and was carried forward via the historically important but little-known Town and Country Planning Act 1943[1] into the Town and Country Planning Act 1947 which established the post-war regime. It is interesting to note that although in theory the 1947 Act generally took away the right to develop land and property in return for a share in a global sum of compensation, it did not remove the right of appeal where the exercise of that theoretically non-existent right was denied. Indeed, the 1947 Act in fact consolidated and extended a variety of rights of appeal in the earlier legislation[2] to a single right of appeal to the minister.[3] So far as ordinary development is concerned, the right of appeal now appears as s.78 of the Town and Country Planning Act 1990. Subsection (1) of this section gives a right

---

[1] S. Crow, 'Development control: the child that grew up in the cold', *Planning Perspectives*, 11 (1996), 399–411.

[2] Under the Town and Country Planning Act 1932, once a 'scheme' was approved, the 'interim' right of appeal to the Minister of Health disappeared. Ministry model clauses provided for no fewer than twelve separate, and by no means comprehensive, circumstances for the making of appeals. Most of these appeals went to the Minister, but there was also provision for arbitration and appeal to the petty sessions in some cases, e.g. refusal of consent to display advertisements or fell trees.

[3] From 1947 to 1951, to the Minister of Town and Country Planning.

of appeal to applicants for planning permission if the application is refused, or granted subject to (unwelcome) conditions. The right of appeal also extends to applications for any approval, consent or agreement which are required in pursuance of a permission already granted, a commonplace example being an application for the detailed plans required to be submitted under an outline planning permission.[4]

Subsection (2) gives a similar right to applicants where no decision is made within the 'prescribed period'. This is prescribed by a development order, the General Development Procedure Order 1995 (GDPO),[5] generally as within eight weeks unless the time is extended by agreement, or application is 'repetitive' (s.70A), or has been referred to the Secretary of State.

Similar rights for applicants for consent to alter or demolish buildings of special architectural or historic interest – 'listed building consent' – are conferred by ss.20–2 of the Planning (Listed Buildings and Conservation Areas) Act 1990, and to applicants for consent to display advertisements by reg. 15 and part III of Schedule 4 of the Town and Country Planning (Control of Advertisements) Regulations 1992.[6]

For the sake of completeness, it may also be noted that there are similar provisions in respect of enforcement proceedings. A person having an interest in land to which an enforcement notice relates, or a 'relevant occupier' (that is ordinarily someone who occupied the land when a notice was served and is still there) may appeal to the Secretary of State under s.174 of the 1990 Act. There is similar provision in respect of listed-building enforcement appeals to be found in ss.39–41 of the Planning (Listed Buildings and Conservation) Act 1990. In enforcement appeals, the question may be raised as to whether permission or consent should be granted, as it were retrospectively, once it is decided that it was needed. This then raises similar[7] considerations to those in the parallel 'ordinary' appeal processes.

The award of costs in respect of planning appeals in England and Wales is governed by s.250(5) of the Local Government Act 1972. Government policy on costs is that all parties to an appeal should normally bear their own costs. Nevertheless, inspectors, or the Secretaries

---

[4] That is, an application for the approval of all or any of the 'reserved matters': siting, design, external appearance, means of access, or the landscaping of the site in accordance with Article 4 of the GDPO (see n.5). Other conditions requiring approval, consent etc. may also be applied to other permissions.

[5] The Town and Country Planning (General Development Procedure) Order 1995 (SI No.419), Article 20.

[6] The Town and Country Planning (Control of Advertisements) Regulations 1992 (SI 1992 No.666).

[7] Department of the Environment/Welsh Office Circular 8/93 (WO 23/93).

of State, may make an award of costs where 'unreasonable behaviour' has caused the other side unnecessary expenditure.

It has been a feature of all modern planning legislation in the United Kingdom that it treats rural and urban areas alike so far as legislative content and administrative procedures are concerned. Only its subject matter is different, as will be later noted.

2 Appeals: Fair to All?

On the face of it, the right of appeal is quite comprehensive, covering all the circumstances in which an applicant for permission could be disappointed with a local planning authority's decision. The right is, however, confined to disappointed *applicants*. Ordinary members of the public in the United Kingdom who may be disappointed in a decision to grant permission have no such right of appeal. As members of the public at large they may feel that they should have a voice in influencing the affairs of their local community, not only in the local political debate but also where these affairs are decided in an independent tribunal. This is a view recognized in the Republic of Ireland and in the Isle of Man, where there are well-established systems of third-party appeals.

Against this commonly held view it should be recalled that, in origin, the right of appeal stems from the perception that 'planning restrictions' took away a right of property, which in the interests of natural justice should not happen without the hearing of those with an interest in that property. And there are other objections which may be thought of greater contemporary significance. All appeals take jurisdiction of generally local matters away from the local planning authority, so extension of the right of appeal would further reduce their jurisdiction. Moreover, as this writer has observed elsewhere, there are also practical considerations.[8] One such is the inevitable delay that would occur in the implementation of any approval whilst waiting for the appeal deadline to pass, whether or not there was an appeal. Another is the potential for almost unlimited numbers of appeals which is restrained in the Isle of Man by a rigorous test of standing and in the Republic of Ireland by a £100 fee.

The judicial perception of the right of appeal as essentially a property right in the early days of the 1947 Act at one time even threatened to affect the rights of third parties as objectors to an appeal. This can be seen in the notorious 'Chalk Pit' case.[9] Here, a proposal to quarry

---

[8] Stephen Crow, 'Third party appeals: will they work? Do we need them?', JPEL [1995] 376.

[9] *Buxton* v. *Minister of Housing and Local Government* [1961] 1 QB 278.

chalk in rural Essex was refused in 1957 by the local planning authority on the grounds that crops and livestock on adjoining land would be
harmed by dust from the working. There was an appeal, and in the
inquiry the inspector allowed a neighbouring landowner, a Major
Buxton, to speak. Subsequently, after the close of the inquiry, officials
of the ministry making the decision had discussions with colleagues in
the Ministry of Agriculture who advised that there was no real problem
about dust. On this basis the appeal was allowed and permission
granted for the quarrying. In Major Buxton's view here was clear
injustice because new expert evidence had been taken into account
without the chance of it being either questioned or rebutted. He applied
to the High Court for redress, but the substance of the case was never
decided because the Judge, Mr Justice Salmon, refused him standing,
saying:

> The scheme of Town and Country Planning legislation, in my judgment, is
> to restrict development for the benefit of the public at large, *and not to
> confer new rights on any individual members of the public,* whether they
> live close to or far from the proposed development. (Italics added)

There was much disquiet at this judgment, not least among the newly
formed Council on Tribunals, to whom the Major complained, and
newly proposed Inquiry Procedure Rules which allowed third parties to
appear by discretion made provision for the reopening of the inquiry if
the Minister received new technical or factual evidence.

Today, third parties frequently make their voices heard where
appeals are considered at inquiry, or in hearings and written representations. Although there is still no general right to 'appear' at an inquiry
(that is to present a case, give evidence and question and rebut that of
others), the current Inquiry Procedure Rules[10] provide that inspectors
may permit them to appear, and that such permission should not be
unreasonably withheld. In practice, ordinary people are always heard,
though as a matter of policy and practice every encouragement is given
for people with a common cause to find a single spokesman, in the
interests of avoiding undue repetition.

Once permission has been given for someone to appear at an inquiry,
he or she has the same rights to present evidence and cross-examine the
evidence of others. This principle was established in the case of
Nicholson v. *Secretary of State for Energy.*[11] Here, the applicant to the

---

[10] Town and Country Planning Appeals (Inquiries Procedure Rules) 1992 (SI 1992
No.2038), Rule 11; Town and Country Planning Appeals (Determination by
Inspectors) (Inquiries Procedure Rules) 1992 (SI 1992 No.2039), Rule 11.

[11] *Nicholson* v. *Secretary of State for Energy* (1977) 76 LGR 693; (1977) 245 EG
139; [1978] JPL 39.

Court, Mr Nicholson, had been allowed to give evidence at the inquiry, but the inspector had refused to allow him to cross-examine the representative of the local planning authority concerned, on whose evidence the planning issues had been determined. This was wrong, said the judge: at an inquiry all permitted to appear must be treated equally. As to the conduct of an inquiry, in a House of Lords case, *Bushell* v. *Secretary of State for the Environment*,[12] judicial comment has warned against their 'over-judicializing'. The most important consideration is that objectors are given a full opportunity of adequately presenting their cases. Given that, procedure does not have to be the same as in a court of law.

It is interesting to note that, some forty years after the Chalk Pit case began, and after a series of judicial review cases in which the issue of standing has been argued out,[13] one judge at least seems to have followed the time-honoured example of planning inspectors in hearing ordinary responsible members of the public, whether or not they have a statutory right to appear. Coincidentally, it is also a quarrying case, this time in Somerset.[14] Here, although on the merits of the application before him the judge, Mr Justice Sedley, refused leave for judicial review of a planning permission granted, he would have been content to grant standing to Mr Dixon, the applicant to the court, on the basis that he was a responsible local resident and parish councillor.

Surprisingly, a recent government proposal[15] seeks the curtailment of third-party participation in inquiry proceedings in order to speed up the process.

3 Other Public Rights

A procedure which lay people sometimes confuse with the right of appeal is that in which an application may be 'called in' by the Secretary of State[16] under s.77 of the Town and Country Planning Act 1990. This section enables the Secretary of State to direct a particular

[12] *Bushell* v. *Secretary of State for the Environment* [1980] 2 All ER 608; [1980] JPL 458.

[13] This subject is, of course, outside the scope of this chapter, except to note the parallel movements on standing between the courts and inquiry practice. It is, however, considered in the reference following.

[14] *R.* v. *Somerset County Council and ARC Southern Ltd, ex parte Dixon* [1997] JPL B138.

[15] Department of the Environment, Transport and the Regions Consultation Paper, *Modernising Planning – Improving Planning Appeal Procedures*, para.40 (London: DETR, August 1998).

[16] The Secretary of State for Wales, or in England, the Secretary of State for the Environment, Transport and the Regions, and in Scotland the Secretary of State for Scotland.

local planning authority or local planning authorities generally to refer to him a particular application or all applications in a particular class. In practice, it works like this. A circular containing a general direction is issued requiring the Secretary of State to be notified of all applications in a particular class, for example, retail developments of over 10,000 m² of floorspace.[17] This notification is then considered by the Welsh Office or the Government Office for the Regions, and a decision taken as to whether a further direction is to be made requiring that the decision be taken by the Secretary of State (to 'call in' the application) or whether he does not intend to intervene in the case concerned. Sometimes an interim 'holding' direction is made preventing the local planning authority making its own decision whilst the decision whether to 'call in' is considered. Although official sources have often stressed that the power of 'call-in' is to be used only where more than local issues are at stake, the decision is purely an administrative one, in which persuasive voices in the locality may well be of significance.

S.77 of the 1990 Act has an interesting parallel in Northern Ireland. Here, in contrast with the discretion given to the Secretaries of State in Britain, a Statutory Order provides for a special procedure for major applications which are defined by express criteria. These are: that the development, if permitted, would involve a substantial departure from the relevant development plan; be of significance to the whole or a substantial part of the province; affect the whole of a neighbourhood; or involve access to a trunk road or be sited within 67 m of the middle of one.[18]

If public rights of access to the appeal machinery in the UK are limited in the context of development control, they are almost unlimited in the context of making objection to a statutory development plan. This is an important right, especially bearing in mind the importance attached to the development plan following the enactment of s.54A of the 1990 Act and the introduction of the 'plan-led' development-control system. Under the current Development Plan Regulations, a local planning authority is required to put on deposit proposals for a statutory plan or the alteration or replacement of a statutory plan for a minimum period of six weeks, during which time anybody may make objections to it.[19] The local planning authority is required to consider the

[17] It is currently proposed that this threshold be lowered to 50,000m². P. Baber, *Planning*, 19 September 1997, 1236.

[18] The Planning (Northern Ireland) Order 1991, Article 31. For a full account of planning law in Northern Ireland, see J. A. Dowling, *Northern Ireland Planning Law* (Dublin: Gill and MacMillan, 1995). A short account may be found in J. Trimbos, 'Planning in Northern Ireland', JPL [1997] 904.

[19] Town and Country Planning Act 1990, s.42; The Town and Country Planning (Development Plan) Regulations 1991 (SI 1991 No.2794); regs. 11 and 12.

objections to a deposited plan and they must hold an inquiry into the objections unless the objectors waive their rights in that respect; similarly, if the deposited plan is the unitary development plan (which the new single-tier local authorities in Wales, as in Scotland, are required to prepare).[20]

In England, in those parts where county and district authorities remain, the situation differs in that county councils prepare a structure plan which, broadly speaking, sets out the broad strategy for planning in the county, whilst the district authorities prepare local plans which detail the expression of that strategy so far as their area is concerned. So far as local plans are concerned, public rights of objection and hearing are similar to those concerning unitary development plans, but are starkly different in the case of structure plans. Here, whilst anyone can make objection to a deposited structure plan, and the local planning authority is under an obligation to consider the objection, there is no general right of hearing. Instead the local planning authority is obliged to hold an 'examination in public' at which discussion is limited to topics selected by the authority, and those taking part in the discussion do so only by the invitation of the authority. Not surprisingly, much opinion regards the examination in public as a very second-rate means for considering objections, the principal merit of which is expediency.[21] It can be, however, an effective way of airing diverse views on policy matters prior to the making of decisions.

4 Methods of Determining Appeals

The modern inquiry is used for a variety of purposes, from ad hoc inquiries hearing allegations into public scandal to railway accidents. But by far the majority of inquiries are related to town and country planning.

The inquiry system as an administrative system outside the scope of the courts of law had its origin in medieval administrative procedures. A report of an 'inquisition'[22] taken in 1290 by one Malcolm de Harleigh, who as the king's escheator was the feudal administrator responsible for the proper conduct of the king's tenancies in chief, could, with a little imagination, be a modern inspector's report, save that it is in Latin. It tells of the unauthorized construction by Isabella,

[20] Ibid., regs. 14, 16 and 17.

[21] S. Crow, S. Essex, H. Thomas, C. Yewlett and A. Brown, 'Slimmer and Swifter': A Critical Examination of District Wide Local Plans and UDPs (London: Royal Town Planning Institute, 1997).

[22] Cassells Compact Latin English Dictionary (London: Cassell, 1927) tells us that the Latin inquisitio is nothing more than one of the words for a judicial type of inquiry. Inspectors still have their ways of getting at the truth!

Countess of Devon, of a weir across the River Exe below Exeter to the distress of the city's merchant trade.[23] The location is still known as Countess Weir.

Later, the inquiry process was developed into its modern form in proceedings under early nineteenth-century enclosure legislation. In the Enclosure Act of 1801 is a code for the proving of the several facts by a 'commission' of inquiry, normally one man, reporting to Parliament on the private Bill. This was followed in the 1845 General Inclosure Act by an inspector reporting to a government department, the Board of Trade. Similar provision was made in nineteenth-century charities, education, public-health and housing legislation.[24] Rules for housing inquiries published in 1909, the year of the first town-planning legislation in this country, could be used today with little variation. The coming of statutory town planning in Britain therefore found in the inquiry process a ready-made instrument for the mediation of private rights and public necessity.

Both the appellant and the local planning authority have a right 'to be heard', though this right is often waived in the commonplace written-representations method of determining appeals. This offers the option of a faster decision through the principal parties forgoing their right to be heard, and has, since its introduction informally in 1965, grown to be the majority procedure in quantitative terms. Its conduct is now governed by regulations.[25]

Hearings, which take the form of a structured meeting chaired by the inspector in accordance with a published code of practice,[26] have much grown in popularity compared with the more formal inquiry. Their use in simple cases is strongly pursued by the inspectorate except for cases where a large number of third parties wish to speak or the ability to cross-examine witnesses is considered desirable.[27] A recent judgment has laid emphasis on the 'inquisitorial burden' carried by the inspector in these informal proceedings where the adversarial testing of evidence is generally absent.[28]

---

[23] Hooker, *The Description of the Citie of Excester* (1919–47 edn). The writer thanks Mr Nicholas Hammans for his research in the Exeter City Library in this regard.

[24] R. E. Wraith and G. B. Lamb, *Public Inquiries as an Instrument of Government* (London: Allen & Unwin, 1971), ch. 2.

[25] The Town and Country Planning (Appeals) (Written Representations) Regulations 1987 (SI 1987 No.701).

[26] Department of the Environment Circular 15/65, *Planning Appeal Procedures*, Annex 2.

[27] Ibid., para.18.

[28] *Dyason* v. *Secretary of State for the Environment and Chiltern District Council* [1998] JPL 778; see also Stephen Crow, 'The Inspector as Inquisitor? Some reflections on *Dyason* and the Informal Hearing' [1998] JPL 825.

The current popularity of the informal hearing may be judged from the fact that in England in the twelve months 1996–7, 13 per cent of appeals were decided after an (informal) hearing, compared with 7 per cent after a (formal) inquiry and 80 per cent after the consideration of written representations. In Wales, the informal hearing is proportionately even more popular, the corresponding figures being 15 per cent by hearing, 12 per cent by inquiry and 73 per cent after the consideration of written representations.[29]

Although all appeals are made to the relevant Secretary of State, in practice the determination of all but the most important (over 98 per cent) is by inspectors appointed by the Secretary of State, to whom the power of decision is transferred by virtue of powers now set out in Schedule 6 of the Town and Country Planning Act 1990 and in regulations made thereunder.[30] This provision began with the Town and Country Planning Act 1968 and regulations which provided for a relatively small proportion of appeals to be transferred. As confidence in the system has increased, successive issues of the regulations have provided for more and more classes of appeal to be transferred, until the situation was reached that all classes of s.78 appeal are transferred, and only those which are 'recovered'[31] are determined by the Secretary of State.

Although uninformed speakers frequently refer to 'inspectorate appeal decisions', it is the case that the inspectorate does not determine any appeals, or any other casework. It is *inspectors* who determine appeals under the powers transferred them as individuals.

5 The Planning Inspectorate

In comparison with the long history of inquiries, the inspectorate is a newcomer, for all that it is proud of its own history. It began with the appointment in 1909 of Thomas Adams, later to become the founding president of the Town Planning Institute, as the first planning inspector. The work in the early days was mainly holding inquiries into planning 'schemes'. Appeals came in only as development control grew in importance.[32]

Possibly the event that has been most formative of modern practice

---

[29] Information kindly provided by the Planning Inspectorate.

[30] The Town and Country Planning (Determination of Appeals by Appointed Persons) Prescribed Classes Regulations 1981 (SI 1981 No.804). These regulations were of course made under the relevant provisions of the statute then in force, Schedule 9 of the Town and Country Planning Act 1971. Similar provisions apply to appeals now made under the Listed Buildings and Conservation Areas Act 1990.

[31] Town and Country Planning Act 1990, Schedule 6, para.3.

[32] Crow, 'Development control', 399–411.

was the report of the Franks Committee in 1957.[33] This report, after some unenthusiastic deliberation by government, led to the enactment of the Tribunals and Inquiries Act of 1958[34] and the establishment of a permanent Council on Tribunals to oversee the tribunals and public-inquiry systems. The report of the Franks Committee is most remembered today for what are commonly known as the three 'Franks' principles – that is, the qualities of openness, fairness and impartiality which are the marks of good administration and judicial procedures alike. Franks's analysis recognized that there are two, equally valid, ways of looking at an inquiry, from the point of view of those wanting to be heard by the decision-maker or his representative, and from that of the decision-maker who wants to be acquainted as quickly and efficiently as possible with sufficient facts to make a good decision. Of course, these two are often in tension, but it is from the mediation of this tension that all the rules of good practice proceed.

When inspectors determine appeals or make recommendations on non-transferred cases, they are beholden to no one as to their professional judgement. For this to be otherwise would be for them to take into account opinion which has not been before, at the inquiry or otherwise, rehearsed by the parties. This independence of professional judgement was crucial in a recent case before the European Court of Human Rights.[35] This case concerned enforcement action against a Mr Bryan by a United Kingdom planning authority. After an unsuccessful appeal, and an equally unsuccessful application to the High Court to have the appeal decision quashed, Mr Bryan complained to the European Court that his treatment under English law did not comply with the European Convention on Human Rights, which requires that 'in the determination of his civil rights and obligations . . . everyone is entitled to a fair and public hearing . . . by an independent and impartial tribunal'. In the event, the court was satisfied that the hearing Mr Bryan had received before an inspector was, but for one narrow point, impartial and independent. That point was that at any time the inspector could be removed from the case by the Secretary of State. This deficiency, such as it was, was made up for by the review of the inspector's decision on legal grounds by the High Court. What impressed the European Court were the numerous but largely extra-legal safeguards by which the integrity of all the Inspectorate's work is maintained.

These long-standing safeguards, which stem largely from the Franks report, are described in an important memorandum which is annexed

---

[33] Report of the Committee on Administrative Tribunals and Enquiries 1957 (Cmnd. 218).

[34] Tribunals and Inquiries Act 1958, c. 66.

[35] *Bryan* v. *the United Kingdom*, judgement of 22 November 1995 (44/1994/491/573) [1995] TLR 8 December, p.32; [1996] JPL 386.

(Annex B) to the Framework Document under which the inspectorate was set up as an executive agency:

> When Inspectors are instructed to hold inquiries on behalf of the Secretary of State, or appointed to determine appeals, they stand in the shoes of the Secretary of State and have the same regard to the Secretary of State's policies as does the Secretary of State.
>
> Each Inspector in exercising the duty of making a recommendation or determining an appeal is technically a tribunal.[36] It is a basic principle that in an appeal, or other case to which an Inspector is instructed or appointed, there should be no material relevant to the case before the Inspector which is not available to the parties. It follows that Government policy in relation to any case before an Inspector must be as presented to Parliament or otherwise published through the usual channels. Each Inspector must exercise independent judgment and must not be subject to any improper influence, nor must it appear that the Inspector may be subject to any such influence.

Although, as has been noted, inspectors are regarded by the courts as tribunals, and do work which is done in some overseas administrations by their courts, an inspector, whether holding an inquiry or otherwise, is not a judge sitting in court, but an administrator, responsible to the Secretary of State (who is accountable to Parliament). Moreover, whilst an inquiry superficially resembles a court in its form and practice, the matter before it is not a *lis inter partes* but a decision to be made in the public interest in the light of declared public policy. Franks, unaware of the opinion of more recent commentators,[37] called this situation 'quasi-judicial'.

In the context of the work of the inspectorate, the 'Franks' principle of openness entails taking into account only that which is in the public domain, and known to the parties. Fairness, among other things, means always giving either side a fair opportunity to put their case and respond to the points against them. Impartiality largely means the inspector having no prior connection with the case, or the people concerned with it, and so partial to neither one side or the other. It cannot mean, as Franks noted, being impartial as to the application of government policy for which the Secretary of State is accountable to Parliament.

---

[36] The expression 'technical tribunal' comes from Forbes J in *Westminster Renslade* v. *Secretary of State for the Environment* [1983] JPL 750; [1983] 127 SJ 444; [1984] 48 P & C R 255. This case has also a number of other interesting points on the role of the inspector at a planning inquiry.

[37] De Smith, Woolf and Jowell, *Judicial Review of Administrative Decisions* (5th edn) (London: Sweet and Maxwell, 1995).

6 *The Organization and Status of the Planning Inspectorate*

Today, the Planning Inspectorate is an executive agency jointly owned by the Welsh Office and the Department of the Environment, Transport and the Regions. This means that its management is largely autonomous, responsible for the administration of its own estimates and accounts, and for the attainment of the targets announced by the two Secretaries of State in Parliament.

Although the inspectorate's reputation is largely built up on its appeal work, as numbers of appeals have dropped in recent years well below 15,000 and local plan inquiry work has multiplied since the enactment of s.54A (of which more later), this work no longer predominates, and has now dropped to less than half of total expenditure and deployment of the inspector resource.[38]

In 1995/6, the average number of people employed by the Inspectorate through the year was 602, made up of 209 inspectors, 374 administrative staff and nineteen in senior supervisory grades. Supplementing the work of salaried inspectors are inspectors engaged on short-term or consultancy contracts, equivalent to over a hundred full-time salaried.

In the appeals administration, a key role is played by case officers. These are administrators who have the responsibility of ensuring that everything done during the handling of a case is legally and procedurally correct, and that the determination of the case is not unduly delayed. The administrative handling of cases involves the making of procedural and other decisions at every stage. These are decisions made in the name of the Secretary of State under the relevant statutes and regulations. Administrators making procedural decisions on appeal cases therefore must act in a quasi-judicial manner, observing the same principles of openness, fairness and impartiality as the person who ultimately determines the appeal.

Linking work with suitable inspectors is a key task at the offices in Bristol and Cardiff. This is known as 'charting' and consists of allocating each case as it arrives to a position in a matrix which brings together complexity and professional specialism. Every inspector also is classified by seniority and specialism, just as every case is ranked according to complexity and specialism.

To avoid prejudice, or suspicion of prejudice, inspectors are not allocated to work in areas where they live or have worked, or with which they have otherwise become familiar, professionally or socially. These areas are known as inspectors' 'precluded areas'.

If, rarely, an inspector cannot be found for an unusually specialized case, a specialist assessor is appointed to assist the inspector. Two or

---

[38] Source: Inspectorate Business Plans.

more inspectors may be appointed to the most lengthy and complex inquiries. In Wales, where the number of inspectors allocated to Welsh Office work is limited, specialist inspectors may be 'borrowed' from the English chart if need be.

As well as matching up the allocations of case and inspector, avoiding precluded areas, whilst at the same time making up an ongoing diary of inquiries, hearings and site visits, it is also necessary to set up the most economical travelling etc. arrangements. Inspector time is too valuable to be spent on excessive travelling!

Inspectors are recruited from time to time by open competition. They are experienced professional people, mainly chartered planners, but also include chartered surveyors, chartered engineers, architects, barristers and solicitors. On joining, inspectors are subject to a period of two years' probation, during which they receive training, including six weeks of formal instruction. Thereafter, continuous professional development is obligatory.

Whilst most inspectors are civil servants, some are appropriately qualified professionals engaged on a contract or consultancy basis. They all owe their legal standing in the casework for which they are responsible to being 'appointed by the Secretary of State', as can be seen in the 1990 Act at s.42(3) in respect of local plan inquiries, at s.79(2) in respect of general planning appeals, at s.175(3) in respect of enforcement appeals, in Schedule 6 as respects the transfer of cases for determination and numerous places elsewhere, including the relevant parts of related legislation. It is only in recent years that the title of inspector has been formerly recognized, as in the present series of Inquiry Procedure Rules, and that only as a shorthand reflecting common usage for the expression 'a person appointed by the Secretary of State'.

In practice, inspectors are appointed to their work by a minute signed on behalf of the Secretary of State by a chartroom administrator. The legal basis of this practice derives from the sections of statute outlined above, and the chartroom administrators, notwithstanding their location in an executive agency, act on the same basis as any other departmental officials making executive decisions on behalf of a minister, in accordance with the 'Carltona' doctrine.[39]

7 The Inspectorate in Wales and the Welsh Assembly

As has been noted, the Planning Inspectorate is jointly owned by both the Welsh Office and the Department of the Environment, Transport and the Regions. Although its 'jointly owned' status is all but unique,

[39] *Carltona Ltd* v. *Works Commissioners* [1943] 2 All ER 560, CA.

there are clear lines of responsibility between the two departments. Whilst the inspectorate is responsible to the Secretary of State for Wales for all its operations in the Principality, it is responsible to the Secretary of State for the Environment, Transport and the Regions not only for activities in England, but also for all matters concerning the operation of the agency as a whole.

Indicative of the inspectorate's joint ownership, it has joint head-quarters in Tollgate House, Bristol, and at Cathays Park, Cardiff, from which all work in Wales is organized.

In its present role as an executive agency in the (joint) ownership of the Welsh Office, the Welsh arm of the inspectorate, the Welsh Agency Group, has its own identity, which it cultivates assiduously. The group is responsible for all the inspectorate's business in Wales, except high-ways and local-plan inquiries (which are organized on an England-and-Wales basis). The administrative unit at Cathays Park uses the Welsh language when properly called upon to do so, in accordance with statute and Welsh Office policy. There is also a small number of Welsh-speaking inspectors who are able to conduct an inquiry in the Welsh language.[40]

The relative scales of the operations in England and in Wales can be ascertained by a comparison of the expenditure on each. In 1995/6, the total expenditure chargeable to the agency was £26,897,000, almost all on running costs, staff pay and fees. Included in this sum was the £1,125,000 expenditure incurred in Wales, which was recovered from the Welsh Office.[41] This amounts to the proportion England to Wales of roughly 23:1.

The size of the Welsh group is adjusted as required to the demand for its services. Currently, it has thirteen inspectors, ten salaried, and three on contract and consultant bases. They are supported at Cathays Park by fourteen administrative staff.[42]

The White Paper, A Voice for Wales,[43] says little about the role of the proposed Welsh Assembly in respect of the determination of planning appeals, other than to note in Annex A that they, with 'call-in powers', are currently a function of the Secretary of State for Wales. Whether their determination would pass to the Assembly on the basis that 'the Assembly will take over the responsibilities that the Secretary of State exercises in Wales'[44] is therefore a matter of speculation, on

[40] [1995] Planning Inspectorate Journal, 13.

[41] Information from the Planning Inspectorate Executive Agency Annual Report and Accounts for the year ended 31 March 1996.

[42] Information current at October 1997 from the Planning Inspectorate at Cathays Park.

[43] Cm. 3718.

[44] Ibid., para.1.7.

which this writer is unable to comment until the announcement of a firm proposal. At this uncertain stage all that can be remarked is that as well as more obvious political considerations such as the location of accountability, there are some practical considerations, which it is to be hoped will be addressed in the composition of any firm proposal.

The first practical question concerns the future of the Welsh Agency Group. In this writer's opinion it does not follow that transfer of function would of itself necessitate the separation of the Welsh arm of the executive agency from the larger remainder. Part-ownership could simply be passed from the Secretary of State for Wales to the Assembly, if that were desired. But what if some voices were to be raised in favour of separation?

At the present time, whilst the administrative arm is fairly self-contained, it is able to benefit both from its physical location within the Welsh Office as well as from links with administrative developments at Tollgate House. Moreover, the inspector team undoubtedly benefits from cross-fertilization with the larger body of inspectors. This is particularly important for the inspectors themselves, who value the opportunities for career advancement offered by association with the larger body.

Of course, this is not to say that smaller organizations cannot be viable. The Reporters Unit of the Scottish Office undertakes its business with twenty full-time reporters and can call on the services of up to twelve part-timers.[45] The Planning Appeals Commission in Northern Ireland is much smaller, currently with nine full-time and three part-time commissioners.[46] But their reporters and commissioners cannot be specialists in particular subjects as inspectors in England and Wales can be. Whether this drawback carries much weight is, of course, a matter of opinion. It is not one which in the experience of the writer ranks for much in these parts of the UK, though perhaps it ought.

A question that needs to be given serious thought (in the writer's opinion) is how an assembly would go about deciding appeals, or at least those which are not determined by the inspectors themselves. There is some precedent for inspectors' reports, those in respect of objections to local plans, being debated in council chambers. But it is not a precedent without danger, as shown by the record of legal challenges to the adoption of plans where inspectors' recommendations have been disregarded.[47] For example, in the case of *Stirk* v. *Bridgnorth District Council*, the local planning committee had before it the inspector's report on objections to its deposited local plan. The committee had very strong views on one of the issues, the rolling-back of the Green Belt around the village of Albrighton, and as the Deputy

---

[45] Information as at October 1997 from the Scottish Office Reporters Unit.
[46] Information as at October 1997 from the Planning Appeals Commission.
[47] *Stirk and others* v. *Bridgnorth District Council* [1997] JPL 51.

Judge, Mr Gerald Moriarty QC, concluded, they came to their decision not to roll back the belt without properly considering what the inspector's report had to say. The affected part of the plan was quashed. Commenting on this case, Professor Michael Purdue referred to 'the problem of a political body . . . having to grapple with very complex and technical matters'.[48]

Moreover, if an appeal decision is to be debated, it is almost inevitable that matters will be raised by one member or another which were not before the inquiry. Who is to say whether these matters were material to the decision which is ultimately made?

Two examples where planning decisions have been debated in Parliament, although undoubtedly unusual cases, well illustrate the potential pitfalls and the need for care. When in 1978 it was desired to give Parliament the opportunity to debate the question of a nuclear-fuel reprocessing plant at Windscale (now known as Sellafield), an unusual device was used. Although the called-in application had been before a public inquiry and was recommended for permission by the inspector, it was refused by the Secretary of State. Instead, the development was permitted by way of a special development order which was placed before Parliament.[49]

A somewhat different procedure was followed a few years later in the case of the called-in application for the nuclear power station at Sizewell. After the inspector's report was received, both Houses of Parliament were given the opportunity to debate it and the issues involved. But in the Commons, the Secretary of State made it clear that he was there only to listen to the debate but had no intention of commenting or making observations on the report. Shortly after the debates, he granted the permission sought, as recommended by the inspector.[50]

How procedures would have had to be adapted if Parliament, rather than the Secretary of State, were to make the decision can only be guessed at. Private Bill procedure possibly comes to mind. Of course, this is not to raise objection to a proposal which in any case has yet to take shape. It is simply to draw attention to some of the problems of practice which may need to be taken into account, and indeed are currently concerning the National Assembly Advisory Group set up to advise on Assembly procedures. Their present proposal is for appeals and the like to be determined by a specialist, cross-party panel.[51]

[48] Ibid. at p.62.
[49] Victor Moore, *A Practical Approach to Planning Law* (London: Blackstone Press, 1987), 13.
[50] Ibid.
[51] National Assembly Advisory Group, *National Assembly for Wales. A Consultation Paper* (1998) and *Recommendations* (1998) paras.7.22ff also: Robert G. Lee, *Devolution and the Environment – Wales*, paper delivered at the annual conference of the United Kingdom Environmental Law Association, Belfast, April 1999.

8 The Determination of Appeals

The 1990 Act, at s.79, provides that the Secretary of State (or by virtue of Schedule 6 and regulations, an inspector) may allow an appeal, or dismiss it, or reverse or vary the local planning authority's decision. He may also decide it as though it were made to him in the first instance. The advantage of this last power is that the decision is not bound by the local planning authority's reasons for refusal or the grounds of appeal as to the scope of his decision.

The grant of planning permission both by local planning authorities and on appeal is governed by two important previsions of the 1990 Act. The first is s.70(2), which requires the decision to 'have regard to the development plan, so far as material to the application, and to any other material considerations'. This is an important provision which gives almost unlimited flexibility to local planning authorities in the consideration of development proposals. It is, however, limited, at least outwardly, by the addition[52] to the 1990 Act of s.54A. This says: 'Where, in making any determination under the planning Acts, regard is to be had to the development plan, the determination shall be made in accordance with the plan unless material considerations indicate otherwise.'

Much has been said and written about the genesis of 's.54A' and what it means in practice.[53] Undoubtedly it has provoked much thought about the nature of decision-making in planning practice, and it has taken several years to expunge from the popular view what it is not.

Except in the sense that all legislation is necessarily a reflection of the policy in the mind of those who introduced it into Parliament, s.54A does not in itself express a policy stance, and it is quite right that it should not. There was much talk in planning circles at the time of its passage that it expressed what was said to be the 'primacy of the development plan', that is to say, that the development plan would carry much greater weight than hitherto *vis-à-vis* 'the other material considerations'. This view was firmly scotched in the judgment of David Widdicombe QC, sitting as a Deputy Judge in the case of *St Albans District Council* v. *the Secretary of State for the Environment and Allied Breweries Ltd*.[54] In this case, the district council had leaned heavily on the then current version of PPG 1, and in particular the sentence 'an applicant who proposes a development which is clearly in conflict with

[52] Planning and Compensation Act 1991, s.26.

[53] For example, Michael Purdue, 'The impact of s.54A' JPEL [1994] 399; Nicholas Herbert-Young, 'Reflections on development control and "plan-led" decision making', JPEL [1995] 292.

[54] *St Albans District Council* v. *Secretary of State for the Environment and Allied Breweries Ltd* [1993] JPL 374; [1993] 1 PLR 88.

the development plan would need to produce convincing reasons to demonstrate why the plan should not prevail'. In other words (as one commentator has put it)[55] it was suggested that the development plan had to prevail unless there were 'strong contrary planning grounds'. But the court was not prepared to attach such weight to the wording of the Act as a matter of law. The weight to be attributed to the relevant factors in a decision is first and foremost a matter for the decision-maker.

Of course, decision-makers have necessarily to have regard to all relevant policy considerations, but even here the general view among legal commentators[56] is that a decision-maker's interpretation of policy may be overturned by a court only when the interpretation is perverse or inconsistent with previous interpretation of the policy. This is to be expected, bearing in mind the courts' general reluctance to become involved in policy matters; still less in planning merits. In the apt expression of a Dutch colleague,[57] our planning legislation is 'empty', that is, in providing for the making and implementation of plans it stops short of specifying their substance. This point was amplified by Lord Hoffman in a recent House of Lords judgment in frustrating another attempt to conflate law with policy and practice.[58]

> The distinction between whether something is a material consideration and the weight which it should be given is only one aspect of a fundamental principle of British planning law, namely that the courts are concerned only with the legality of the decision making process and not with the merits of the decision. If there is one principle of planning law more firmly settled than any other, it is that matters of planning judgment are within the exclusive province of the local planning authority or the Secretary of State.

All this in fact makes life simpler and easier for decision-makers whom this writer from the earliest days of s.54A has advised as to

---

[55] Ian Gatenby and Christopher Williams, 'Interpreting planning law', ch.9 of *British Planning Policy in Transition*, ed., Mark Tewdwr-Jones (London: UCL Press, 1996), 139.

[56] Herbert-Young, 'Reflections', 303.

[57] Erik Bussink, 'Physical planning systems in the EC Member States: a global survey', first published in *Europe 2000* (European Commission, Directorate General for Regional Policy, 1991) and also included in the *Proceedings of the Seminar on Planning Legislation: The European Experience* (Bucharest: Ministry of Public Works and Regional Planning (Romania)/Council of Europe/European Council of Town Planners, 1995); also *PlanningWeek* [1994] vol.2, No.48, p.8 (this comment unreported).

[58] *Tesco Stores Ltd* v. *Secretary of State for the Environment* [1995] 2 All ER 636 at 657f.

practice,[59] with the subsequent approval of leading legal practitioner-commentators, Ian Gatenby and Christopher Williams,[60] as follows. There are essentially two steps to be taken, and they must not be conflated. The first is to consider how a proposal measures up to the plan, and reach a view on that. Secondly, the decision-maker must consider the other material considerations that almost always exist, and decide whether they override the provisional consideration already in mind about the proposal in relation to the plan. The amount of weight to be put on the conclusion of the first step against the material considerations evaluated in the second is a matter of policy and of professional judgement, bearing in mind the individual merits of the case.

9 Planning Appeals: A Rural Question?

For all that the coverage of public rights to be heard in the context of planning decisions is limited here and there, as has been noted, there can be little doubt that the issues thrown up in planning practice by the tensions between the need for development, the conservation of the built and natural environment and the protection of neighbourhood amenities are thoroughly exposed and debated in the appeal and analogous processes. Nowhere is this tension more apparent than in rural areas.

It is the writer's recollection of over twenty years of hearing and determining appeals[61] that something like half of them have been sited in the countryside. This recollection is borne out by an analysis of the appeal decisions reported in the weekly journal *Planning* for the six months March–September 1997. Of the 431 cases reported in this period,[62] all, or almost all of them, cases determined following an inquiry, 47 per cent were located either in the countryside or in rural villages[63] of England and Wales. The exact figures in this small and imperfect sample are scarcely worth reporting, but they do support the author's experience that very few of the appeals reported directly

---

[59] For example, see S. Crow, 'The development plan, the Planning Inspectorate, and decision making', *Town and Country Planning Summer School Proceedings* (London: Royal Town Planning Institute, 1993).

[60] Gatenby and Williams, 'Interpreting planning law', 146.

[61] The author served with the Planning Inspectorate in England and Wales from 1976 to 1994, and continues to hear appeals in the Isle of Man.

[62] Although the cases are selected for editorial interest, the journal advises that there is no conscious bias or selection as between urban and rural locations. The sample appears to be roughly one-third of all inquiry appeal decisions.

[63] As identified from the reports, or, in the case of named locations, from the description 'village' in *Bartholomew's Gazetteer of Britain* (Edinburgh: John Bartholomew and Son, 1977).

concern agriculture or traditional rural activities. Here is to be found (for example) an unsuccessful appeal concerning the re-roofing of a slated barn with sheet material,[64] and a successful appeal giving an unhappy indicator of a contemporary agricultural problem – a chimney to serve a bovine incinerator.[65] A greater number of the appeals noted concern seldom upheld claims, on the basis of 'agricultural need', for houses in the countryside. Yet more are for urban peripherals such as an airport extension, telecommunications masts, garden centres, cemeteries, sports fields and facilities for horse-riding, or for urban developments themselves; housebuilding and superstores.

It is clear from the appeals considered and the writer's own experience that the countryside is to a very large extent the battleground on which are deployed the rival interests of development, the conservation of the built and natural environment and the protection of neighbourhood amenities. This should not be a surprise for, as is shown in the table taken from a recently published survey,[66] the countryside in recent years is the seat of by far the greater part of land-use change.

Changes within and between urban land use (England)

Percentage of land changing use	1985	1992
Within rural uses	50	38
Within urban uses	24	34
From rural uses to urban uses	23	25
From urban uses to rural uses	4	3
All changes	100	100

It can be seen from the table by adding the figures of change within rural uses to those from rural uses to urban that in 1985 no less than 73 per cent, and in 1992, 63 per cent of all land-use change took place in what were, or had been, rural areas. This is the case notwithstanding the remarkable increase in the period (from 38 per cent to 47 per cent) in the reuse of previously developed urban land for residential development.[67] Although the figures relate only to England, there is no reason to suggest that a similar picture would not appear in Wales.

Planning appeals can therefore very much be regarded a rural question, and their importance increases year on year as the commercial

---

[64] Appeals News, *Planning*, 18 April 1997, p.9.

[65] Appeals News, *Planning*, 15 August 1997, p.7.

[66] JPL [1997] B136, reproduced by permission. The statistics are based on changes in land use recorded by the Ordnance Survey during their map-revision work between 1985 and 1996.

[67] Ibid.

pressures on the rural land resource meet increasing resistance not only from traditional rural interests but also from an increasingly vocal and increasingly better-organized conservation movement. As the value of land depends pre-eminently on the kind of planning permission that can be got for it, and permission once granted normally runs with the land, every owner except the most altruistic has the incentive for seeking the most generous grant of planning permission which it is possible to obtain. As the sample studied shows, this may be for overt urban uses, or it may be for urban uses disguised as rural uses in order to give them a better chance of success. Ostrich farms, and barns designed (and in one instance actually built) remarkably like private dwelling-houses are among the more enterprising attempts to buck the system.

For indeed, arrayed against most development in rural areas are not only the opposition of conservation bodies and rural residents, not least those who have their origins and livelihoods in the towns, but also several tiers of conservation policies. At national level are policies such as those related to Areas of Outstanding Natural Beauty and Green Belts,[68] whilst most development plans, that is unitary development plans, structure and local plans, contain batteries of policies directed at the preservation of the openness of the countryside, whilst attempting to a greater or lesser degree to provide for what are seen as legitimate rural activities.

Nevertheless it is the writer's experience that appeals in the rural areas frequently present the greatest challenges to the professional skills of an inspector. This remains true despite batteries of development-control policies and the disciplines imposed by s.54A. Thanks to the present rigour in the costs regime, obvious losers, for example shopping developments in the Green Belt, are rare. What are more commonplace are situations which require not just the application of policy to a case, but a real exercise of professional planning judgement. This can be seen in a quite simple case such as that reported at Sychdyn near Mold.[69] Here (as it seems from the press report) a proposal to build a house on the edge of the settlement had been refused on the basis of structure and local plan policy prohibiting housebuilding in the 'open countryside'. The site was within an existing residential curtilage but lay outside the settlement boundary in the local plan. Nevertheless the inspector, whilst generally supportive of the policy, was unconvinced about its application to the case because his appraisal of the situation told him that the proposal would do no harm to the character and appearance of the area, and so the general objective of the policy

[68] In England only.
[69] Nigel Packer, 'County's definition of open countryside overturned', *Planning*, 15 August 1997, p.7. Case ref. APP/P0119/A/97/277691.

would not be jeopardized. He allowed the appeal. In terms of the application of s.54A, one might say that the local planning authority had applied the first limb of argument, and fairly found the proposal at odds with the plan, but as to the second limb, the other material considerations – in this case what went on the ground – they had either failed altogether to consider them or had not attached to them the weight that the inspector thought right.

This case is a typical example of rural appeal. There are many like it. Especially in rural areas, such work requires inspectors to display skills of discerning fact from fiction, of assessing all sorts of differing technical considerations and weighing their relative importance against the policy background, but above all of applying a touch of common sense bred of professional experience.

In conclusion, it is the writer's experience that rural areas are not only the battlefield on which the conflicting interests meet head on, but, more than anywhere else, where the professional skills of inspectors are fully exercised. Appeals are undoubtedly a rural question, and often a ticklish one at that.

10

Legal Aspects of Development and the Church in the Countryside

J. D. C. HARTE

1 The Significance of the Rural Church for Development and Public Amenity

Church denominations, and especially the national Church embodied in the Church of England, own important sites in the countryside on which they may on occasion wish to carry out development. The Church of England covers the whole of England and virtually the entire landscape is divided into some 28,487 parishes.[1] These are grouped into forty-two dioceses, each centred on a cathedral. Although the Church in Wales is disestablished[2] the ancient parish churches of the Principality, like churches of other denominations, are also covered by some distinctive law.

A parish church and its churchyard are the responsibility of the incumbent and of the elected parochial church council. The principal administrative committee in every diocese is the Diocesan Board of Finance.[3] Clergy houses are largely the responsibility of the Parsonages Board.[4] This may be a distinct body or its functions may be exercised by the Diocesan Board of Finance. Major reserves of Church land controlled by the dioceses consist of glebe, scattered throughout the parishes and originally part of the property of each rector or vicar.[5]

---

[1] *Times*, 12 November 1997.
[2] Welsh Church Act 1914.
[3] Diocesan Boards of Finance Measure 1925.
[4] Repair of Benefice Buildings Measure 1972.
[5] Whether a parish has a rector or a vicar is largely a matter of historical accident. A 'rectory' was the benefice of a parish priest with control over all the endowments of

Much Church land, and especially ancient church buildings with their surrounding churchyards, enjoys special legal protection in respect of development nearby. At the same time, they are exempt from a number of regulatory regimes which apply to most other land. This exemption was granted essentially because the churches run their own parallel systems of control. This chapter considers the special Church controls, particularly the faculty jurisdiction which applies to the parish churches of the Church of England. It also discusses how Church controls interrelate with general planning law and with other secular systems of control designed to protect the national heritage.

Although the Church and the various structures through which it operates are not, for the most part, heritage organizations, the Church of England, especially, is the steward of a major part of the national heritage. Indeed, some agencies of the Church of England, notably the Council for the Care of Churches,[6] and the Churches Conservation Trust,[7] are primarily concerned with the protection of church buildings as part of the national heritage. The Council for the Care of Churches originated in 1923 as a central council of diocesan advisory committees for the care of churches. It was reconstituted by the General Synod in its present form, as the Council for the Care of Churches, in 1981.[8] This acts as an advisory body on church buildings and their contents and on churchyards. Alterations to parish churches require the approval of a faculty from the bishop's judge, the chancellor. The council has a formal statutory role in faculty proceedings before the diocesan consistory court, wherever the chancellor considers that an application might concern or involve an article or matter of historic or artistic interest, including any part of a building and anything fixed to land or a building.[9]

the parish. Originally, vicars were substitute clergy provided by a monastic house which had acquired the endowment of the parish. After the Reformation, these endowments were distributed to various laymen or corporations or retained by the Crown. The incumbents of parishes created in the nineteenth century or more recently are also called vicars. The old terms have been given new meaning in some modern groupings of parishes into team ministries under the Pastoral Measure 1983. This provides for a team to be headed by a team rector with a number of vicars sharing the work of several parishes, but each based in a particular parish. See, too, Team and Group Ministries Measure 1994.

[6] Technically, a permanent commission of the General Synod, appointed under Synodical Government Measure 1969, s.2(1) and Schedule 2, Article 10(2).

[7] Previously the Redundant Churches Fund, established under the Pastoral Measure 1983, s.44 and renamed by Pastoral (Amendment) Measure 1994, s.13.

[8] See Donald Findlay, *The Protection of Our English Churches: The History of the Council for the Care of Churches 1921–1996* (Council for the Care of Churches, 1996).

[9] Faculty Jurisdiction Rules 1992, SI 1992 No.2882, r. 14. The council has six weeks in which to prepare a report for the chancellor. Under r. 21 the council may apply to give evidence in any faculty case.

The Churches Conservation Trust was originally set up as the Redundant Churches Fund under the Pastoral Measure 1983.[10] The present name was substituted in 1994.[11] A church building, or part of such a building, which is no longer required for parish use may be declared redundant under a pastoral scheme.[12] If no other suitable use can be found for it,[13] it may be demolished and the site cleared.[14] However, if it appears that the building is 'of such historic and archaeological interest or architectural quality that it ought to be preserved in the interests of the nation and the Church of England', and provided the Trust has sufficient resources to meet the cost of repair and maintenance, a pastoral scheme may entrust to it the care of the building and the land attached.[15]

The requirement that there must be funds available underlines the finite resources of the Church of England in providing for its ancient buildings where these no longer have active congregations. The message is somewhat ominous in parts of the countryside where old church-going communities may be increasingly replaced by emigrants from urban Britain who do not identify with the Christian faith and are not prepared to contribute towards its work. On the other hand, incomers who are not prepared to pay towards the Christian ministry of the Church may be prepared to support an old church building as an interesting and attractive historic monument. The Trust provides a vehicle for preserving significant redundant churches, both by looking after them and by raising funds from people with secular conservation interests.

A country church will normally be accompanied by a parsonage house. Even if it no longer houses the rector or vicar it is still likely to form a visual companion to the church. Where the Church of England retains an ancient parsonage it will benefit from statutory provisions whereby the Diocesan Parsonages Board is responsible for maintaining the houses of all incumbents, that is the clergymen primarily responsible for each parish. The responsibility to keep parsonages in good repair is laid down in the Repair of Benefice Buildings Measure 1972. Every parsonage must be professionally inspected at least every five years, and repairs carried out in accordance with the surveyor's report.[16] In the interval between quinquennial inspections,

---

[10] Pastoral Measure 1983, s.44.

[11] Pastoral (Amendment) Measure 1994, s.13.

[12] Pastoral Measure 1983, s.28.

[13] Ibid., ss.47(1) and 51(1)(a).

[14] Ibid., ss.51(1)(d) and (4).

[15] Ibid., s.47(2) as amended by Pastoral (Amendment) Measure 1994, s.3.

[16] Repair of Benefice Buildings Measure 1972, ss.3, 4 and 5. S.8 provides for interim inspections.

the incumbent has a duty to see that the Parsonages Board is notified of any necessary repairs.[17] Parsonage houses therefore share with churches themselves a unique statutory system for ensuring sound maintenance.[18]

The curtilage of a parsonage may be a substantial garden. Beyond this there may be very extensive glebe land. Glebe was originally the endowment given to a parish over the centuries by the founder of the church and by succeeding local benefactors. Originally, it was either farmed directly by the incumbent or, often, would be rented out. Much land, in a central belt from the south-west, north-east to Lincolnshire, was enclosed under some 4,500 Enclosure Acts from the sixteenth to the nineteenth centuries, and especially in the eighteenth century. Previously, individual holdings, including the glebe, would have been scattered in several large fields. On enclosure, individual holdings were consolidated, and fields which still have such names as 'Parson's Meadow' indicate the parson's allocation.[19] Today glebe is vested in the diocese.[20]

Although a high proportion of old country parsonages and much Church land such as glebe has now been sold off by dioceses, the Church often continues to provide some protection. It is normal for a diocese to impose covenants at the time of sale which will restrict possible future damage, including infill building within the curtilage. Such covenants serve primarily to protect the amenity of Church land nearby, particularly church buildings.[21] Where a church building of architectural or historic distinction is no longer needed for parish use and has been transferred to the Churches Conservation Trust, the Trust will be able to enforce any covenants over other land which were made to protect the church.[22]

If a church building itself is to be disposed of altogether it may be sold for some suitable new use, such as a house or an art gallery, and covenants will normally be imposed to ensure that it is not abused in future. In a country location, the diocese is likely to retain some land which will benefit from the covenant, such as part of the churchyard where there have been recent burials. If the church does not retain land

[17] Ibid., s.13.

[18] For church-building inspections see Inspection of Churches Measure 1955, s.1.

[19] Historically, the incumbent's income also depended heavily on tithes, a tenth of the agricultural produce of the parish. With enclosure, tithes were frequently extinguished, in return for extra allocations of land. Often all these allocations would be grouped together near the church and were added to the glebe. See in particular Tithe Act 1842. Remaining tithes were eventually commuted to rent charges and these have now been extinguished; Tithe Act 1936.

[20] Endowments and Glebe Measure 1976, ss.15, 19 and 20.

[21] Ibid., s.22.

[22] Pastoral Measure 1983, s.44.

in the immediate vicinity, the diocesan conveyancers may ensure that the initial purchaser does not sell on the church site without ensuring that his successor enters into a new covenant.

Covenants on the sale of Church land are intended primarily to protect the Christian character of the immediate area where worship has taken place in the past and, except where the church building itself is sold, will continue to take place. However, covenants can also serve as a conservation tool, providing valuable protection for a village or an open area in the countryside around a church. The Church of England is sometimes criticized for updating its church buildings, or for releasing open land, such as glebe, for development. This may be a particular problem where villagers or the public have treated such land as a public open space although they have no formal right to do so.[23] By contrast, a sympathetic alliance between the Church authorities and the local community could use the church and other Church land as a focus for covenants made by owners of properties nearby to protect their homes, gardens and fields from future development which would threaten the character of the area. A parish church could thus serve a function similar to that of the National Trust, in policing covenants made with it to protect amenity land from damaging development.

The Church of England does not have a special statutory power, as the National Trust does,[24] to enter into restrictive covenants to protect from unsuitable future development land in which it has no interest itself. A landowner may make such a covenant with the National Trust to protect any piece of land, even though the Trust does not own any other land in the vicinity.[25] This power has been used extensively, for example, as an aspect of Operation Neptune to protect from future development unspoiled stretches of coastline which are kept in private ownership. However, where the Church of England disposes of property, because it is likely to retain land nearby which will have important qualities for amenity, it can fulfil a similar function to the National Trust by including an ordinary restrictive covenant in the conveyance.

Covenants policed by the Church could help the local community to guard against development which an unsympathetic local government planning authority was intent on encouraging. Covenants can be a much more reliable conservation tool than nuisance actions or public participation in the planning process. Although the grant of planning permission will not override the restrictions imposed upon a developer

[23] R. v. *Oxfordshire County Council ex parte Sunningwell Parish Council*, QB, 11 July 1997, unreported, considering R.v. *Suffolk County Council ex parte Steed* [1997] 10 EG 146.

[24] National Trust Act 1937, s.38.

[25] *Gee* v. *National Trust* [1966] 1 WLR 170, CA.

by the law of nuisance,[26] planning policy can fundamentally change the character of an area and reduce the effect of the law of nuisance by redefining what activities are reasonable in the vicinity.[27] In any event, simple development of land will not in itself constitute a nuisance, even though long-enjoyed views and the general character of a place are destroyed. This is underlined by the clear view of the courts that it is not possible to create an easement for a view.[28] By contrast, restrictive covenants continue to provide a valuable safeguard for residents from being subjected to planning policies which they do not want.

The prospect of development of Church land can inject an explicit ethical dimension into conflicts between competing values.[29] Such conflicts may arise in the planning system, as where the interests of established residents have to be reconciled with the very different life-styles of others who need homes and a share in the material resources of life. The essential character of the Church may suggest ways for resolving such conflicts or anticipating and avoiding them, which could be valuable in helping to establish a framework and a number of helpful models for the wider community.

There are obvious difficulties in the Church becoming involved in potential conflicts between local authorities and the immediate inhabitants of a parish by acting as guardian of a covenant against development on land in a village.[30] Provided the local authority acquired or appropriated the development land it could override a covenant which was hampering development.[31] Nevertheless, in such a case, if the Church were to defend the covenant, it could ensure that the matter was publicly aired by challenging the local authority order, and compelling the Secretary of State to hold an independent inquiry before confirming it.

In practice, a local planning authority could well be reluctant to attack a covenant under which the Church acted as trustee for the amenities of a particular parish. A developer could still seek to have the covenant quashed or modified by the Lands Tribunal, under s.84 of the Law of Property Act 1925. However, the criteria on which the Lands Tribunal may act are restricted and would be unlikely to apply.

[26] *Wheeler* v. *Saunders* [1995] 2 All ER 697.

[27] *Gillingham BC* v. *Medway (Chatham) Dock Co. Ltd* [1992] 3 All ER 923. See further *Hunter Canary Wharf Ltd* [1997] AC 655.

[28] *Phipps* v. *Pears* [1964] 1 QB 76.

[29] *Harries* v. *Church Commissioners of England* [1993] 2 All ER 300.

[30] However, a planning authority committed to approving unpopular development in a village would hardly be likely to acquire a church by compulsory purchase so as to eliminate the covenant. As to the special position of ecclesiastical land which is acquired or appropriated by a secular public body, see Town and County Planning Act 1990, s.238.

[31] Ibid., s.237.

The most commonly invoked criterion is that the covenant has become obsolete, but so long as the land subject to the covenant is near enough to the church to have some impact on its amenity, the covenant would be unlikely to be considered obsolete.

In some circumstances the Church may appear in a very different guise from that of the guardian of local amenities. Surplus parsonage gardens and glebe are often near to the church and serve as a green buffer protecting it from development. Glebe often includes an open space which serves as a village green or is otherwise used for recreation. Financial pressure on the Church of England makes this land vulnerable to development. The danger to amenity is increased because of Church concern to help with social problems, for example, by providing low-cost housing in villages where the housing stock seems to have been taken over by commuters and retired people with higher incomes. Low-cost housing is also one form of development which planning policy tends to encourage in the countryside.[32] There is much scope for resentment, whether the diocese 'spoils' an attractive village and what is regarded as a public recreation area by providing sites for new housing, or whether it sits on its resources and is perceived as a wealthy institution of hypocrites ignoring the needs of the poor. If the Church builds on its own land, it may seem inconsistent to enforce covenants which prevent other people from building nearby, especially if that other development would be less prominent and of a higher standard.

As a trustee, a Church body is normally required to obtain the maximum return on its trust property. This requirement generally applies to charitable trustees as it does to others. Balancing the aesthetic and conservation responsibilities of the Church with its social responsibilities and the need to maximize financial resources for its central spiritual work is unavoidably difficult.[33]

2 The Application of Secular Planning Control to Church Property

The most obvious presence of the Church in the countryside is in the parish churches of the Church of England with their surrounding churchyards. The churches and chapels of other denominations, some being as early as the seventeenth century, also number many fine examples listed nationally. The future of the rural church is likely to affect profoundly the character of the English countryside, its villages and open landscapes, where church towers or spires have been the most striking features for centuries. To these may now be added a growing

---

[32] Department of the Environment PPG 7, *The Countryside and the Rural Economy* (January 1992), para.2.19 and PPG 3, *Housing* (March 1992), Annex A.

[33] *Harries v. Church Commissioners for England* [1993] 2 All ER 300.

number of places for the worship of other faiths. Some places of worship, such as the mosques of Islam, are more likely to be built on prominent urban sites. Others, such as a Hindu Ashram, may constitute a major new development in the countryside, intended as a centre for quiet devotion but able to accommodate large numbers for special festivals.[34] These and large new worship centres for modern Christian sects pose special planning problems because they may be seen as conflicting with traditional concepts of the countryside.[35]

Large religious festivals can pose problems for rural planning whether or not they are associated with an established community. Festivals may be single events which do not require planning consent because they are a temporary use of open land for less than twenty-eight days in a year.[36] They will, however, be subject to other regulations. For example, if there is a noisy musical element they might be restricted as 'rave events'.[37] Some religious festivals are annual events on sites with a permanent infrastructure which will require planning consent.[38]

As an institution, the Church has a wide-ranging role in the planning system. Church bodies such as Church of England dioceses or parochial church councils and their equivalents in other denominations may contribute to the formation or revision of local planning-authority development plans.[39] They may also make representations in the development-control process. For example, in the person of the incumbent and through the diocese, the Church of England will have an interest in retaining the amenity of the land near a parish church. They will be in a position to challenge an application for planning approval of any unsuitable development affecting an old parsonage or generally in the vicinity.

In planning terms, much that is done on Church land appears the same as activities carried out by secular occupiers. In a society which has become increasingly uninterested in organized Church activities since the introduction of modern development control under the Town and Country Planning Act 1947, a planning application will not enjoy an advantage simply because it is made by a Church body.

[34] *International Society for Krishna Consciousness* v. *Secretary of State for the Environment and Hertsmere Borough Council* (1991) 64 P & C R 31.

[35] *Tandridge District Council* v. *Secretary of State for the Environment* [1997] JPL 132; 72 P & C R 83; [1997] JPL 646; 74 P & C R 159; *Barnet London Borough Council* v. *Secretary of State for the Environment* [1990] JPL 430; 60 P & C R 137; [1993] JPL 739 and 761.

[36] Town and Country Planning (General Permitted Development) Order 1995, SI 1995 No. 418 Schedule 2, part 4 Class B.

[37] Criminal Justice and Public Order Act 1994, s.63.

[38] These may be compared with regular sites for special sporting events such as car or horse races and with agricultural shows.

[39] Town and Country Planning Act 1990, part II.

It is a well-established principle that the identity of a developer, by itself, does not determine whether any changes which the developer makes do or do not amount to development.[40] Thus, a new clergy house on the edge of a village is essentially just another dwelling-house. If it is a new building, its construction will be a building operation and will clearly require permission. If it is an existing building, already used as a dwelling by someone else, it will not require permission for a clergyman to live in it, but conversion to a parsonage of a barn or of a building previously used for some other purpose, such as part of the church itself, will need permission.

On the other hand, a Church application may raise special planning grounds which would justify permission being granted. The special needs of a person proposing development can be a planning consideration.[41] Thus, permission to build a new vicarage, of rather ordinary design, may be looked on favourably, even in a protected place such as a conservation area.[42] In the case of a new Church of England parsonage or of a clergy house for another denomination, there may be reasons similar to those raised by a farmer who applies for permission to build a new farmhouse.

Permission for a new rectory or vicarage might be refused altogether if, instead, an existing over-large building could be adapted to modern needs. However, a diocese may claim that it lacks the capital for a conversion and needs to sell an old parsonage to raise money for a new one. Especially if the old building is listed, it may be argued that the best way of ensuring that it is properly renovated and conserved will be to permit the building of a replacement.[43] In any event, planning policies have generally been sympathetic to new housing development within the envelope of a village if there is available land.[44] For a replacement vicarage, there is normally either a large garden or glebe available.

Where planning permission is given on the basis of the special needs of the applicant, conditions are commonly imposed to restrict the change to meeting those needs. This is frequently illustrated by

[40] Lewis v. Secretary of State for the Environment (1971) 23 P & C R 125; Snook v. Secretary of State for the Environment (1975) 33 P & C R 1.

[41] Westminster City Council v. Great Portland Estates plc [1985] AC 661. See too South Lakeland District Council v. Secretary of State for the Environment and Rowbotham [1991] JPL 440 and the discussion of these cases in Victor Moore, A Practical Approach to Planning Law, sixth edn (Blackstone Press, 1997), 207.

[42] South Lakeland District Council v. Secretary of State for the Environment [1992] 2 AC 141.

[43] See Brighton Borough Council v. Secretary of State for the Environment (1979) 39 P & C R 46.

[44] PPG 7, The Countryside and the Rural Economy, para.2.16.

permission for a dwelling required on a farm which is given subject to a condition that future use must be related to agriculture.[45] Permission for a new vicarage could similarly be restricted to future occupation by an ordained clergyman. Such a condition would be easier to frame than one relating to the much more wide-ranging concept of persons working in agriculture or related activities. In practice, however, a new vicarage is unlikely to be sold off to a private occupant and a condition designed to avoid that risk is likely to be thought unnecessary.

Apart from dwellings, Church activities may involve a number of uses. Some of these are treated as essentially the same as one another in planning terms and so will not require planning permission where one is changed to the other. Under the Use Classes Order, various uses are listed in classes and no permission is needed to change to a different use in the same class.[46] Class D 1 consists of non-residential institutions and includes at (h) any use 'for, or in connection with, public worship or religious instruction'. This is interchangeable with a use (b) as a crèche, day nursery or day centre, (c) for the provision of education, (d) for the display of works of art (otherwise than for sale or hire), (e) as a museum, (f) as a public library or public reading room or (g) as a public hall or exhibition area.

These uses in Class D 1, apart from worship, cover a great many of the ancillary uses to which churches may be put. Indeed, they identify the sort of use to which a redundant church might appropriately be made over. Educational and aesthetic uses suggest ways that the rural church could develop its Christian profile. The Church has great potential to make more of its buildings for the mutual benefit of the local community and of visitors. Because of the Use Classes Order, the secular planning system would not necessarily hinder such developments.[47]

On the other hand, there are uses which the Church itself might consider suitable in a village church building but which would require planning consent. Thus, the church building could be used to provide outlets for work and a source of income for local people. Historically, the nave of a church was once often used as a market. Today, in some places, a church could house craft workshops. A church hall could become the base for a mail-order service, perhaps for goods with religious associations.

New business uses, including offices, research or light industry,

[45] *Fawcett Properties Ltd* v. *Buckinghamshire County Council* [1961] AC 636.

[46] Town and Country Planning (Use Classes) Order 1987, SI No.764.

[47] Class D 1 para. (a) is a use for the provision of medical or health services which is not attached to a residence of medical personnel. This suggests a further way in which churches might come to develop new aspects of ministry or find a suitable use for a redundant building.

require planning consent.[48] So also do retail uses,[49] or use for the sale of food or drink to consume on the premises.[50] Thus, a self-contained charity shop or tea room opened by a congregation in a village street near the church or in a room of a large vicarage or manse will clearly be a new free-standing shopping use. However, a lively church may be involved in a variety of activities which it may claim are ancillary to its primary functions as a centre for worship. Typically, a bookstall may develop into a quite substantial shop or the kitchen attached to a church hall may be used for regular catering, perhaps providing visitors with lunch. As the original uses are common in churches, under planning law, they would be treated as ordinarily incidental and so recognized as not requiring planning permission.[51] However, if they were to expand too much, they would become uses in their own right and would require approval.[52] This will be especially true if a use is operated in a distinct planning unit, such as a corner of the church, with its own external door, or one end of the hall, with its own entrance.

A new church will require planning consent. However, it is likely to be proposed in association with new housing, and there should usually be no planning objection to it if housing has been approved. Nevertheless, the planning authorities may influence the design and the character of a new church, for example, by pressing for it to be shared for a range of community uses. In practice, such an approach may be welcomed by the Church. It is likely to make the scheme more viable and will integrate the place for worship more fully into the community.

Like a new church, an extension to a churchyard or other burial ground will constitute a material change of use and so will require secular planning consent. If the land is available, an extension to a churchyard is likely to be approved. It is noteworthy here that cemeteries are regarded by the Department of the Environment as one of a small number of new uses which may be suitable for a Green Belt. The relevant policy guidance indicates that new buildings in association with a cemetery are not inappropriate. This is explained on the basis that a cemetery is a use of land which preserves the openness of the Green Belt and does not conflict with its purposes.[53] Existing church buildings and churchyards may provide a tool whereby the planning system is

[48] Ibid., Class B 1.
[49] Ibid., Class A 1.
[50] Ibid., Class A 3.
[51] Ibid., reg. 3(3). See too *Royal Borough of Kensington and Chelsea* v. *Secretary of State for the Environment* [1981] JPL 50.
[52] *Williams* v. *Minister of Housing and Local Government* (1967) 18 P & C R 514 and *Jillings* v. *Secretary of State for the Environment* [1984] JPL 32.
[53] Department of the Environment PPG 2, *Green Belts* (January 1995), para.3.4.

able to protect focal areas in villages from unsuitable development. Where planning permission is sought for any development which would affect either a listed building or its setting,[54] or the character or appearance of a conservation area,[55] there are express statutory requirements that special attention is to be paid to the desirability of preserving them. Under these provisions, account must be taken of how any proposed new development may affect views of a listed building, looking at it from viewpoints outside.[56] Even without these express provisions, it would seem likely that it is a material planning consideration that the architectural integrity of a church and its setting should be taken into account where development is proposed nearby. In the parallel case of an archaeological site, it has been held that, even where a site is not scheduled, its presence will be a good justification for refusing planning permission for development which could damage it.[57]

Apart from development control, special secular planning regimes are, therefore, significant for Church land in the countryside. Listed building control, designation of conservation areas and scheduling of ancient monuments do not in general directly restrict change to church buildings, because of the special ecclesiastical exemptions which are considered in the next section. However, they may be important in preventing development on other land nearby. Indeed, where a church is listed or in a conservation area, this may hamper the Church authorities from building on their own neighbouring land. Nevertheless, even the statutory requirements for taking account of the effect of development on a listed building or on a conservation area, are limited in what they can do.

In *South Lakeland District Council* v. *Secretary of State for the Environment*,[58] the Court of Appeal and the House of Lords agreed that outline planning permission had been wrongly refused for a new vicarage at Cartmell Priory on the western edge of the Lake District. The site was in a conservation area and the local planning authority had relied on the statutory requirement that in deciding whether to give planning permission it should pay special attention 'to the desirability of preserving or enhancing the character or appearance of the area'. The planning authority argued that, like enhancement, preservation meant some positive benefit, such as reinstatement of a damaged building. However, it was held by the House of Lords, in the words of Lord

---

[54] Planning (Listed Buildings and Conservation Areas) Act 1990, s.66.

[55] Ibid., s.72.

[56] *R.* v. *South Herefordshire District Council, ex parte Felton* [1990] JPL 515.

[57] *Hoveringham Gravels Ltd* v. *Secretary for the Environment* [1975] QB 754. And see now Department of the Environment PPG 16, *Archaeology and Planning* (November 1990).

[58] [1992] 2 AC 141.

Bridge, that it was enough if the development 'leaves the character or appearance unharmed, that is to say, preserved'.[59]

3 Ecclesiastical Exemption from Special Controls

In the case of church buildings, secular listed-building control and conservation-area control do not normally apply, because of what is commonly known as 'the ecclesiastical exemption'.[60] Normally, express consent is required from a local planning authority or from the Secretary of State for the Environment for any works which will affect a listed building,[61] and there are criminal penalties for carrying out such work without permission.[62] There are associated powers for the local planning authority or the Secretary of State to implement emergency repair works which appear to be necessary for the preservation of a listed building.[63] The Secretary of State also has power to authorize the compulsory purchase of a listed building where reasonable steps are not being taken for properly preserving it.[64] An unlisted building which appears to a local planning authority to be of special architectural or historic interest and to be in danger of demolition or of alteration which threatens its character as a building of such interest may temporarily be covered by a building preservation notice. This ensures most of the protection enjoyed by a listed building, for up to six months.[65]

Under s.60 of the Planning (Listed Buildings and Conservation Areas) Act 1990, listed-building controls do not apply to 'any ecclesiastical building which is for the time being used for ecclesiastical purposes'. Similarly, conservation-area consent, which is normally required for the demolition of any building in a conservation area, does not apply to listed buildings or to 'ecclesiastical buildings which are for the time being used for ecclesiastical purposes', whether they are also listed or not.[66]

[59] Ibid., at p.150, applying words of Mann LJ at [1991] 1 WLR 1326–7.

[60] Listed-building control and related secular regimes are discussed extensively in Charles Mynors, *Listed Buildings and Conservation Areas*, 2nd edn (FT Law and Tax, 1995) and Roger W. Suddards and June M. Hargreaves, *Listed Buildings: The Law and Practice of Historic Buildings, Ancient Monuments and Conservation Areas*, 3rd edn (Sweet and Maxwell, 1996).

[61] Town and Country Planning (Listed Buildings and Conservation Areas) Act 1990, ss.7–9.

[62] Ibid., ss.9 and 57.

[63] Ibid., s.54.

[64] Ibid., s.47.

[65] Ibid., ss.3 and 4.

[66] Ibid., s.75(1). Generally as to central government policy on historic buildings, see PPG 15, *Planning and the Historic Environment* (September 1994). Part 2.8 deals with churches and the ecclesiastical exemption.

Normally, where a building is listed, the protection applies also to 'any object or structure fixed to the building' and to 'any object or structure within the curtilage of the building which, although not fixed to the building, forms part of the land and has done so since before 1st July 1948'. With ecclesiastical buildings, the churchyard would normally coincide with the curtilage. Thus, if it were not for the exemption, in the churchyard of a listed church, ancient preaching crosses, village stocks, free-standing family mausoleums and indeed the churchyard wall and pre–1948 gravestones would be subject to listed-building control. Because of the exemption, the control does not normally apply to these any more than to the church. However, they can be made subject to listed-building control by being separately listed.

The reason for the ecclesiastical exemption was that, when controls for historic buildings were first introduced, buildings of the Church of England were excluded because of the national Church's existing arrangements for protecting the buildings for which it was responsible. It was also recognized that control over the use of church buildings could interfere with religious freedom. Therefore, exemption was made general, so as to apply to all churches. Subsequently, the word 'ecclesiastical' would probably have been considered to apply to all religious buildings, including those of other faiths beside Christianity.

'Ecclesiastical uses' was interpreted by the courts to include use of a house as a vicarage, and, for a time, all parsonages were recognized as free from listed-building and conservation-area control.[67] Indeed, 'ecclesiastical use' would appear to apply to any use to which a building is put by a church or other religious body, such as use as diocesan offices or a theological college or a church shop or restaurant. It is not confined to use for worship. However, the exemption was soon withdrawn from clergy houses; any 'building used or available for use by a minister of religion wholly or mainly as a residence from which to perform the duties of his office shall be treated as not being an ecclesiastical building'.[68]

The ecclesiastical exemption has now been cut back much more fundamentally. The Secretary of State has been granted power to withdraw the exemption by statutory instrument in respect of listed-building control,[69] or in respect of conservation areas.[70] The way this power has been used in practice has been to confine the exemption to actual

[67] *Phillips* v. *Minister of Housing and Local Government* [1965] 1 QB 156.

[68] Now provided by Town and Country Planning (Listed Buildings and Conservation Areas) Act 1990, s.60(3) in respect of listed buildings and s.75(5) in respect of buildings in conservation areas.

[69] Ibid., s.60(5).

[70] Ibid., s.75(7).

church buildings of denominations which have their own systems of control, notably the faculty jurisdiction of the Church of England which is considered more fully below. However, there is also power for such orders, removing the exemption, to be made in respect of buildings generally, descriptions of buildings or particular buildings.[71] For example, an order could be made withdrawing the exemption in respect of all grade I and grade II* buildings or the exemption could be withdrawn in respect of chapels and mausoleums attached to parish churches which are not used by the church for congregational purposes.

There is power for orders to be made in respect of particular areas of the country. For example an order could apply to churches in National Parks,[72] and in Areas of Outstanding Natural Beauty.[73] There is also power for orders withdrawing the exemption to be tailored to deal in different ways with different parts of a building or with different types of works. Thus, works of a particular description might be specified, such as changes in roofing materials, or works of a particular extent such as the removal of walling of more than a certain length.

The power to withdraw the exemption has been applied in the Ecclesiastical Exemption (Listed Buildings and Conservation Areas) Order 1994.[74] This removes the exemption completely in respect of denominations which do not operate a system of control complying with a Department of the Environment Code of Practice. The major denominations do operate such systems and therefore continue to have the benefit of the exemption. As well as the Church of England and the disestablished Church in Wales, these include the Roman Catholic Church, and the Methodist and United Reformed Churches.

Where it remains, the exemption is now confined to buildings whose primary purpose is as places of worship and to objects or structures attached to their exterior or standing within the curtilage, which are not separately listed. Apart from parsonages, many historic ecclesiastical buildings are associated with a parish church, and may be physically within its curtilage, such as an ancient schoolroom over the porch or a library attached to an aisle. Such ancillary buildings will only be subject to listed-building control if separately listed.

Although the exemption from listed-building control may now appear vulnerable, it seems unlikely to be abolished. The threat of secular planning authorities seizing control is a major incentive for denominations to take care of the important buildings for which they are responsible. Church people may grumble about the expense of

---

71 Ibid., s.60(6) and 75(8).
72 As defined in National Parks and Access to the Countryside Act 1949, s.4.
73 As defined in ibid., s.87.
74 SI 1994 No.1771.

conservation and the bureaucracy of the faculty jurisdiction and of parallel arrangements in other denominations, but they are aware that the cost and the level of interference with Church activities by secular planning authorities could prove very much greater. The secular planning authorities themselves may be happy to be spared a major area of controversial and time-consuming work.

In those cases where more secular control is considered desirable to protect features in a churchyard, separate listing would seem a much simpler device than making complex orders to withdraw the exemption. In churchyards, detailed control by planning authorities would be expensive, time-consuming and very inconvenient for all concerned, especially where regular burials still take place. Significant alterations to the outside of a church itself are in any event likely to require planning consent. Also, secular planning authorities and other special amenity bodies, such as English Heritage, have now been given a substantial consultative role in the Church of England process. Furthermore, where English Heritage gives a grant to a church for restoration work this will often be subject to a right to veto any future alterations to the building.

A fundamental qualification of the exemption is that it is restricted to any ecclesiastical building 'which is for the time being used for ecclesiastical purposes'. To avoid a catch-22 situation, it is provided that 'a building shall be taken to be used for ecclesiastical purposes if it would so be used but for the works in question'.[75] Thus, where a church is temporarily out of use whilst rebuilding is carried out, the exemption continues to apply.[76]

There is a further, far-reaching, exemption from listed-building control, where a redundant Church of England church is demolished under the Pastoral Measure 1983.[77] This does not apply to listed churches of other denominations. If they become redundant they can only be demolished under secular listed-building consent.[78] Roman Catholic churches in the countryside are relatively few in number and are usually unlikely to be made redundant. However, one which is not needed for worship may be a fine building, perhaps provided for by a wealthy Roman Catholic landed family and regarded as an encumbrance if the family is no longer there to support it. Nonconformist chapels are often prominent features in a village or at the roadside away from any village, built to be out of sight of the parish church, at a time when Nonconformity reflected antipathy to the established

---

[75] Ibid., s.60(4) and 75(6).

[76] As to the special control under the faculty jurisdiction in such cases, see Care of Churches and Ecclesiastical Jurisdiction Measure 1991, ss.17 and 18.

[77] Ibid., s.60(7).

[78] *Attorney-General* v. *Howard United Reformed Church* [1976] AC 363.

Church.[79] Such a building is often in a simple classical style which can relatively easily be converted to a different use. A chapel may have belonged to an independent congregation which is now defunct. Even where it is attached to a major denomination, its members may have little commitment to preserving buildings. They may positively object to conservation as an unspiritual preoccupation. This contrasts with the concern for preserving an ancient parish church which is often shared by churchgoers and non-churchgoing members of a village community. Even if an Anglican congregation consider its local church an encumbrance, the diocesan structure will normally enable those beyond the immediate congregation to ensure its conservation.

The Pastoral Measure 1983 allows parish churches which are taken out of commission and declared redundant to be put to other suitable uses or retained by the Churches Conservation Trust. Only if no alternative is available and if the building is not important enough to save will its demolition be allowed.[80] This is very rare with a church which is listed. In the countryside, an old but undistinguished church which is redundant may be made safe, with the removal of the roof, and left as a ruin, rather than being demolished outright. Sometimes such churches may later be found to have very valuable features and may be rescued.[81]

Apart from special protection under Town and Country Planning legislation, listed-building and conservation-area control, significant historic buildings in the countryside may be safeguarded by scheduling as ancient monuments under the Ancient Monuments and Archaeological Areas Act 1979. Here, churches in use are again excluded from secular control because they may not be scheduled.[82] On the other hand, other structures in a churchyard, or indeed a churchyard itself, could be scheduled as an ancient monument. Scheduling as an ancient monument takes priority over listing[83] and any alteration or work affecting a scheduled monument must be approved by central government.[84] Permission is unlikely to be given for work on a scheduled structure standing above ground in a churchyard, except where it is necessary for the purpose of conservation or safety. Permission may be given for works which would disturb features below ground but only

[79] Over 1,500 Nonconformist chapels in England are listed; Mynors, *Listed Buildings and Conservation Areas*, 315.

[80] Pastoral Measure 1983, s.51(1)(d).

[81] The return to parish or other use of churches vested in the Churches Conservation Trust is envisaged by Pastoral Measure 1983, s.58.

[82] Ancient Monuments and Archaeological Areas Act 1979, s.61(8).

[83] Planning (Listed Buildings and Conservation Areas) Act 1979, ss.61 and 71(5)(b).

[84] Ancient Monuments and Archaeological Areas Act 1979, s.2.

after careful consideration and on condition that a proper archaeological dig is carried out first.[85]

4 The Faculty Jurisdiction and Other Control by the Church of England

From a conservation point of view, the most significant body of Church
law is the specialist planning system known as the faculty jurisdiction,
which has been developed by the Church of England for protecting its
ancient parish churches.[86] Cathedrals are not covered by the faculty
jurisdiction and neither are a small number of other special churches,
technically known as 'peculiars', such as Westminster Abbey and
ancient Oxford and Cambridge colleges with their chapels.[87] From a
distance, many of the great cathedrals, such as Durham, Ely or
Lincoln, which are set in prominent positions continue to dominate the
rural landscape. Others, like Winchester rising from adjacent meadows,
are linked with the surrounding countryside by open amenity land.
Constable's rural views of Salisbury, for example, may still be recognized today. However, barring some disaster such as fire, no alteration
to these views is at all likely, and cathedrals will not be considered in
detail here. They are covered by their own special system with individual fabric advisory committees and the national Cathedrals' Advisory
Commission for England.[88]

Peculiars which wish to retain the ecclesiastical exemption from
secular controls are now required to submit to the faculty jurisdiction in
any event.[89] A number of independent school chapels, may be peculiars
and are features in the rural landscape.[90] The legal status of Tonbridge
School chapel was raised when[91] it was sought to rebuild it, after it had
been reduced to a shell in a fire. Initially, listed-building consent was

---

[85] For central government policy and guidance on the relationship between planning law and archaeology generally, see PPG 16, *Archaeology and Planning*.

[86] Major decisions of the ecclesiastical courts dealing with the faculty jurisdiction
are published in the main series of law reports. Valuable short reports on other decisions are included in the *Ecclesiastical Law Journal*, which is published twice a year
by the Ecclesiastical Law Society. The main textbooks on the subject are Mark Hill,
Ecclesiastical Law (Butterworths, 1995) and Lynne Leader, *The Ecclesiastical Law
Handbook* (Sweet and Maxwell, 1997).

[87] Paul Barber, 'What is a peculiar?' 3 Ecc LJ 299.

[88] Care of Cathedrals Measure 1990 and Care of Cathedrals (Supplementary
Provisions) Measure 1994.

[89] Ecclesiastical Exemption (Listed Buildings and Conservation Areas) Order
1994, SI 1994 No. 1771.

[90] An example is the domed chapel of Giggleswick School reopened after restoration in 1997; *Church Times*, 10 October 1997.

[91] *Re Tonbridge School Chapel* [1993] 3 All ER 350.

sought, but the application was withdrawn by the governors, who proceeded instead with an application for a faculty. The chancellor accepted jurisdiction and granted the faculty, after rejecting arguments against the scheme by the local planning authority. That authority, by implication, would have refused listed-building consent.

The faculty jurisdiction is mainly concerned with parishes scattered across the towns and countryside of England. It applies to the parish churches themselves and also to satellite churches and chapels. Thus, in large parishes, one or more 'chapels of ease' were often built to provide services for those who lived at a distance from the parish church. Frequently, such chapels of ease later became daughter parish churches.

The basis of the faculty jurisdiction is that any alteration to a church within the jurisdiction of a diocesan bishop may only be made under the authority of a faculty granted by the bishop or his judge. In practice, today, that means the chancellor.[92] Any operation or change of use amounting to development will require planning consent and a faculty as well. However, the faculty jurisdiction is much wider. It applies to all parish churches, whether they are listed or not, and it covers works, such as repairs, which do not constitute a change, as well as removal or additions to contents which are not part of the building at all.

The faculty jurisdiction, therefore, serves as a major safeguard against inappropriate alterations to church buildings. These include churches which are listed and are often of very considerable architectural and historic importance.[93] They also include buildings which are not of sufficient importance to be listed and which may not be recognized by any other special secular designation, such as a conservation area, but are, nevertheless, an important visual focus for the surrounding community and landscape. In a rural area, often the parish church is simply the biggest structure in sight. Also, it is usually surrounded by a churchyard which ensures that it is seen in an open setting and can be viewed with the perspective of distance.

A significant aspect of the faculty jurisdiction is how the criteria which chancellors apply relate to those of secular planning authorities or to those which are advocated by conservation bodies.[94] In particular,

[92] The last attempt by a bishop to take over a case was publicly attacked by his own chancellor in a later case; *Re St Mary's Barnes* [1982] 1 WLR 531. Today such an initiative by a bishop could put at risk the whole ecclesiastical exemption.

[93] Mynors, *Listed Buildings and Conservation Areas*, ch. 11, gives recent statistics. Some 8,500 churches, half of the churches belonging to the Church of England, date from before the Reformation. These and a further 4,500 later Church of England churches are listed. At the beginning of 1994, 3,000 churches, the great majority belonging to the Church of England, comprised nearly 50 per cent of all grade I listed buildings in England.

it might be expected that chancellors would be more sympathetic to change and to allowing an ancient building to be used in new ways. Certainly, chancellors are Church men and women who see church buildings, primarily, as living places for divine worship by contemporary people. However, they are also sensitive, in a way that local congregations may not always be, to the historic and aesthetic importance of church buildings, not least as an expression of continuity and beauty.

There is a tension here, but it can be creative. It can enable church buildings to be adapted and reused in such a way that they are less likely to become redundant and really at risk. Also, it may allow for more innovative design than is often possible in a secular building. In this respect, the amount of change needed to maintain viable worship for a modern congregation may be greater than would be needed to ensure the continuing life of, say, a country house.

Changes to country churches which give rise to controversy are often made inside, but they may also include extensions, or alterations, to doors and windows, which make an impact on the exterior view. These exterior changes are likely to require planning permission. However, planning control normally takes relatively little account of aesthetics.[95] It is not entirely clear to what extent a planning authority would be justified in refusing planning consent for, say, a church extension, essentially on aesthetic grounds. With a significant secular building, such an application would be dealt with by the same authorities, as an aspect of listed-building control. In the case of a church, if a chancellor approved an extension or other external change, it would seem very unsatisfactory from the point of view of the local community which the church represents if planning permission were refused on the basis that the secular authorities considered that the chancellor was wrong.

Because internal alterations will not normally need planning permission,[96] the faculty jurisdiction is crucial in providing protection for a historic church interior which, for a secular building, would be provided by listed-building control. In a rural context, church interiors are often of particular interest because they may have been less subject to change than those in towns. A country church is also often a particularly significant focus for the community. Churchgoing in the country side is often still much higher in proportion to population than in most urban areas. Conversely, where a village church expands or a new

---

[94] See generally PPG 15, *Planning and the Historic Environment*, especially Annex C, 'Guidance on alterations to listed buildings'.

[95] *Winchester City Council* v. *Secretary of State* [1978] 36 P & C R 455.

[96] There are exceptions. For example, planning permission would be required for a new crypt or underground storage area; Town and Country Planning Act 1990, s.55(20)(a).

incumbent arrives with fresh ideas, demands for change may lead to significant tensions.

The Church of England faculty appeal courts are the Court of Arches and, in the Northern Province, the Chancery Court of York. They share a senior judge who sits as Dean of the Arches in the South and as Auditor in the North. The present occupant is Sir John Owen, who is also a High Court judge. These Church appeal courts have recently been reconstituted to form exceptionally strong tribunals for dealing with Church heritage cases, such as would provide a model for a more general environmental appeal court. As secular appeal courts increasingly draw on trial judges to sit with specialist appeal judges, so the Dean of Arches and Auditor sits with two chancellors drawn from the relevant province.[97] Although the number of faculty appeal cases is very small, this arrangement serves to diffuse expertise and insights from different parts of the country and to combine them in dealing with difficult and sensitive cases.

The practice for faculty appeals has also been improved by another initiative of the Dean of the Arches,[98] in giving English Heritage, the local planning authority, and relevant national amenity societies the right to be formally cited as parties to faculty proceedings where they have an interest. These are cases where a chancellor considers that the character of a listed church as a building of special architectural or historic interest is likely to be affected, where the archaeological importance of the church or archaeological remains within its curtilage are likely to be affected or where demolition is proposed which will affect the exterior of an unlisted church in a conservation area.[99] English Heritage, along with the Council for the Care of Churches, is given a right to adduce evidence.[100]

Where a church is listed, there has been a tendency for the Church courts to avoid provoking a confrontation with the secular system, by basing decisions on the criteria which would be taken into account for listed-building consent. Ultimately, the conservation of any listed building is likely to depend on it continuing to be used by people prepared to pay for its upkeep. Here, Church authorities may have a more realistic awareness than secular planning authorities of the need to authorize change if a church building is to continue in use. As Sir

[97] Ecclesiastical Jurisdiction Measure 1963, s.47, as substituted by Care of Churches and Ecclesiastical Jurisdiction Measure 1991, Schedule 4, para.8. The first case heard by the newly constituted court was *Re St Luke the Evangelist, Maidstone* [1994] 3 WLR 1165.

[98] See his recommendations in *Re St Mary's Banbury* [1986] Fam. 24; [1987] 1 All ER 247.

[99] Faculty Jurisdiction Rules 1992, SI 1992 No.2882, r. 12(3).

[100] Ibid., r. 23.

John Owen has commented, 'an abandoned church is little use to the Church or to conservationists'.[101] Nevertheless, the chancery courts follow the principle that

> although the exemption is necessary so that in such cases the dead hand of the past shall not prevent the proper use of a building consecrated to the worship of God, a listing does indicate that a faculty which might affect the special nature of the architectural or historic interest [of a listed church] should only be allowed in cases of clearly proved necessity.[102]

The leading case first emphasizing this principle was concerned with a proposal to reorder the important church of St Mary's Banbury, and in particular to replace late eighteenth-century pews.[103] The principle was expressed *obiter dicta* but the opportunity was taken to spell out guidelines on reordering and on the relationship between the competing criteria which apply in such cases. 'The faculty jurisdiction must and does treat churches such as St Mary's Banbury as treasures not only for the people of the parish, whether churchgoing or not, not only for the Anglican Church, but also for the country at large.'[104] However, where there is a conflict between the interests of worship and the interests of conservation, 'it must never be forgotten that a church is a house of God and a place of worship. It does not belong to conservationists, to the state or to the congregation but to God.'

In deciding whether to allow a reordering, the court should have in mind a number of matters:[105]

> (i) the persons most concerned with the worship in a church are those who worship there regularly although other members of the church may also be concerned; (ii) when a church is listed as a building of special architectural or historic interest a faculty which would affect its character as such should only be granted in wholly exceptional circumstances, those circumstances clearly showing a necessity for change . . .[106] A reordering of such a church solely to accommodate liturgical fashion is never likely to justify such a change; (iii) whether a church is so listed or not a chancellor should always have in mind not only the religious interests but also the aesthetic,

---

[101] *Re St Luke the Evangelist, Maidstone* [1994] 3 WLR 1165 at 333.

[102] *Re St Mary, Banbury* [1986] Fam. 24; [1987] 1 All ER 247.

[103] The decision, affirming that of the Chancellor of Oxford, Peter Boydell QC, was in fact based on the proprietary rights of pew holders which the courts did not have power to override.

[104] [1987] 1 All ER 247 at 285.

[105] The Dean of the Arches referred also to the criteria set out by Spafford Ch. in *Re Holy Innocents, Fallowfield* [1982] Fam. 135 at 137–8.

[106] In the light of the later decision of *Re All Saints, Melbourn* [1990] 1 WLR 833 at 844, the Dean appears to have had in mind only adverse affects; see Mark Hill, *Ecclesiastical Law* (Butterworths, 1995), 447n.

architectural and communal interests relevant to the church in question; (iv) although the faculty jurisdiction must look to the present as well as to the future needs of the worshipping community a change which is permanent and cannot be reversed is particularly to be avoided.

The approach of the consistory courts, and especially of the Court of the Arches, has been rather more sensitive to secular conservation interests than has that of the parallel Court of Ecclesiastical Causes Reserved. This is the appeal court from the dioceses where doctrinal matters are involved, and sits with two senior judges and three diocesan bishops.[107] In dealing with a doctrinal question as to the permissibility of a huge stone altar in place of a communion table, it also had to consider the aesthetic appropriateness of the altar.[108] The altar had been carved by Henry Moore to form a new centrepiece in one of the most distinguished churches by Sir Christopher Wren. The chancellor had rejected a petition for the altar to stay in the church after allowing it to be installed temporarily at a cost of £33,000. In reversing the chancellor's decision and allowing the altar to stay, the Court of Ecclesiastical Causes Reserved discussed the significance of the church being listed and doubted whether a faculty should only be given for work affecting a listed building in cases of 'proved necessity'. No such limitation was imposed on secular planning authorities in deciding whether to authorize changes to a secular listed building.[109]

Despite the comments of the Court of Ecclesiastical Causes Reserved, the Dean of the Arches, who is not bound by that court, has reiterated the test of proven necessity in *Re All Saints, Melbourn*,[110] but added that his previous observation, that alterations to a listed church which would affect its character should only be given in wholly exceptional circumstances, should be changed to refer only to where the effect would be an adverse one. In the *Melbourn* case, the Dean allowed an appeal against a refusal to allow parish rooms to be built in the churchyard on the north side of 'an impressive building of typical Cambridgeshire appearance – flint and pebblestone with clunch'. The Chancellor had refused permission because of the adverse affect on the setting of the church and on its unimpeded view from the north. The Dean of the Arches considered that the possibility of adverse affect had been exaggerated, but that in any event the development was necessary

---

[107] Ecclesiastical Jurisdiction Measure 1963, s.5.

[108] *Re St Stephen Walbrook* [1987] Fam. 146. There has been only one other case heard by the Court of Ecclesiastical Causes Reserved, *Re St Michael and All Angels Great Torrington* [1985] Fam. 81; [1985] 1 All ER 993.

[109] In a secular context, comparison may be drawn with the approach to an innovative piece of modern architecture replacing a listed building in *Save Britain's Heritage* v. *No. 1 Poultry Ltd* [1991] 1 WLR 153; [1991] 2 All ER 10.

[110] [1990] 1 WLR 833.

for the pastoral well-being of the church. The test of necessity was also applied by the newly reconstituted Court of Arches in *Re St Luke the Evangelist, Maidstone*,[111] and chancellors in the Province of Canterbury, who are bound by the decisions of the Court of the Arches, have followed the Dean on this point.[112]

The Church courts which deal regularly with faculty cases would, therefore, appear to apply an essentially conservation-minded test in rejecting proposals for change which are unnecessary, whilst, in practice, being sympathetic to change which is pastorally desirable. This helps to protect the Church's position in retaining the freedom to run its own affairs under the ecclesiastical exemption. The case must be made out that any proposed change is necessary and the burden of proving this is on the petitioners seeking change. However, what is 'necessary' has to be decided very much as a matter of discretion for the Church courts. Here the Court of Arches plays a crucial role. Like any appeal court, it will be reluctant to reject a trial judge's findings of fact. But it will be prepared to draw different inferences, to make different judgements on aesthetics and to strike the balance as to what is necessary in a different way from the chancellor below.

Under the Care of Churches and Ecclesiastical Jurisdiction Measure 1991, 'due regard should be had to the role of the church as a local centre of worship'.[113] However, this emphasis on pastoral need is actually directed at those concerned with conservation and not at the ecclesiastical judges who have to strike the balance between both types of concern. It has been held that judges are not obliged to apply this test, although it is a factor which they ought to and, in any event, would take into account.[114] The worship and mission factor is not in any way paramount.[115] A practical test propounded by one chancellor is: 'Have the petitioners proved on the evidence in relation to each proposal that there is a good and adequate reason for change?'[116] An aspect of the faculty system is that the archdeacon for the relevant

[111] [1990] 3 WLR 1165.

[112] *Re St James, Shirley* [1994] Fam. 134, Winchester Consistory Court, Clark QC Ch.; *Re St Helen's Bishopsgate*, 26 November 1993, unreported, London Consistory Court, Cameron QC, Ch.; *Re St Michael Tettenhall Regis* [1995] 3 WLR 301, Lichfield Consistory Court, Shand Ch.; *Re Sherborne Abbey* [1996] 3 All ER 769. Cf. *Re St Chad, Romiley, Chadkirk*, 4 Ecc LJ 769, Chester Consistory Court, Lomas Ch.

[113] Care of Churches and Ecclesiastical Jurisdiction Measure 1991, s.1.

[114] *Re St Luke the Evangelist, Maidstone* [1995] 1 All ER 321, at 326.

[115] *Re St Michael Tettenhall Regis* [1993] 3 WLR 301 per Shand Ch.

[116] *Re St James, Shirley* [1994] Fam. 134. The case was concerned with authorizing a baptistery for total immersion. The test had originally been propounded by the advocates and adopted by the same chancellor in the earlier unreported case of *Re St Mary's Ealing*.

parish has a responsibility to see that possible objections are fully aired even where there is no other formal opposition.

5 Churchyards

In considering the necessity for change, a matter which is given considerable weight is concern not to disturb remains. This may result in a petition being refused, even where secular authorities support it and would readily have approved it. A striking example was in *Re St Michael and All Saints, Tettenhall Regis* in the diocese of Lichfield.[117] A proposal for a church extension with teaching rooms and other facilities had been supported enthusiastically by a large and active congregation. It was also supported by the archdeacon,[118] the Diocesan Advisory Committee and English Heritage. However, there was strong opposition from the relatives of a number of people whose remains were interred in the churchyard.

The vicar and other proponents of the scheme had understated the large number of burials likely to be affected and had apparently been party to the unauthorized cremation of those remains excavated in a trial archaeological excavation. The trial had been sanctioned by the chancellor and was carried out by professional secular archaeologists who then reported that there were no archaeological reasons why the extension should not be built. The archaeologists failed to notify the chancellor of the discovery of the burials, despite a clear condition of the trial dig that they should do so.[119] The chancellor refused a faculty for the main works even though he accepted that the extension actually was 'necessary' for the expanding life of the parish.

The traditional country churchyard serves as a setting for the church and is itself an important focus for the local community. It may also be an important habitat for flora and fauna, and of landscape and amenity value in its own right. Increasingly, demands are made to protect the archaeological evidence in ancient churchyards.

Churchyards enjoy a large measure of special protection because they are Christian resting places for the remains of the dead.[120] As the

---

[117] [1995] 3 WLR 299, Shand Ch.

[118] The chancellor commented that the archdeacon should more actively have ensured that objections were aired.

[119] The remains were cremated on the grounds that because the churchyard had been formally closed by Order in Council no reburial was lawful. But the chancellor expressed the clear opinion that the statutory restriction on using a closed churchyard was simply on grounds of public health and did not apply to reburial.

[120] The exclusive right of burial in a churchyard or other consecrated ground in England may, however, only be reserved for one hundred years at a time; Faculty Jurisdiction Measure 1964, s.8. The period may be extended but, in practice, faculties reserving future burial spaces now tend to be for a much shorter period. Reburying

curtilage of a parish church and as consecrated ground, a churchyard will be protected under the faculty jurisdiction. Indeed, other burial grounds which have been consecrated by an Anglican bishop are subject to the faculty jurisdiction and this will include large parts of municipal cemeteries. Churchyards and other burial grounds, whether they are consecrated or not, are largely protected from future development. The Disused Burial Grounds Acts prohibit any building on burial grounds which are no longer in use, except by way of additions to a church.[121] There are statutory powers under which secular building or other development may be authorized on a burial ground, but, in the case of land still belonging to the Church, this is only likely where essential public works are needed, such as a new road.[122]

Nowadays, extensive additions may be permitted to a church, such as meeting rooms and parochial offices.[123] A churchyard may be cleared and redeveloped under the Pastoral Measure 1983. There are detailed safeguards here which are designed to protect the sensitivity of relatives of those whose bodies may need to be moved.[124] In particular, a redundant churchyard may not be built on if there is opposition from any of the surviving relatives of anyone whose remains were interred there within the previous fifty years.[125] These safeguards are also important because they may be used to protect the amenity value of a churchyard. Thus, even if a scheme provides for the removal of monuments, relatives are to be given the opportunity of resiting them. Otherwise they may be re-erected elsewhere on the direction of the bishop.[126]

Development of a redundant church site which is authorized under the Pastoral Measure will require planning consent as well. Equally, extensions to a churchyard will involve a material change of use requiring planning consent. However, either sort of development may be prevented if the churchyard or land nearby, which the church authorities wish to incorporate into it, is protected by one of the other special secular legal regimes. Thus, it may be scheduled as an ancient monument under the Ancient Monuments and Archaeological Areas Act

---

may be carried out on land with previous interments, but if a memorial has been erected, a faculty will be needed to remove the memorial.

[121] Disused Burial Grounds Acts 1884 and 1981.

[122] But see here *Norfolk County Council* v. *Knights* [1958] 1 All ER 394.

[123] Cf *London County Council* v. *Dundas* [1904] P. 1, where a hall, lavatories and a kitchen were not allowed, followed in *Re St Sepulchre, Holborn Viaduct* [1903] 19 TLR 723, with the more permissive approach in *Re St Mary's Luton* [1968] P. 47, Sir Henry Willinck, QC, Dean of the Arches and *Re St Anne's Kew* [1977] Fam. 12.

[124] Pastoral Measure 1983, s.65 and Schedule 6.

[125] Ibid., s.30(4).

[126] Ibid., Schedule 6, para.6 But cf. para.9.

1979 or designated as a Site of Special Scientific Interest under the Wildlife and Countryside Act 1981, s.28 or s.29. Churchyards are often rich in wildlife, especially natural plant life which is likely to have been wiped out on surrounding agricultural land by modern intensive farming and herbicides. Designation as an SSI may help to ensure that overenthusiastic parishioners do not suburbanize a churchyard by too intensive weeding and grass cutting.

Normally, the distinctive character of a churchyard will depend upon its monuments. These are carefully controlled by diocesan chancellors under the faculty jurisdiction. In practice, chancellors delegate the power to approve standard forms of memorial to the parish clergy. This will be done by a formal legal instrument. The scope of memorials which an incumbent may approve on his own initiative varies from diocese to diocese. For example, the delegation may include wooden crosses in parts of the country where there is an abundance of local timber. It may include slate where that is a local material. Generally, incumbents are authorized to approve simple headstones of a standard size, such as 750–1200 mm high and 500–900 mm wide, of natural stone and with a straightforward inscription.[127]

The regulation of memorials helps to prevent the character of the churchyard being damaged by unsightly or incongruous memorials. However, it makes for monotony. Chancellors encourage applications for distinctive memorials to be approved by faculty and these are not necessarily much more expensive than an off-the-peg stone from a large firm of monumental masons. But the cost of petitioning for the faculty and pressures from the funeral industry mean that individual designs are rare. Also, the system does not always stop firms of masons from selling stones for churchyards which are more suitable for municipal cemeteries, for example of polished red or black granite or white marble. Even though the incumbent may have no authority to allow these, it may be pastorally invidious to order their removal. Cases where the rules are enforced can cause great distress and unhelpful publicity for the Church.[128]

The future of the English churchyard is unclear. The remains of a large proportion of the dead are now cremated, and with emerging technology there may cease to be any physical material left after cremation. At present, the calcified remains left after cremation are then often buried in churchyards. Those people who die in the parish or die when resident there or who are on the electoral role of the parish

---

[127] The practice of churchyard management and policies on monuments are discussed in P. Burman and H. Stapleton, *The Churchyards Handbook*, 3rd edn (Church House Publishing, 1988).

[128] *Re Holy Trinity, Freckleton* [1994] 1 WLR 1588. See too *Re St Luke's Holbeach Hurn, Watson* v. *Howard* [1990] 2 All ER 749.

church as regular worshippers when they die, are entitled to have their remains interred in the churchyard. For this purpose, remains include cremated ones.[129] However, the Church has not yet developed a satisfactory approach to cremated remains and they are often tucked away in a separate part of the churchyard with miniature stones reminiscent of a pets' cemetery.

In the past, old memorials have gradually been replaced by new ones, as the ground is reburied, with the result that in many churchyards there are monuments of many different ages and styles. However, today churchyards in populous parishes have often been closed for new burials by Order in Council.[130] The appearance of a closed churchyard may become fixed at an increasingly remote time in the past. Especially where local stone is soft, old memorials erode without being replaced. In less populous parishes, where the churchyard is still in use, modern, very hard, stones may increasingly predominate. Nevertheless, there are considerable opportunities. Families may have forebears buried in a churchyard and this may provide a continuing link with the area. Such families may be persuaded to become friends of the parish church and to contribute to its upkeep and to the maintenance of the churchyard. New forms of memorial for families and for groups, perhaps including major new sculpture with Christian themes, or incorporated in rebuilt walls or paths, may help to build new personal links. Such initiatives can help to maintain churchyards as key features in the countryside and give them a new relevance.

6 Conclusion

This chapter has focused on Church property which is visibly being used by the contemporary Church and which provides a focus for rural communities. The heritage of ancient church buildings and their surroundings, especially Anglican parish churches and their churchyards, contributes a wealth of priceless features in the countryside. However, especially with escalating financial pressures, constant vigilance and new ideas are needed for using church buildings more effectively in the work of the Church and of the wider community.

Where the Church uses its land for non-religious purposes it may run into controversy. Sometimes it may be criticized for failing to make available sites for social needs such as low-cost housing.[131] Sometimes it is at least as strongly criticized for developing open land which local people consider a public amenity and want to see kept open. In

---

[129] Church of England (Miscellaneous Provisions) Measure 1992, s.3.
[130] Burial Act 1853 s.1.
[131] See David Faull and John Rees, 'The Church and Housing', 3 Ecc LJ 313.

practice, such controversies tend to occur ad hoc, perhaps where money is needed for a capital project, such as a new church building or extension.

The Church of England is currently undergoing a structural re-organization and it remains to be seen whether this will include changing the approach to how central assets are used. At present, they are managed primarily so as to maintain their value and to maximize income. Without sacrificing their long-term value, it may be that they could be seen more as resources for meeting social needs, including the improvement of the environment. At a local level, since parish land is now held by dioceses, there may be scope for more imaginative plans to use it for the benefit of the local community. Rather than reacting to current Church needs, it may be that dioceses could produce long-term plans for their undeveloped land in conjunction with local authorities, so as to produce more planning gain than an ordinary commercial developer would be prepared to consider. This would still allow for the realization of capital sums which could partly be reinvested in other amenity land. But it could help to ensure that development envisaged in development plans would do more to enhance amenity in the area rather than degrade it. Where new housing is needed in a rural area, an ancient church in open country can provide an obvious focus for a well-designed new community. The new community will restore the true purpose of the church building.

11

Planning Law and Policy in Wales: The Production of a Rural Cacophony?

NICHOLAS HERBERT-YOUNG

Mr Carlile:	What is it about Ceredigion in your view that has entitled it to ignore the fact that there has been town and country planning legislation in force for over 40 years? ...
Councillor Lloyd-Evans:	No, we have not ignored town and country planning legislation.[1]

Introduction

Nathaniel Lichfield observed in 1956 that in 'even the most static areas of the country, the remoter Welsh counties ... many different kinds of development take place'.[2] This chapter has been prompted by two factors: the range of developments during the 1990s affecting the town and country regime, law and policy in Wales *and* the challenges facing planning in rural Wales. To what extent can, and should, a new system of creating national policy and secondary legislation affect and effect town and country planning law and policy in Wales? How readily can, and should, law and policy accommodate and represent the diversity of interests in, and concerns about, planning in rural Wales?

The Labour government's White Paper, *A Voice for Wales*, proposed a National Assembly for Wales (the Assembly) for election in May

---

[1] House of Commons Welsh Affairs Committee 1992–3 Third Report, *Rural Housing* (HC 621–I and II 1992–3). See HC 621–II 1992–3, p.71, Q.322.

[2] Nathaniel Lichfield, *Economics of Planned Development* (London), 12.

1999 and in due course, this body may provide substantial answers to the questions raised above. The Government of Wales Act 1998 (the 1998 Act), enacted on 31 July 1998, provides for the establishment of the Assembly. The Government's stated aim is that

> within the framework of a strong United Kingdom, the Assembly will give the people of Wales a real chance to express their views and set their own priorities. It will reinforce Wales's distinctive place in the United Kingdom, and provide leadership to reinvigorate all aspects of Welsh life and culture.[3]

Planning and local government in Wales had not been ignored by Westminster and Whitehall before the 1997 general election. First, both Westminster and Whitehall observed certain characteristics in local development planning and control common to parts of rural Wales and, for example, north Cornwall.[4] Questions were raised, and opinions aired, about planning and local government upon the temporal cusp of local-government reorganization and about the consequent concentration of statutory planning functions into the hands of a reduced number of local authorities. Second, until 1996 planning functions were vested in eight county councils and thirty-seven district councils; now twenty-two authorities and three designated National Park authorities exercise them. Important planning policy requirements, however, including the mandatory preparation of district-wide local plans, are still to be fulfilled in some rural areas of Wales, and such plans will be only transitional. Third, national planning for Wales was made the responsibility of the Welsh Office in early 1996. Add to these points the small matters of devolution and standards of conduct in local government and the pertinence of a full consideration of the town and country planning regime, law and policy in Wales, and rural Wales, particularly, becomes apparent.

This chapter does not afford sufficient scope for a panoramic consideration of planning in Wales, even if this could be undertaken properly at this transitional stage. It offers a snapshot of some recent, and some prospective, changes in planning, particularly with reference to Lichfield's 'remoter counties' and the rural areas of Wales. How can a planning voice be produced for rural Wales on the basis of those changes? Local, and devolved, government powers will be considered. Mention will be made not only of the 1998 Act but of two recent White Papers, the last Conservative government's *A Working Countryside for Wales*[5] and Labour's *A Voice for Wales*, and two reports, the 1993

---

[3] Cm. 3718 at p.31, 5.4.

[4] See, e.g., Department of the Environment, *Enquiry into the Planning System in North Cornwall District*, Audrey Lees (London: HMSO, 1993). See also above n.1.

[5] Cm. 3180.

report of the House of Commons Welsh Affairs Committee (WAC), *Rural Housing*,[6] and the Nolan Committee report on *Standards in Public Life: Standards of Conduct in Local Government in England, Scotland and Wales*.[7] First some attempt must be made to introduce a working idea of 'rural Wales'.

1 Rural Wales

A precise definition of rural Wales is elusive. Ethnographic studies, undertaken coincidentally with enactment of 1947 planning legislation, identified rural Wales as west Wales and based rurality upon limited criteria of language and culture, ignoring apparently all those areas of the Welsh countryside where English was the popular first language.[8] Conceptions of rurality have become more sophisticated since, and recent studies of rural Wales have been less exclusive, referring also to areas of government and administration. This brings its own difficulties, however, particularly in the reduced number of local government authorities, the concomitant spatial expansion of individual local authority areas and the variety of data. Cloke, Goodwin and Milbourne point out that

> When we speak of rural Wales in a general context, we refer to those . . . District Councils characterised as 'remote rural' in Cloke's and Edwards's (1986) Index of Rurality. In some chapters, however, the spatial area referred to by the term will vary depending on the type and source of data used. Thus in some cases 'rural Wales' means the area under the jurisdiction of the Development Board for Rural Wales (DBRW), and in others it means the . . . county councils of Dyfed, Gwynedd and Powys.[9]

Does the area for which the DBRW had statutory responsibility offer a suitable yardstick? It spans mid-Wales entirely from the coast of Cardigan Bay to the border between England and Powys;[10] it includes

---

[6] See above n.1. Note also previous expressions of concern by WAC, e.g., the report on Affordable Housing, HC 581–I, 1990–1.

[7] Third Report of the Committee on Standards in Public Life (July 1997), Cm. 3702–I and II. See also, e.g., Charles George QC, *Probity and Planning* [1997] JPL 181.

[8] See, e.g., Elwyn Davies and Alwyn D. Rees (eds.), *Welsh Rural Communities* (Cardiff, 1960) (studies of Aberporth, Tregaron, Aberdaren and Glan-llyn during the 1940s and 1950s).

[9] Paul Cloke, Mark Goodwin and Paul Milbourne, *Rural Wales: Community and Marginalization* (Cardiff, 1997), 10, n.1, referring to Paul Cloke and Gareth Edwards, 'Rurality in England and Wales 1981: a replication of the 1971 index', *Regional Studies*, 20(4), 289–306.

[10] See s.1(2) Development Board for Rural Wales Act 1976 (Powys, Ceredigion and Meirionnydd) and *Municipal Yearbook 1997* (Municipal Journal Ltd), 2, 689. Ss. 129–33 and Schedule 15 of the 1998 Act provide for the process of abolition of the DBRW.

the aforementioned ethnographic rural Wales and the English-speaking county of Powys and so accounts spatially for some 40 per cent of the total land area, while accommodating less than 8 per cent of the total population, of Wales. Land use and employment in rural Wales, by this reckoning, is dominated by agriculture, forestry and, to a lesser degree, small-scale manufacturing. Sixty per cent of the population of the area live on isolated farms or in small hamlets.[11] The former DBRW area of responsibility is not a reliable yardstick of rurality however; prior to abolition of the DBRW, the scope of the area was variable by order of the Secretary of State from time to time[12] and its rural qualities are shared by other Welsh areas. Furthermore, other sources and criteria suggest that a broader spatial approach should be taken in terms of the town and country planning regime, law and policy, to include local government areas to the south and north. The WAC report, *Rural Housing*, included the former district/borough councils of Carmarthen, Dinefwr and South Pembrokeshire, to the south and those of Ynys Môn (Anglesey) and Delyn, to the north. The 1996 White Paper, *A Working Countryside for Wales*, included in its 'Planning' section the following perspective of 'the rural scene': 'The greystone walls and slate of Snowdonia, the black and white homes of the Severn Valley and the whitewashed farms of Carmarthenshire . . .'[13]

Rurality may be found also in the variety of countryside land uses and economic activities. A recent study of farming and rural policy in Wales by Bateman and Ray (a) acknowledged the importance of agriculture in the rural economy, (b) emphasized a 'very considerable variation' in 'the level and type' of diverse activities undertaken by farming households on and off farm in order to maintain economic viability and continued occupation of land[14] and (c) addressed language and culture factors in agriculture and land use in rural Wales.

In the rural areas, particularly Mid Wales, the West and the north-west, Welsh speakers can form the majority of the population while the language is also highly correlated with those who earn their living in the agricultural sector. Whilst the ability to speak the Welsh language does not ethnically define the indigenous population of rural Wales (many have been raised in households and communities whose sole language has been English), the growing interest in its maintenance justifies the identification of this part of the indigenous population as being of academic interest and a target of rural policies.[15]

[11] *Municipal Yearbook 1997*, 2, 689.
[12] S.1(2) Development Board for Rural Wales Act 1976.
[13] See 'The Built Environment', 89.
[14] 'Farm pluriactivity and rural policy: some evidence from Wales' [1994] 10 *Journal of Rural Studies* 1.
[15] Ibid., 9.

The authors argued that the main objective of rural policy in Wales should be to create conditions for indigenous farmers and their families to afford to live and work at their farm holdings whilst allowing for the 'greater tendency' of regional incomers to establish their own diversified sources of income.

So rural Wales may be understood in a wide-ranging, inclusive manner, covering a significantly larger land area than that for which the DBRW was responsible, extending it north and south, accommodating Welsh- and English-speaking communities and including agricultural, light-industrial, forestry, tourism and other land uses. Recent, and prospective, developments in the town and country planning regime, law and policy of Wales must be able to accommodate, reflect and even encourage the diversity that exists within rural Wales if 'the people of Wales', indigenous or immigrant, Welsh-speaking or English-speaking, are to have a 'real chance to express their views and set their own priorities' and so fulfil the government's aim to 'reinforce' distinctiveness and 'reinvigorate all aspects of Welsh life and culture'.[16]

2 Local Government: Continuity and Change

The first point is that the structure of local government in Wales has been abruptly, and comprehensively, reorganized while transition from two-tier to unitary local government has taken place across the United Kingdom. The number of local authorities in Wales charged with planning responsibilities has fallen with the demise of the two-tier system from forty-five (eight county planning authorities and thirty-seven district/borough planning authorities) to twenty-two, pursuant to the Local Government (Wales) Act 1994 (LGWA 1994).[17] Statutory planning responsibilities have been affected also by the creation of National Park Authorities, under the Environment Act 1995 (EA 1995), when the Brecon Beacons, Pembrokeshire Coast and Snowdonia National Park authorities were established on 23 November 1995 and assumed those responsibilities fully in April 1996.[18] The provisions of EA 1995 were not exclusive to Wales.

[16] See above n.3.

[17] See ss.1(1B), 10A (1), 23 A–C, 27A and 28 A, Town and County Planning Act 1990 as amended by LGWA 1994.

[18] See esp. ss.63, 64 and 65 EA 1995 and National Park Authorities (Wales) Order 1995 (SI 1995 No.2803). Note, for example, that of twenty-four members of the Brecon Beacons National Park Authority, sixteen may be appointed by local authorities in the 'principal area' and eight by the Secretary of State: see Articles 4 and 6 and Schedule 2, parts 1 and 2.

The second point is that the expression of a rural voice and, more particularly, the setting of priorities called for by the Labour Government, can be achieved in theory, at least, at local level in rural areas by local planning authorities, most obviously through the production of development plans and the determination of development control issues; it is interesting to note that *A Voice for Wales*, referred to a 'real chance' for the people of Wales to express views and set priorities[19] through the Assembly almost as if local authorities have not, and could not be expected to have, produced them without an Assembly. The relationship between local government and the Assembly will be considered below (see the 'National Assembly' section of this chapter). One of the most evident challenges for the rural planning regime in Wales in the 1990s has been to ensure the maintenance of high standards in the creation and application of development-plan policies.

2.1 Development plan-making

Since April 1996 the long-term goal of development planning throughout Wales has been the creation of unitary development-plan coverage for the whole of the Principality. Urban and rural local planning authorities alike are required to prepare a unitary development plan for their area within such period as the Secretary of State for Wales may direct, pursuant to ss.10A and 12(1), Town and Country Planning Act (TCPA) 1990. The target year for completion of unitary development plans in Wales is 2000 and, under Part II, TCPA 1990, the appropriate development plan in all areas of Wales should consist then of unitary development-plan provisions for the time being in force in the relevant area together with the necessary resolution of adoption and/or notices of appeal.[20]

Present development planning is affected adversely by at least two important qualifications. The first qualification is delay in the creation of unitary development plans. By late 1997, the Welsh Office could report little progress in the creation of unitary development plans, only the receipt of early plan drafts from some local planning authorities.[21] Meanwhile every plan properly made in relation to any part of Wales immediately before 1 April 1996 continued, and continues, in force until replaced by a unitary development plan. A structure plan continues until revoked, in whole or in part, by the Secretary of State for Wales upon approval, in whole or in part, of part I of the relevant

[19] See above n.3.
[20] See further *Planning Guidance (Wales): Unitary Development Plans* (May 1996), esp. para. 2, and s.27A TCPA 1990.
[21] Information supplied by John Saunders of the Welsh Office.

unitary development plan.[22] The susceptibility of transitional arrangements to any delay in making unitary development plans extends the potential for discrepancy between existing plan policy, prospective plan policy, national planning guidance/technical advice[23] and, of course, local development circumstances. This difficulty may be common for transitional planning but any idea that the new structure of Welsh local government is best able to provide a planning voice for Wales will decline as delays increase. There is no reason to suspect that *all* rural planning authorities will be slower than their urban counterparts in producing plans but, in the light of what follows in this chapter, one may wonder whether it is too much to require that all Welsh planning authorities produce both strategic and local policies for their area. The possibility of continued changes in law and policy to expedite plan-making may lead one to ask whether or not too many attempts at expedition have been made already.[24]

A second qualification on unitary development-plan progress will compound the effects of delay. Cloke[25] has pointed out that, although amendments to TCPA 1990 by the Planning and Compensation Act 1991 (PCA 1991) 'made it mandatory for planning authorities to prepare district-wide (and national park-wide) local plans . . . many areas in rural Wales were not covered by local plans in 1994'. Cloke identified specifically six rural local authorities lacking any local plan coverage (Carmarthen, Ceredigion, Glyndwr, Montgomeryshire, Preseli–Pembrokeshire and South Pembrokeshire) and he observed that the county structure plan remained the statutory development plan 'for very many rural areas'. Three years later, in late 1997, the transition to unitary development planning was inhibited still; planning authorities faced a plan backlog of similar proportions to that of 1994 as twenty-five plans awaited adoption across thirteen new unitary authorities under statutory transitional provisions for the completion and adoption of local plans and for proposals to alter or replace structure and local

[22] Schedule 2, Part IA. TCPA 1990.

[23] Welsh Office Technical Advice Notes were introduced in 1996 as part of what Malcolm Grant described as the Welsh Office's bid for independence in planning policy' (*Encyclopaedia of Planning, Law and Practice*, Monthly Bulletin, July 1996, p.7). They are to be 'taken into account by local planning authorities in Wales' in preparing development plans and by relevant bodies determining plan applications/appeals.

[24] See n.20 above. The expectation in PPG 1 (1992), para.18 that district-wide local plans be adopted by 1996 was noted by WAC at HC 621–II, 1992–3, p.1, para.7 (Memorandum by the Welsh Office) and Q.2.

[25] See Paul Cloke, 'Housing in the open countryside' (1996) 67 *Town Planning Review*, 291 at 297. As for the six authorities without local plans, see also HC621–I, p.xii, para.17.

plans 'prepared or in the course of preparation on April 1st 1996'. The adoption of four transitional plans was awaited in the DBRW area in late 1997, including the local plan for what is now the Ceredigion County Council area, while a further seven remained for adoption within the wider area of rural Wales countenanced by the Secretary of State in *A Working Countryside for Wales*.[26]

None of this should come as a great surprise, given the vexed history of development plan-making, but the uniform system of unitary planning authorities in Wales is unlikely to produce a uniform and coherent body of development plans for years to come. Considerable efforts need to be made to minimize outdatedness, nonconformity, conflict and irrelevance in development plan policies, as well as prematurity, but these efforts will be worthwhile to establish and sustain the operational effectiveness and reputation of unitary authorities in Wales. These considerations apply with at least as much force to rural planning authorities in Wales as they do to urban authorities in the light of concerns over local government standards and planning in parts of rural Wales, most recently investigated by WAC and by the Nolan Committee (Nolan).[27] WAC in particular raised two broad issues on development planning considered in the context of unitary development planning as a Welsh rural planning voice. The first issue may be labelled 'plan policy formulation'; the second, plan reputation, serves as a caution on local needs issues and on excessive delay.

Rural development plan policy formulation in Wales under transitional and unitary provisions must be monitored to prevent recurrence of some planning approaches taken before April 1996 by rural planning authorities, the more so now because the new authorities have both strategic and local responsibilities in producing plans. The first example is pertinent to local plans and unitary development plans. In 1993, WAC found that land parcels were included within proposed development boundaries under draft local plans contrary to planning officers' recommendations in two of the six authorities with which WAC was concerned. Further, as Cloke has pointed out,[28] written information supplied to WAC by local planning authorities was indicative rather than strictly accurate, and the scope of the problem could not be gauged

---

[26] See Welsh Office, *Development Plan Position at 30 November 1997*, esp. table 5, Local Government (Wales) Act 1994: 'Schedule 5 development plans – carried forward under the transitional provisions and not yet adopted.' The 'wider area' includes Carmarthenshire County Council and two local plans within its area. WAC foresaw the problems of delay and the opportunities available for some local planning authorities to exploit it: HC 621–I, 1992–3, p.xxix, paras.79–81.

[27] See above nn.3 and 7.

[28] Cloke, 'Housing in the open countryside', 294.

easily. The problem having been identified,[29] one could infer that the practice was more widespread than the evidence showed. Dinefwr Borough Council and Delyn Borough Council were the two planning authorities in which the problem was found, their areas now being the responsibility of Carmarthenshire County Council and Flintshire County Council respectively. The practice was more evident in Dinefwr than in Delyn; in the former, twenty parcels of land were included and only two in the latter. WAC would have been 'surprised' if all twenty inclusions 'could be justified . . . on strict planning grounds' and made two recommendations: the first urged examination and assessment of draft local plans by the Welsh Office with reference to the inclusion of land parcels against planning officers' advice, in addition to a recommended six-monthly review of local plan-making; the second was that the Welsh Office should ask for landowners' identities in order to check that draft local plan development boundaries were not drawn upon the basis of improper considerations.[30]

The response of the Welsh Office to these recommendations is perhaps the most interesting aspect of the issue as an indicator of future development-planning problems. The Head of the Transport, Planning and Environment Group at the Welsh Office appeared to suggest that the Welsh Office's lack of awareness that land parcels were being so included in the development plan meant that it was a relatively minor problem. Second, the Welsh Office took the view that

> it is really in the first instance for the local authorities themselves to have mechanisms in place so that kind of problem does not arise . . . we have subsequently written to local authorities . . . to press home to them the importance of the Monitoring Officer's role in this kind of situation.

Third, on the issue of land-parcel ownership and planning impropriety, 'ownership is not the most relevant consideration of a piece of land . . . not necessarily the only factor to be considered and I would still believe that most cases go through without any impropriety'.[31]

WAC did not challenge these comments but, given the purely indicative basis of WAC's information, it is interesting to note the Welsh Office response. To adopt an approach whereby an unacknowledged problem must be minor or insignificant hardly inspires confidence that national planners will seek directly to prevent it arising again in new plans for rural areas. Reliance on existing mechanisms 'so that the problem does not arise' seems especially bizarre when 'the problem'

[29] See above n.1 at p.xix, para.43 and WAC's Rural Housing: Follow-Up Minutes of Evidence, 16 February 1994, HC234, 1993–4, at p.9, Q.53–Q.55.
[30] Ibid., p.xix, para.43.
[31] See above n.29, Rural Housing: Follow-Up, at p.9, Q.56.

has arisen already.[32] The Welsh Office should be careful to see that new rural authorities' transitional and unitary plans are not tainted in this way and to ensure that development planning is as transparent as possible for the Welsh Office, at least.

A second example was raised by WAC, namely the treatment of plan policies in relation to local occupancy and s.106 agreements in the specific context of local housing exceptions policies and open country-side development. WAC criticized the adoption of plan policies that required in s.106 agreements that a named individual must reside at a 'property' for a minimum period, and held up for example residence requirements of five years (Dinefwr) and ten years (Ceredigion).[33] Banks and building societies had inclined to the view that these resi-dence requirements made houses unmortgageable, valueless as security for the duration of the requirement unless an occupier was able to reside therein for the duration. The vexed issued of development plan drafting and local occupancy in rural Wales cannot be discussed exten-sively here but its persistence should caution planners and the Welsh Office; it is sufficient to note that local plans for Ceredigion and the former district council area of Dinefwr, at least, had still to be adopted by late 1997.[34]

Plan reputation, more accurately described as the view of the devel-opment plan held by members of a local planning authority, should be a factor also in assessing the contribution of development plans to estab-lish any coherent rural planning voice. WAC found that reputations attached to existing development plan policies gave some rural local planning authorities considerable scope to decide whether or not to apply policies in certain cases. Two concerns should be recognized: first, the attachment by some rural authorities of greater significance to 'local needs' than to current structure plan policies, and, second, the outdatedness of plan policy[35] – these concerns are linked inextricably to earlier discussion about current transitional and unitary planning diffi-culties and plan formulation.

The danger that informal 'local needs' policies or rule-of-thumb criteria may persist, in spite of s.54A, was anticipated by Cloke who, writing in 1996, put the point neatly:

Although there is a likelihood that the preparation of local plans could be delayed by the transition from district to unitary authorities, the resultant

[32] Ibid.
[33] HC 621–I, 1992–3, at pp.xix–xx, para.45.
[34] See above n.26.
[35] See, e.g., HC 621–I, 1992–3, at p.xii, para.18 (incl. references therein to local planning authority informal development policies, and to an out-of-date structure plan, in Montgomeryshire) and p.xiii, paras.19–22.

plans will at least bring the acceptance of strategic statements and boundaries and the decisions on specific development proposals within the same
local authority decision-making structure. However, the evidence presented
to the Welsh Affairs inquiry suggests that many issues arising from decision-
making authorities in rural Wales will be carried through into unitary
authorities.

Cloke highlighted the submission of Councillor Lloyd-Evans to WAC
because the latter stressed that the then existing practice of Ceredigion
District Council's planning committee 'will be in line with what we
will be doing after the plan has been approved and accepted'.[36]
Ceredigion District Council's planning committee had favoured some
planning applications on narrow, yet intriguing, local needs criteria and
marginalized structure-plan policy where it conflicted with this
approach.

One might hope that there will be little or no room for policy
discrepancy, informal local needs criteria and conflict between strategic
policies and specific development decisions in the production and operation of unitary development plans when only one local planning
authority makes structural/strategic policy and local policy within one
overall plan. Unitary planning *per se* cannot necessarily eliminate
entirely either the scope for discrepancy between national, 'Anglocentric' policies applicable to plans and local views, as understood by
planning-authority members, or the potential that this has for unusual
development control decisions. As for transitional plans, the traditional
reluctance of the Secretary of State to intervene in development planning and control may yet be tested again where signs emerge, or
re-emerge, that 'local needs' afford rural local planning authorities an
opportunity to make determinations without the existing plan.

The possibility that outdatedness might taint plans in the future has
been raised already and some rural local planning authorities might
continue to make some planning determinations in spite of existing
statutory development plan policies, relying on their own claims that
plan policies are out-of-date; delayed development plan-making and the
stigma of outdatedness have been exploited thus so that the observation
of development plan policies where ss.70 and 54A apply, for example,
varied from authority to authority and from case to case. This problem
is not simply historical in rural Wales, for the Dyfed County Structure
Plan remains as *the* development plan for Ceredigion, at least; the
problem is also prospective, for how far can authorities be required
effectively and expeditiously to revise planning policies in future?

---

[36] Cloke, 'Housing in the open countryside', 305. See HC 621–I, 1992–3, at
p.xxix, para.80 and HC 621–II, 1992–3, Q.326.

WAC cited Montgomery District Council as an example of a rural authority applying or ignoring the county structure plan on housing almost at whim; plan policies were used to support grants of planning permission for retiring farmers' housing against government guidance but were ignored where they conflicted with the Council's interpretation of subsequent government guidance, for example, on affordable housing.[37]

Opportunities to exploit perceived irrelevance, lack of local content and outdatedness in plan policies are most apparently available to a local planning authority in development-control cases, but the contention that matters can be improved, and plan policies observed, by central setting of deadlines for plan adoption, or by the Welsh Office pointing out to rural authorities what plan-making they should have done, is and will be of little practical value.[38] Exhortation, the existence of statutory provisions for transitional and unitary plan-making, and growing familiarity with the terms of s.54A might help to improve the treatment of development plans by local planning authorities; however, two years after the introduction of s.54A, WAC was neither satisfied with the Welsh Office argument that Ceredigion District Council and Dinefwr District Council should have prepared local plans (that for Ceredigion, at least, remains outstanding for adoption under transitional provisions) nor optimistic that plan-making would be completed by the end of the century. WAC asked rhetorically whether some rural local authorities would consider themselves less bound by 'not-so-up-to-date' local plans within five or ten years (1998–2003);[39] yet, given more recent delays in local plan adoption, the most tardy local authorities may find themselves with the most up-to-date local plans. So rural development plans alone should not be treated as the vehicle for expressing a contemporary planning 'voice' for rural Wales: rural development plans are varied in age; where rural local planning authorities have not seen fit to treat development plans as the proper vehicle, they have made their own, informal policies; WAC accepted criticisms by some local councillors that the structure plans for Dyfed and Powys had not reflected particular area characteristics, especially in terms of suitable policies for monitoring settlement patterns.

---

[37] HC 621–I, p.xxi, para.51. See also the practice of Dinefwr Borough Council and Ceredigion District Council on the homes-for-retiring-farmers issue: HC 621–I, p.xvi, para.30.

[38] See e.g. WAC's expression of scepticism at HC 621–I at p.xxii, para.53.

[39] HC 621–I, p.xxii, para.55. Note generally WAC at HC 621–I, p.xxi, para.50: 'the performance of many rural planning authorities is very good. We would not wish it to be thought that all are as bad as the worst we have found.'

2.2 Development control

The evidence gathered by WAC on the treatment of development plans in development control determinations made by some rural authorities in Wales hardly encourages a belief that s.54A was applied successfully by those authorities in the first years after its enactment. Claims that councillors in England and Wales were unfamiliar with the operation of s.54A might have been accepted by some as sufficient excuse for a less than complete observation of the section, though such claims were hardly likely to be indulged by the courts.[40] Consideration of the Nolan hearings, held in Wales in early December 1996, allows further scope for assessing development control in rural Wales; the relevant evidence given at those sessions is highlighted here, particularly the evidence of Elwyn Moseley, the local government ombudsman for Wales.[41]

Moseley's evidence was especially significant not just by virtue of his office at the time of the Nolan hearings but because he held it also at the time of the WAC investigation into rural housing; his evidence to Nolan offers an element of impartiality as well as continuity of analysis. Moseley pointed out the susceptibility of rural planning authorities to certain development control 'concerns', notably, in relation to rural housing permissions, absence of formality in decision-making systems and the susceptibility of rural councillors to lobbying. Susceptibility to lobbying in rural areas reflected a clear urban–rural planning split for, whereas planning authorities in Cardiff, Newport and Swansea are alive to the dangers of secrecy, suspicion of abuse and arbitrary decision-making, 'the mischief has tended to arise in rural areas where an individual applicant, say the local farmer, has lobbied his local Councillor'. Moseley recommended that local planning authorities be obliged to give reasons for all decisions, including reasons for their rejection of professional planning advice.[42] Consistent susceptibility to lobbying is clearly contrary to the thrust of s.54A.

Moseley commented further on alleged 'deficiencies' in local authority decision-making in the light of the WAC report, circumstances following in its wake and Welsh local government reorganization:

> I had thought that the position would have changed sufficiently for the problem not to recur . . . but there are indications that the problem is recurring, and my impression is that some new councillors, for example in the

[40] Cf. the distinction between a misdirection as to s.54A by a planning officer, to a planning committee, where it is clear that the correct approach is applied and such a misdirection by someone expected to be well versed in planning statutes: *North Yorkshire County Council* v. *Secretary of State for the Environment and Griffin* [1996] JPL 32.

[41] Cm. 3702–II, at pp.17–23.

[42] Ibid., 18, para.63.

planning field, where the problem does tend to occur, simply do not understand their obligations and what are relevant considerations.[43]

In 1993, Moseley expressed the view that certain Welsh local authorities acted in 'negation' of the planning process, since when an initial improvement occurred, especially a reduction in rural development contrary to published development plans, but, according to Moseley, a more recent tendency to take account of applicants' private information, canvassers and lobbyists means that some local planning authorities have accorded weight to 'not necessarily material' issues in their determinations.[44]

Other witnesses referred to the use of a 'local lad' principle, the importance attached to the local councillor's opinion of a proposal, and a lack of concern for development plans and policy guidance in determinations by Ceredigion District Council and its successor authority,[45] but Moseley's comments reflect their author's breadth of experience and familiarity with the range of local planning authorities in Wales. The substance of Moseley's evidence to Nolan is instructive also when assessing the effectiveness of the Welsh Office response to the WAC report. The Welsh Office response outlined for Nolan was an all-Wales approach, not limited to rural areas only, whereby *inter alia* the Secretary of State for Wales wrote to local planning authorities on propriety in planning, called in councillors and officers from Ceredigion and Anglesey to discuss rural housing and planning complaints and required Ceredigion District Council to send to the Welsh Office for vetting any rural-housing departure applications which the Council was, and its successor is, minded to approve.[46] Moseley's concerns indicate that in development control determinations, at least, the application of development plans will have to be monitored just as much in the future as in the past, and probably more so, given increased public consciousness of the exercise of statutory planning functions by local government, the importance of s.54A and the Nolan recommendations.

The extent of local government responsibility for statutory planning appears to be settled, given Nolan's recommendations for proper training for councillors, an effective code of best practice, increased use of call-in powers and a possible redrafting of planning obligations legislation.[47] The views of certain local councils and councillors given to WAC and Nolan, though attracting criticism, should be heard,

---

[43] Ibid., 18–19, para.64.

[44] Ibid., 23, paras.82 and 83.

[45] Ibid., 7–10, paras.7 (Carole McKeown) and 28–39, esp. 34 (Susan Miller).

[46] Ibid., 37, paras.153–5 and p.43, paras.177–9 (Jon Shortridge and Peter Roderick).

[47] Cm. 3702–I, ch.6, R34, R35, R39 and R36–7, respectively.

however; complaints of Anglocentricism in national policy and requests for more region-related policy, and for greater concern for local settlement patterns, have been acknowledged.[48] To what extent is the statutory system failing to account for local needs and if it is, how should it be changed? Councillor Lloyd-Evans, of Ceredigion County Council (by 1996), followed his appearance before WAC's investigation into rural housing with one before Nolan to state *inter alia* that 'planning guidance was drawn up with certain areas of England perhaps in mind, where you have vast areas with no development in sight . . . we have no such situation in Wales, especially in Ceredigion'.[49]

It may take more than a translation of national policy-making to Cardiff to answer such a complaint; meanwhile, the reorganization of local government, and consequent concentration of planning powers in any given local authority area, could exaggerate the planning phenomena already mentioned. So, should not more region-related planning policies be accompanied by legislation to address the range and variety of substantive and procedural planning issues in rural Wales? Could this be achieved without requiring another bout of development planning?

If not, there must be a danger that rural Welsh local planning, and the control of development in rural Wales, will become less able to conform to statutory type at the very time when local government will have to establish a relationship with the new representative body exercising planning powers devolved from central government.

3 The National Assembly

The production of a rural planning voice through local government, however fraught, should not be treated in isolation; the establishment of the Assembly in 1999 will raise important questions for planning law and policy-making in Wales, particularly as to the accommodation of local government planning policies with those of the Assembly. *A Voice for Wales* treated the reorganization of Welsh local government as part of a 'process of reform' which 'the establishment of an Assembly will complete'. There is 'to be a new relationship between central and local government founded on mutual respect for the legitimate role of both parties' whereby, *inter alia*, local authorities will have a role in influencing decision-making by public bodies *and* in the creation of secondary legislation. The result will be 'a new, more inclusive and

[48] Note, e.g. WAC's observation in 1993 that 'guidance which reflects the settlement patterns in the home counties is unlikely to be equally applicable to rural Wales', referring to village-envelope restrictions on development. WAC recommended a greater reflection in guidance of traditional Welsh settlement patterns without reducing development controls and aesthetic values: HC 621–I, p.xiv, para.26.
[49] Cm.3702–II, p. 27, para.100.

participatory democracy'.[50] The existing relationship between central and local government in town and country planning is described by Victor Moore as 'a hierarchy of central pontification' where, 'despite many attempts made over the years to shift more of the responsibility for planning decisions from central to local government', the Secretary of State for the Environment, Transport and the Regions is 'the supreme central pontiff'.[51] In 1996, the shift in Welsh national planning policy-making to production by the Welsh Office alone might not have been seen as anything more than a variation within Moore's point; it seems that the shift should been seen now as part of a reforͫ process that the present government wishes to complete with the establishment of the Assembly.

The Government of Wales Bill (GWB) included clauses for the transfer of central government powers to the Assembly, and these appear largely unchanged in the 1998 Act.[52] It would be foolhardy to anticipate exactly how an accommodation will be achieved in practice between central government, the Assembly and local government to allow each to express, or contribute to, coherent planning law and policy within Wales, but some tentative observations are offered here. Two areas will be considered: first, the extent of the Assembly's opportunity to make its own rural planning law and policy in Wales; and second, the formal channels in the 1998 Act through which Welsh local authorities may contribute to Assembly-made law and policy.

3.1 The Assembly's rural planning law and policy

Three factors will be considered: subject matter, powers and means of exercising powers. The extent of the subject matter is set out in the list of eighteen 'fields' under Schedule 2 of the 1998 Act; it is from these 'fields' that functions exercised/exercisable by ministers of the Crown in Wales may be transferred to the Assembly 'as the Secretary of State considers appropriate', subject to Parliament's approval.[53] Town and country planning is the fifteenth field listed in Schedule 2, with

[50] See p.15, paras.3.1 and 3.4–3.5.

[51] See *A Practical Approach to Planning Law,* 6th edn, 10.

[52] See ss.21–6 of the 1998 Act and part II, GWB. The GWB was criticized for proposing a committee-based structure for decision-making without clear allocations of responsibility. A system of appointed Assembly secretaries, each having defined functions, may provide a more practical system for decision-making, linking specific functions to a specific office in an arrangement more akin to cabinet government than to local government. See ss.56 and 57 of the 1998 Act.

[53] S.22(1)–(4). The National Assembly Advisory Group has recommended that key planning decisions should be made by a 'small panel' of Assembly members: see *Planning,* 4 September 1998, pp.1 and 2.

connected fields including ancient monuments and historic buildings (no.2), culture (no.3), economic development (no.4), the environment (no.6), highways (no.8), housing (no.9), local government (no.11), tourism (no.14), transport (no.16) and the Welsh language (no.18). Schedule 2 is not the only guide in the 1998 Act to the issues awaiting the Assembly: statutory provisions allow Assembly support for *inter alia* buildings of historical or architectural interest, or other places of historical interest, in Wales, the Welsh language and 'other cultural or recreational activities in Wales'.[54] The government referred also to sustainable development and environmental-protection goals in *A Voice for Wales* and to the 'special need for imaginative and sensitive policies that will promote the regeneration of towns and villages across urban and rural Wales'.[55]

The 1998 Act gives both general and subject-specific Assembly powers in relation to many of these policy areas. Where power to make secondary legislation[56] is transferred to, or made exercisable by, the Assembly by an Order in Council, the Assembly may have extensive scope to make substantial changes to planning law without necessarily having to submit to parliamentary resolution procedures. The precise scope to make changes will depend initially upon the terms of the Order as approved by Parliament.[57] So, for example, in a rural planning context, the Assembly may become able to amend, even abolish, the list of those Welsh areas included in Article 1(5) land and to alter provisions affording those areas protection from permitted development. The latter power is more extensive than an Article 4 direction as it allows repeal of exceptions to Article 4 directions found in Article 4(3) and (4) of the Town and Country Planning (General Permitted Development) Order 1995. National Parks, areas of outstanding national beauty and areas specified under s.41(3) of the Wildlife and Countryside Act 1981 (enhancement and protection of the natural beauty and amenity of the countryside), for example, fall within Article 1(5) land; Welsh rural areas outside National Parks, listed as article 1(6) land, could be affected also by reforms to permitted development rights. Any exercise of secondary legislative powers in this vein might indicate a substantially different approach to rural planning in Wales from that in England. The Assembly could either increase or reduce the protection available.

The Assembly's powers will not be purely legislative, of course; 'virtually all the functions of the Secretary of State for Wales' will be

---

[54] S.32.
[55] See p.12, para.2.4, s.121.
[56] Ss.22 and 44.
[57] Ss.42(1), (2) and (4) and 44. Note restrictions at s.44(2)–(5).

transferred by Order in Council 'soon after the Assembly is established'.[58] So Welsh Office administrative and judicial powers will be
transferred including, presumably, appeal functions and the production
of Welsh national planning policy. Exploitation of the opportunity for
an elected body to produce planning policy nationally will need careful
consideration by Assembly, local government, developers and others,
and it may provide for greater transparency in national policy-making.
Discrepancies between national policy and local policy/practice, for
example, may be exposed in a more public forum after April 1999
than previously, debated in the Assembly rather than confined to
correspondence between local authorities and the Welsh Office. Rural
complaints about 'Anglocentric' national policies could be reduced by
the production of national policy more specific to rural-area needs, so
reducing the scope for some local planning authorities to depart from
development-plan policies as well as national planning policies.

A number of Schedule 2 fields connected to planning have been identified above and the 1998 Act provides extra emphasis for most of these
fields by allowing the Assembly power to do anything it considers
appropriate to support them.[59] The objects of this power include specifically, as we have seen, buildings of historical or architectural interest,
or other places of historic interest, in Wales, the Welsh language and
cultural or recreational activities in Wales. Quite what 'support' the
government has in mind, and what will be appropriate, is not made
clear, but all of these subjects have important existing status in the
development planning and control of rural areas, notably with regard to
the Welsh language and to tourism, and have been addressed in
national planning-policy documents. The precise scope of the provision
is not clear for the further reason that the 1998 Act offers no statutory
context in surrounding clauses, in a schedule or by reference to other
legislation; in a rural planning context, however, the very existence of
the provision could conceivably be invoked by rural members urging
the Assembly to exercise its powers to make new national policy on
those subjects within the provision or to exercise powers in such a
manner, and to such ends, as may affect planning law and rural policy
directly or indirectly.

The extent of the Assembly's powers to create a rural planning voice
is ultimately beyond the Assembly's direct determination,[60] though it
may contribute by advising the Secretary of State for Wales. The allocation of new statutory powers created after the Assembly is established
will be determined outside Wales also: 'the Government will consider,

---

[58] *A Voice for Wales*, 8, para.1.8 and see ss.21ff.
[59] S.32.
[60] See, e.g. the 1998 Act, Parts II and V.

in drafting each Bill that it introduces into Parliament, which of the new powers it contains should be exercised in Wales by the Assembly'.[61] The Assembly's powers will be limited by a variety of external factors including Parliament, central government, Community law, courts and tribunals, for example, and so the means by which those powers will be exercised may prove to be of great importance to the rural context of the Assembly's work. Certain Assembly decisions may be susceptible to legal challenge in the same manner that a decision made currently by the Secretary of State for Wales may be challenged. A court or tribunal may decide, for example, that the Assembly has acted beyond its legislative powers but the 1998 Act allows the court or tribunal to suspend that decision 'to allow the defect to be cured' or to remove or limit any retrospective effect of the decision (s.110).[62]

Instead of mounting legal challenges to Assembly decisions, rural bodies and individuals outside government are likely to attend to the deliberations of Assembly subject committees addressing planning, and related fields, as these committees will be vital to the formulation and effective promotion of the Assembly's version of a rural planning voice in Wales. Subject committees will undertake the 'day-to-day work on such matters as developing policies, monitoring the performance of public bodies, preparing secondary legislation and considering Bills going through Parliament'.[63]

An executive committee, made up of an elected Assembly First Secretary and Assembly Secretaries appointed by the Assembly First Secretary, will perform 'functions . . . similar to those of the Cabinet' and will provide the 'overall political direction of the Assembly'. All subject committees will include the Assembly Secretary allocated 'accountability' in the particular Schedule 2 field (see further s.56). The planning subject committee and the executive committee 'will be responsible for the preparation, and submission to the Assembly for debate and approval, of secondary legislation' on town and country planning matters. Draft secondary legislation will be made only after it has been agreed by either committee;[64] both committees will be able to pursue the 'clear priorities' set out at para.2.4 in *A Voice for Wales*, including the 'special need for imaginative and sensitive policies that

---

[61] *A Voice of Wales*, 20, para.3.39.

[62] Note also s.109 and Schedule 8 where the 1998 Act provides for judicial determination of devolution issues, e.g. whether or not functions are within Assembly powers.

[63] *A Voice for Wales*, 26, para.4.18 and s.57 of the 1998 Act. See also nn.52 and 53 above.

[64] *A Voice for Wales*, 27, para.4.22. Secondary legislation 'must be laid before the Assembly after the relevant committee has agreed to it': *A Voice for Wales*, 27, para.4.22.

will promote the regeneration of towns and villages across urban and rural Wales', by setting planning policy and drafting secondary legislation. Furthermore, the Assembly itself is likely to be designated to make regulations, pursuant to s.2(2) of the European Communities Act 1972, to implement Community obligations in Wales.[65] All draft secondary legislation will be submitted for scrutiny to a subordinate legislation-scrutiny committee; this committee will report to the Assembly before the latter considers the merits of the draft legislation.[66]

So what opportunities will exist within the Assembly's legislative and policy-making processes for Welsh rural areas to contribute on rural planning issues? Regional committees within the Assembly[67] may well provide a basis from which rural Assembly members could advise, urge secondary legislation or planning-policy developments, particularly in those subject areas which the 1998 Act allows the Assembly to support in any way it considers appropriate, given the goals of sustainable development and environment protection specified in *A Voice for Wales*.[68] Access to members, or membership, of the planning subject committee, associated subject committees and the executive committee, as well as to subcommittees of any of these to which functions have been duly delegated, will be essential to the creation and content of secondary legislation and policy. Rural Assembly members will need to influence Assembly secretaries, committee members and Assembly staff and to enforce committee-membership safeguards.

Membership safeguards are treated in party political terms.[69] Most of the members of subject committees, but none of the executive committee, will be elected by Assembly members. Subject-committee membership is to reflect 'the balance of parties in the Assembly', as far as is practicable, and subcommittees created by subject committees are to be elected by the latter from their own membership, so that not all members of subcommittees are drawn from one political party. These safeguards could prove to be particularly important where powers of delegation are exercised pursuant to ss.62 and 57, but the delegation of functions by a subject committee to its Assembly secretary member might reduce effective minority-party representation.[70]

---

[65] S.29. 'The Assembly will have an obligation to ensure the implementation and enforcement of relevant EU obligations': *A Voice for Wales*, 22, para.3.48.

[66] SS.58 and 59. See also *A Voice for Wales*, 28, paras.4.26 and 4.27.

[67] S.61.

[68] See pp.9 and 10, paras.1.22 and 1.24.

[69] See, e.g. ss.57(4) and (8) (subject committees); cf. *A Voice for Wales*, 26–8, paras.4.15 (executive committee), 4.19 (subject committees) and 4.26 (scrutiny committee).

[70] S.62(3)(b); cf. *A Voice for Wales*, 26, para.4.19: 'the principal political leadership for the committee's work ... usually a member of the majority party'.

Furthermore, membership of the cabinet-style executive committee will be made up of appointed Assembly Secretaries and an elected Assembly First Secretary.[71]

It appears, prior to the first Assembly elections, that assembly membership is likely to be dominated by Labour. Members will be returned to represent constituencies created on a mixed basis: all current Westminster parliamentary constituencies will return one member each; the five European parliamentary constituencies in Wales will be subdivided into twenty Assembly seats.[72] Labour electoral dominance is based substantially upon the urban and suburban electorate, whereas the diversity of rural Wales, outlined earlier in this chapter, is reflected to some extent in its parliamentary and local-government representation. In Parliament, Liberal Democrat and Plaid Cymru MPs represent eastern and western halves respectively of the former DBRW area, while rural areas to the north reflect a Plaid Cymru/Labour split and those to the south are Labour. In local government, independent representation dominates mid-Wales but, elsewhere, the pattern of parliamentary affiliation is evident in the political balance of local authority councillors.[73]

The expression of a rural Labour interest in Westminster offers the hope that at least some rural concerns will be expressed adequately in the Assembly. The worst consequence of rural political diversity for an Assembly-made rural planning voice, and its expression in secondary legislation and national policy, would be resurrection of development planning and control problems in the exercise of planning functions by certain rural unitary authorities. A Labour-dominated Assembly, returned by a substantial urban/suburban electorate and a less substantial rural vote, might prove to be as incapable of eliminating bad practices as the succession of 'Anglocentric' Conservative Secretaries of State of Wales. Potential difficulties are easy to foresee: (a) the evolution of a planning-policy regime that assists in perpetuating sentiments that the new political centre does not, or cannot, reflect local perceptions of local planning needs and interests; (b) the creation and reform of secondary legislation that has the same popular effect as in (a); and so (c) a return to localized development planning and control approaches and practices, by some rural planning authorities, of the type that brought their predecessor authorities to the attention of WAC and the Nolan Committee. These difficulties may arise particularly if the Assembly fails to bear in mind and act upon WAC recommendations and Bateman and Ray's point that the main objective of Welsh rural policy should be to create conditions for indigenous farmers and

[71] *A Voice for Wales*, 26 para.4.15, and see ss.53 and 56.

[72] Ss.2 and 4 and Schedule 1, esp. paras.1–4 and 8. See also *A Voice for Wales*, 24.

[73] See further, e.g. *The Wales Yearbook 1997*, ed. D. Balsom (Cardiff, 1997).

their families, for example, to live and work on their farm holdings while regional incomers establish diversified sources of income.[74] To adapt Moore's papal analogy, one pontiff (the Secretary of State for Wales) may be replaced by another, albeit one created upon a popular election; rural accusations of planning-policy Anglocentricity may be replaced by accusations of an urban-orientated national planning policy.

No doubt the Government has considerable faith in the capacity of the Assembly to advance the 'priorities' of rural planning for Wales and to establish the 'new relationship between central and local government founded on mutual respect of the legitimate role of both parties'; after all, the Assembly's initial standing orders will be drafted to the Secretary of State's guidance, they will have a major effect upon the operation of Assembly committees (for example) and the initial standing order will have the Secretary of State's approval in order to have any effect.[75] The former Secretary of State, Ron Davies, might have held himself out as a bridge across any industrial/urban and rural divide in planning matters by reiterating his interest in rural issues, had he been a contender for Assembly First Secretary.[76]

3.2 A voice for rural planning authorities?

It is clear that in the establishment of a new relationship between central and local government, a process which we have been told is to be completed by the creation of the Assembly,[77] Welsh local planning authorities will have no direct statutory contribution to enacting secondary legislation or making national planning policy. Rural areas and rural planning authorities will have to exert their views and priorities through the influence of Assembly members and, particularly, through relevant regional committees and sympathetic members of relevant subject committees and subcommittees; in an irony to be savoured by opponents of the Assembly, local planning authorities might wish even to address their concerns to the Secretary of State for Wales, who will retain a seat in the Cabinet, rather than rely on the Assembly and its members. The power to create primary legislation for Wales will remain with Parliament, and the Secretary of State for Wales will be in a key position to seek to influence and to effect it; the Secretary of State could inform the Assembly of rural concerns conveyed to him during mandatory consultations on the Government's legislative programme for the parliamentary session.[78]

[74] See above n.14 at pp.12–13.
[75] See, e.g. ss.46 and 50.
[76] See above n.73 at p.132.
[77] A Voice for Wales, 15, paras.3.4, 3.5 and 3.6.
[78] S.31.

The most direct formal channel in the 1998 Act by which any local planning authority could influence the Assembly is likely to be the Partnership Council for Wales (Cyngor Partneriaeth Cymru) (PCW), a body of local government–Assembly membership where local authority members will be appointed in numbers sufficient to balance, at least, the number of Assembly members. In general, appointments will be made by the Assembly from those nominated by Welsh local authorities and their associations after consultation between all three of these groups.[79] Rural planning authorities can hope to contribute, not least because local authorities are defined in the 1998 Act to include county councils and National Park authorities,[80] but the extent of their representation lies within the power of the Assembly, appointments are for the Assembly to make as it 'considers appropriate', and there is no statutory provision to secure either a party-political balance or an area-representative balance or special provision for rural authorities.[81]

The Assembly's 'local government scheme' offers no channel of influence directly to law- and policy-making, only a method by which the Assembly can aim to sustain, promote and respect 'local self-government' and to appoint 'more local authority members' to boards of public bodies.[82] Appointments to public bodies' boards may offer local authorities greater influence over planning law and policy; perhaps the most substantial means afforded by the 1998 Act to increase rural local authorities' powers over development has far less to do directly with statutory planning than with the reallocation of statutory functions, conferred or imposed by primary and secondary legislation, from public bodies to local authorities. The identity of the public bodies in question echoes the objects, specified by the 1998 Act, to which the Assembly may give any appropriate support; they include the Welsh Development Agency, the Ancient Monuments Board for Wales, the Historic Buildings Council for Wales and the Welsh Language Board.[83] The particular significance of the Welsh Development Agency here is that rural local authorities may find themselves exercising former DBRW functions transferred to the Welsh Development Agency prior to the establishment of the Assembly; it is not apparent that these functions will be made available to rural local authorities beyond the former DBRW

[79] S.113 and Schedule 11. Note that PCW may make representations to the Assembly about local-government matters and concerns and advise local government: s.113(4)(b) and (c).

[80] S.113(7)(a) and (b).

[81] Schedule 11, paras.1(1) and 2(1).

[82] The Assembly 'shall have regard' to advice given, or representation made, by the PCW: s.113(5). See also S.113(1) and *A Voice for Wales*, 15, para.3.6 and p.19, paras.3.30 and 3.31.

[83] S.28 and Schedule 4, Part 1.

areas of Ceredigion, Meirionnydd and Powys (such as Gwynedd, Conwy, Carmarthenshire and Pembrokeshire), but the government's rejection of a separate rural development board suggests that they might well be. How far will rural local authorities wish to assume transferred functions when individual councillors may exert a direct influence over the revamped economic and social development agency? Much may depend on the percentage of the Assembly's annual budget likely to be made available to rural authorities, together with the estimated annual savings in running costs made by merging the DBRW, the Welsh Development Agency and the Land Authority for Wales and by winding up Housing for Wales.

4 Conclusion

The consideration given in this chapter to the planning regime in Wales, to planning law and policy, has been limited deliberately to aspects of planning for rural areas in Wales. The context of this consideration has been provided by the reorganization of Welsh local government and by the current devolution process. Devolution and a greater regional emphasis to planning in the United Kingdom has been called for by some planners for a considerable time;[84] now the government purports to treat local government reorganization as part of a devolutionary process for Wales culminating in the establishment of the Assembly.

The production of a rural planning voice, even if one accepts the idea of a 'voice', faces considerable challenges within the context of devolution. The state of local government planning in large parts of rural Wales during the 1990s, and the current transitional spasms of plan-making, do not encourage hope that a unified Welsh rural planning voice will be produced by Assembly and local government without difficulty. Further, the decision-making processes proposed for the National Assembly are opaque; for example, demarcations of responsibility and the precise scope for rural representation in the Assembly are not clear enough to show how that representation might be made effectively and to the satisfaction of rural local authorities and other interested parties. There is, therefore, a strong possibility that discrepancies may arise between Assembly and local government generally and between Assembly-made planning law and policy and the approaches taken by some rural planning authorities to observing and implementing such law and policy (and to the treatment of their own development plans).

[84] See, e.g. Andrew Blowers (ed.), *Planning for a Sustainable Environment: A Report by the Town and Country Planning Association* (London, 1993), esp. 7–8 and 16–18.

Constitutional and structural aspects of local and regional planning responsibilities are not likely to be the only telling factors in the production of a rural planning voice for Wales. The diversity of rural Wales and its land-use-related issues must be a further factor; the evolution and substance of Welsh planning policy guidance for rural areas, its distinctiveness or lack of it, may prove to be a key indicator of the extent to which Assembly and local government can co-operate in planning for rural Wales. In the short term, the prospects for coherent planning in rural Wales are even more open to doubt than they have been at any time in recent years.

Index